CONTENTS

Quick Reference Specifications For Your Vehicle

Fill in this chart with the most commonly used specifications for your vehicle. Specifications can be found in Chapters 1 through 3 or on the tune-up decal under the hood of the vehicle.

 Tune-Up

Firing Order_____

Spark Plugs:

    Type_____

    Gap (in.)_____

Point Gap (in.)_____

Dwell Angle (°)_____

Ignition Timing (°)_____

    Vacuum (Connected/Disconnected)_____

Valve Clearance (in.)

    Intake_____   **Exhaust**_____

Capacities

Engine Oil (qts)

    With Filter Change_____

    Without Filter Change_____

Cooling System (qts)_____

Manual Transmission (pts)_____

    Type_____

Automatic Transmission (pts)_____

    Type_____

Front Differential (pts)_____

    Type_____

Rear Differential (pts)_____

    Type_____

Transfer Case (pts)_____

    Type_____

FREQUENTLY REPLACED PARTS

Use these spaces to record the part numbers of frequently replaced parts.

PCV VALVE   **OIL FILTER**   **AIR FILTER**

Manufacturer_____   **Manufacturer**_____   **Manufacturer**_____

Part No._____   **Part No.**_____   **Part No.**_____

General Information and Maintenance

HOW TO USE THIS BOOK

Chilton's Repair and Tune-Up Guide for the Toyota Carina, Corolla, Tercel, and Starlet is designed for the Toyota owner who wishes to do some of the service on his/her own car. Included are step-by-step instructions for maintenance, trouble-shooting, and repair or replacement of many components of the car.

Before attempting to perform any of the service procedures outlined in this guide, thoroughly familiarize yourself with the steps of the procedures which you are going to perform. Read each step carefully being sure to note the tools which you will need for each procedure.

Safety is an important factor when performing any service operation. Areas of special hazard are noted in the text; but common sense should always prevail.

Here are some general safety rules:

1. When working around gasoline or its vapors, don't smoke, and remember to be careful about sparks which could ignite it.

2. Always support the car securely with jackstands (not milk crates!) if it is necessary to raise it. Don't rely on a tire changing jack as the only means of support. Be sure that the jackstands have a rated load capacity adequate for your car.

3. Block the wheels of the car which re-main on the ground, if only one end is being raised. If the front end is being raised, set the parking brake as well.

4. If a car equipped with an automatic transmission must be operated with the engine running and the transmission in gear, always set the parking brake and block the *front* wheels.

5. If the engine is running, watch out for the cooling fan blades. Be sure that clothing, hair, tools, etc., can't get caught in them.

6. If you are using metal tools around or if you are working near the battery terminals, it is a good idea to disconnect it.

7. If you want to crank the engine, but don't want it to start, remove the high tension lead which runs from the coil to the distributor.

TOOLS AND EQUIPMENT

Before attempting service procedures, it is important to have at least some basic tools and equipment on hand. Toyotas use metric nuts, bolts, and fittings. A basic tool kit is supplied with the car, but it will be necessary to purchase more tools for more complex jobs.

Remember to use the proper tool for each nut, bolt, or fitting. If a torque wrench is called for and torque specifications given, use them.

Be sure not to force things. If a part won't come off, a hammer and a pair of locking pliers is not the solution; patience and care are. It is much easier to do something right the first time than to repeat it or replace a damaged part.

The following is a recommended list of basic tools and equipment for anyone wishing to perform maintenance or tune-ups on their car:

Tools:
• Assorted screwdrivers, including a magnetic one;
• Assorted allen keys;
• Socket wrench set (include a spark plug socket);
• Torque wrench;
• Assorted crescent wrenches (or several adjustable wrenches);
• Oil filter (band) wrench;
• Wire feeler gauges (spark plugs);
• Flat feeler gauges (points);
• Pliers.

Equipment:
• Hand-operated grease gun;
• Timing light;
• Dwell/tachometer;
• Tire pressure gauge;
• Vacuum gauge;
• Remote starting switch;
• Jackstands and wheel blocksIf you wish to perform more complex service procedures, you will probably find it necessary to buy or borrow more tools. Check the procedure before beginning it, to see what tools are necessary.

SERIAL NUMBER IDENTIFICATION

Vehicle

All models have the vehicle identification number (VIN) stamped on a plate which is attached to the left side of the instrument panel. This plate is visible through the windshield.

The VIN is also stamped on a plate in the engine compartment which is usually located on the firewall.

The serial number consists of a series identification number (see the following chart) followed by a six-digit production number.

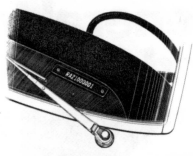

VIN plate on the left-side of the instrument panel

VIN plate on the firewall

Engine

The engine serial number consists of an engine series identification number, followed by a six-digit production number.

Vehicle Identification

Year	Model Type	Series Identification Number
1972–79	Carina	TA12L
1971–79	Corolla 1600 Sedan	TE31L
	Hardtop	TE37L
	Station Wagon	TE38LV
	Sport Coupe	TE51
	Lift Back	TE51
1970–79	Corolla 1200	KE30L
1980–81	Corolla	TE72
1980–81	Corolla Tercel	AL-10, AL-12
1981	Starlet	KP61G

Engine Identification

Year	Model	Engine Displacement		Number of Cylinders	Type	Engine Series Identification
		cu. in.	(cc)			
1972–73	Carina	96.9	(1588)	4	OHV	2T-C
1970–79	Corolla 1200	71.2	(1166)	4	OHV	3K-C
1971–79	Corolla 1600	96.9	(1588)	4	OHV	2T-C
1980–81	Tercel 1500	88.6	(1452)	4	OHV	1A-C, 3A, 3AC
1980–81	Corolla 1800	108.0	(1800)	4	OHV	3T-C
1981	Starlet	78.7	(1290)	4	OHV	4K-C

OHV Overhead valve
OHC Overhead cam

The location of this serial number varies from one engine type to another. Serial numbers may be found in the following locations:

3K-C, 4K-C

The serial number on the 3K-C and 4K-C engine is stamped on the right-side of the engine, below the spark plugs.

2T-C, 3T-C, 1A-C, 3A, 3A-C

The serial number is stamped on the left-side of the engine, behind the dipstick.

ROUTINE MAINTENANCE

Air Cleaner

The air cleaners used on Toyota vehicles are of the dry-element, disposable type. They should never be washed or oiled.

Clean the element every 3,000 miles, or more often under dry, dusty conditions, by using low-pressure compressed air. Blow from the inside toward the outside.

CAUTION: *Never use high air pressure to clean the element, as this will probably damage it.*

Replace the element every 18,000 miles, (1970–72); every 24,000 miles (1973–74); 25,000 miles (1975–77); 30,000 miles (1978–81); or more often under dry, dusty conditions. Be sure to use the correct one; all Toyota elements are of the same type but they come in a variety of sizes.

To remove the air cleaner element, unfasten the wing nut(s) and clips (if so equipped) on top of the housing and lift off the top section. Set it aside carefully since the emission system hoses are attached to it on some models. Unfasten these hoses first (if so equipped), to remove it entirely from the car. Lift the air cleaner element out for service or replacement.

Installation is the reverse of removal.

PCV Valve

The positive crankcase ventilation (PCV) valve should be replaced every 12 months/12,000 miles on models made prior to 1972. On 1972–74 models, check the PCV valve every 12 months/12,000 miles and replace it every 24 months/24,000 miles (whichever occurs first). On 1975–77 models, replace the PCV valve every 25,000 miles.

On 1978–81 models, replace the PCV valve every 30,000 miles or 24 months.

NOTE: *For PCV valve removal and installation, See Chapter 4.*

Charcoal Canister
1972–77

Toyota used the charcoal canister storage system for fuel vapor for the first time in 1972. Prior to this, Toyota used a "case" system which had no charcoal canister.

The charcoal canister vacuum lines, fittings, and connections should be checked every 6,000 miles for clogging, pinching, looseness, etc. Clean or replace components as necessary. If the canister is clogged, it may be cleaned using *low-pressure* compressed air, as shown.

The entire canister should be replaced every five years/50,000 miles (60,000 miles on 1978 and later cars).

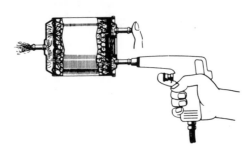

Using compressed air to clean the charcoal canister

Belts
TENSION CHECKING AND ADJUSTING

Inspection and adjustment to the alternator drive belt should be performed every 3,000 miles or if the alternator has been removed.

1. Inspect the drive belt to see that it is not cracked or worn. Be sure that its surfaces are free of grease or oil.

2. Push down on the belt halfway between the fan and the alternator pulleys, with a force of about 22 lbs. The belt should deflect ⅜–½ in.

NOTE: *On models with the 2M or 4M six-cylinder engines, push down on the belt with a pressure of 24 lbs. halfway between the fan and the crankshaft pulleys.*

3. If the belt tension requires adjustment, loosen the adjusting link bolt and move the alternator until the proper belt tension is obtained.

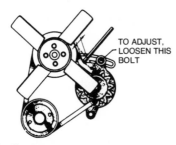

TO ADJUST, LOOSEN THIS BOLT

Fan belt adjustment

CAUTION: *Do not overtighten the belt; damage to the alternator bearings could result.*

4. Tighten the adjusting link bolt.

Air Conditioning

SIGHT GLASS CHECKING

The ambient temperature must be between 70°–110°F in order to perform this test.

1. Start the engine and allow it to reach normal idle speed and operating temperature.

2. Run the engine at fast idle (about 2,000 rpm). Turn the blower switch on "High" and set the air conditioner control on "Cold" (10).

3. Open all of car's doors and windows.

4. Locate the receiver which may be found at the front of the engine compartment, near the evaporator. Lift up the protective plastic cover (if so equipped) on the receiver sight glass.

5. There should be no foam or bubbles visible in the sight glass. If there are, have the air conditioning system checked.

6. If the air conditioning system is not working at all (no cooling), and the sight glass is clear, there is probably no refrigerant in the system.

7. Check the air conditioning lines and fittings for signs of leakage; oil visible on them indicates a leak. Do not attempt to tighten the fittings or replace the lines yourself.

CAUTION: *Your automobile air conditioner has no owner-serviceable parts. Contact with refrigerant could cause severe injury or frostbite. Overcharging the system could result in an explosion.*

Fluid Level Checks

ENGINE OIL

The engine oil level should be checked at regular intervals; for example, whenever the car is refueled. Check the oil level if the red

oil warning light comes on or if the oil pressure gauge shows an abnormally low reading.

It is preferable to check the oil level when the engine is cold or after the car has been standing for a while. Checking the oil immediately after the engine has been running will result in a false reading. Be sure that the car is on a level surface before checking the oil level.

Remove the dipstick and wipe it with a clean rag. Insert it again (fully) and withdraw it. The oil level should be at the "F" mark (Full) or between the "F" and the "L" (Low) marks. Do not run the engine if the oil level is below the "L."

Add oil, as necessary. Use only oil which carries the API designation SE.

CAUTION: *Do not use unlabeled oil or a lower grade of oil which does not meet SE specifications.*

See the chart in the lubrication section of this chapter for proper oil viscosities. Do not overfill.

MANUAL TRANSMISSION

The oil in the manual transmission should be checked every 6,000 miles and replaced every 18,000 miles (24,000 miles 1974 models, 25,000 miles 1975–77 models, and 30,000 miles 1978–81 models) or 24 months, whichever occurs first.

To check the oil level, remove the transmission filler plug. This is always the upper plug; the lower plug being the drain.

The oil level should reach the bottom of the filler plug. If it is lower than this, add API grade GL-4 oil of the proper viscosity. Use SAE 80 oil in all models, except for 1974–77, which uses SAE 90 oil.

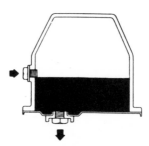

Manual transmission oil level should be up to the bottom of the filler (upper) plug

AUTOMATIC TRANSMISSION

Check the level of the transmission fluid every 3,000 miles and replace it every 18,000 miles (24,000 miles 1974 models, 25,000 miles 1975–77 models, and 30,000 miles 1978–81 models). It is important that these figures be adhered to, in order to ensure a long transmission life. The procedures for checking the oil are given below.

2-Speed Toyoglide

Start the car cold and allow the engine to idle for a few minutes. Set the handbrake and apply the service brakes. Move the gear selector through all of the ranges.

With the engine still running, the parking brake on, and the selector in Neutral (N), remove and clean the transmission dipstick. Insert the dipstick fully, remove it and take a reading. The fluid level should fall between the "L" and "F" marks. If the level is below "L," add type F fluid to the filler tube until the fluid level is up to the "F" mark.

CAUTION: *Do not overfill the transmission.*

If the fluid contains particles or bubbles, or is burnt, the transmission is defective and should be overhauled.

CAUTION: *Never use type A (DEXRON®) fluid or gear oil in the transmission. Do not use engine oil supplements either.*

3-Speed

The procedure for checking and adding fluid is basically the same as that for the two-speed Toyoglide, except that the transmission dipstick has two ranges.

1. COLD-the fluid level should fall in this range when the engine has been running for only a short tiem.

2. HOT-the fluid level should fall within this range when the engine has reached normal running temperatures.

Replenish the fluid through the filler tube with type F fluid, to the top of the "COLD" or "HOT" range—depending upon engine temperature.

All of the other two-speed Toyoglide procedures and cautions apply.

BRAKE AND CLUTCH MASTER CYLINDERS

The brake and clutch (manual transmission) master cylinder reservoirs are made of a translucent plastic so that the fluid level can be checked without removing the cap. Check the fluid level frequently.

NOTE: *There are three reservoirs on most models with dual tandem master brake cylinders and manual transmission.*

If the fluid is low, fill the reservoir with DOT 3 fluid, pouring so bubbles do not form in the reservoir. Use care not to spill any fluid on the car's paint, damage may result.

NOTE: *Do not use a lower grade of brake fluid and never mix different types. Either could result in a brake system failure.*

COOLANT

The coolant level should be checked at least once a week or when the temperature gauge registers "HOT" (H).

CAUTION: *Allow the engine to cool before removing the radiator cap.*

Because the cooling system is under pressure, check the coolant level with the engine *cold* to prevent injury from high-pressure, hot water.

The level should be ¾ in. below the filler neck, when the engine is cold. Replenish with clean, non-alkaline water. If antifreeze is being added, use a type approved for aluminum (*ethylene glycol*). Most Toyota models have alloy heads.

CAUTION: *Never add cold water to a hot engine; damage to the cooling system and engine block could result. On 2T-C engines, bleed the cooling system by loosening the temperature sending unit after filling the radiator. Tighten the sender.*

Some models are equipped with a closed cooling system, with a tube running from the radiator to a thermal expansion tank. On these models, check the level of the coolant in the expansion tank. The main radiator cap should only be removed when cleaning or

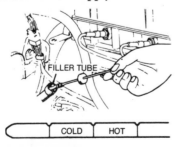

Three-speed automatic transmission dipstick location—insert shows ranges

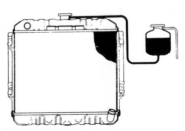

Check the coolant level in the expansion tank on models with a closed cooling system

draining the cooling system or if the expansion tank is empty.

CAUTION: *The cap on the main radiator is not a pressure/vacuum safety cap. Never remove it when the engine is hot. Serious injury could result.*

The expansion tank should be about ¾ full or coolant should reach the "FULL" mark. Add coolant as outlined.

REAR AXLE

The oil level in the differential should be checked every 6,000 miles and replaced every 18,000 miles (24,000 miles—1974, 25,000 miles—1975–77, and 30,000 miles—1978–81) or 24 months, whichever comes first. The oil should be checked with the car on a level surface. Remove the oil filler and upper plug, located on the back of the differential.

NOTE: *The bottom plug is the drain.*

The oil level should reach to the bottom edge of the filler hole. If low, replenish with API grade GL-5 gear oil of the proper viscosity. The viscosity is determined by the ambient temperature range. If the temperature averages *above* 10°F, use SAE 90 gear oil. If the temperature averages *below* 10°F, use SAE 80 oil. Always check for leaks when checking the oil level.

STEERING GEAR

Check the steering gear oil level every 12,000 miles. The level should be up to filler plug hole. Add API GL-4 gear oil of the proper viscosity. All pre-1974 models use

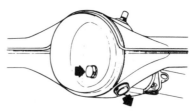

Filler (upper) plug and drain (lower) plug locations on the differential

SAE 80. All 1974–81 models use SAE 90. When checking the oil level, look for leaks.

POWER STEERING RESERVOIR

All six cylinder cars and some other 1978 and later cars use power steering. Check the level of the power steering fluid periodically. The fluid level should fall within the cross-hatched area of the gauge attached to the reservoir cap. If the fluid level is below this, add DEXRON® fluid. Remember to check for leaks.

BATTERY

Check the electrolyte level in the battery frequently. The level should be between the upper and lower level lines marked on the battery case or just to the bottom of the filler well, depending on type. Use distilled water to correct the electrolyte level.

CAUTION: *Do not overfill the battery. It could leak and damage the car finish and battery bracket.*

Tire Care

Toyota models come equipped with various types of tires, depending upon model and

Capacities

Model	Year	Crankcase (qt) W/Filter	Crankcase (qt) W/O Filter	Transmission (qt) Manual	Transmission (qt) Automatic	Drive Axle (pt)	Fuel Tank (gal)	Cooling System w/heater (qt)
Carina 1600	72–73	3.9	3.3	1.6	5.0	2.0	13.2	6.9
Corolla 1200	70–79	3.7	2.9	①	—	2.2	12.0	5.1
1600	75–79	4.6	3.7	1.6	2.5	1.2	13.2	8.8
1800	80–81	4.0	3.5	1.8	2.5	1.1	13.2	8.5
Tercel 1500	80–81	3.7	3.4	3.4	2.3	2.0	11.9	5.4
Starlet	1981	3.7	3.2	2.6	—	2.2	10.6	6.0

①Sta. Wgn.: 10.6

year. Most older Toyotas came equipped
with conventional bias-ply tires and sport
models generally with radial tires. Most 1975
models had radial tires as standard equipment.

There are several precautions concerning
tire use and care:

1. Don't mix tires of different sizes on the
same axle (i.e., if the tire on the right front
wheel is a 6.95 x 14 do not put a 7.35 x 14 on
the left front wheel).

2. Do not mix bias-ply and radial tires. If
radial tires are to be used, it is best to buy a
set of five. The same is true going the other
way (i.e., replacing radial with bias-ply tires).

CAUTION: *Do not mix tires of different
construction on the same axle. Severe handling deterioration may result.*

3. Keep the tires properly inflated. Over
(or) underinflation can shorten tire life. See
the decal in the passenger compartment
(usually attached to the steering column) for
proper inflation pressures. Remember to
check the spare.

4. Check the tires regularly for signs of
uneven wear or tread damange.

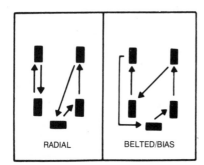

RADIAL   BELTED/BIAS

Tire rotation

Fuel Filter

There are two basic types of fuel filter used
on Toyota vehicles: The cartridge type (disposable element) and the totally "throwaway" type.

CAUTION: *Do not smoke while servicing
the fuel filter. Vapors trapped in it could
ignite.*

Cartridge Type

The cartridge type filter is located in the fuel
line. To replace the element, proceed as follows:

1. Loosen and remove the nut on the filter
bowl.

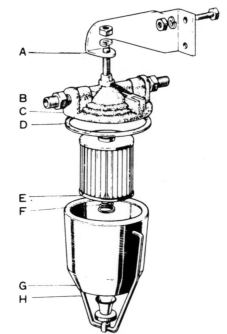

A. Fuel filter bracket E. Filter element
B. Fuel line fitting   F. Element retaining spring
C. Body   G. Filter bowl
D. Bowl gasket   H. Bowl retaining bail

Cartridge-type fuel filter components

2. Withdraw the bowl, element spring,
element, and gasket.

3. Wash the parts in solvent and examine
them for damage.

4. Install a new filter element and bowl
gasket.

5. Install the components in the reverse
order of their removal. Do not fully tighten
the bail nut.

6. Seat the bowl by turning it slightly.
Tighten the bail nut fully and check for leaks.

The above service should be performed if
the clear glass bowl fills up with gasoline or
at the following specified intervals:

NOTE: *Be sure to specify engine and
model when buying the element replacement kit. The kits come in several different
sizes.*

Throwaway Type—1971–74

The throwaway type of fuel filter is located in
the fuel line. It must be completely removed
in order to replace it. The procedure to do
this is as follows:

1. Unfasten the fuel intake hose. Use a
wrench to loosen the attachment nut and another wrench on the opposite side to keep

the filter body from turning (except 1973 and later 3K-C and 2T-C).

2. On 2T-C engines, slip the flexible fuel line off the neck on the other side of the filter. On 1973 and later 3K-C and 2T-C engines, remove the fuel lines from both sides of the filter by loosening the clamp and slipping the rubber hose off.

3. Unfasten the attaching screws from the filter bracket, if so equipped.

4. Install a completely new fuel filter assembly in the reverse order of removal, above.

Throwaway Type—1975–81

Starting 1975, Toyota passenger cars use a "see-through" type, disposable fuel filter. This filter should be replaced every 2 years or 25,000 miles on 1975–77 vehicles, and 30,000 miles or 2 years on 1978–79 vehicles, or if the filter appears clogged or dirty. To replace it, proceed as follows:

1. Remove the hose clamps from the inlet and outlet hoses.

2. Work the hoses off the filter necks.

3. Snap the filter out of its bracket.

Installation is performed in the reverse order of removal. Be sure to install the filter in the proper direction. The arrow on top should point towards the carburetor.

"See-through" fuel filter

Battery Care

Maintain the battery electrolyte level, as outlined in the fluid level section.

CAUTION: *Don't smoke near the battery; it produces highly explosive hydrogen gas.*

If the terminals become corroded, clean them with a solution of baking soda mixed with water. Wash off the top of the battery with this solution and then rinse it off using clean, clear water.

NOTE: *Be sure that the filler caps are on tight or the electrolyte in the battery may become contaminated.*

Use petroleum jelly or silicone lubricant to protect the battery terminals. Check to be sure that the cables are fastened securely at both ends. Also, be sure that the battery

hold-down bracket nuts are secure and free of corrosion.

When installing a new battery, be sure that its amp/hour capacity is at least as high as that of the battery which was removed. Its physical size should be the same as that of the battery which it is replacing.

When hooking up the battery cables, be careful to observe proper polarity. The positive (hot) cable should be connected to the positive (+) terminal of the battery and the negative cable (ground) should be connected to the negative (−) terminal.

LUBRICATION

Oil and Fuel Recommendations

Use a good quality motor oil of a known brand, which carries the API classification SE. The proper viscosity of the oil to be used is determined by the chart below.

CAUTION: *Do not use unlabeled oil or a lower grade of oil which does not meet SE specifications. If 5W, 10W, or 5W-20 oil is being used, avoid prolonged high-speed driving.*

Change the oil at the intervals recommended in the lubrication chart below. If the vehicle is being used in severe service such as trailer towing, change the oil more frequently than recommended.

It is especially important that the oil be changed at the proper intervals in emission-controlled engines, as they run hotter than non-controlled engines, thus causing the oil to break down faster.

All Toyota models made from 1972–74 are designed to run on regular grade gasoline, with an octane rating of 90 or higher.

The 1970–71 fuel recommendations, are as follows:

Model	Type of Fuel Used	Minimum Octane
Corolla 1200	Regular	92
Corolla 1600	Regular	92
Corona 1900	Premium	98

If the engine pings, knocks, or diesels, either the fuel grade is too low or the timing is out of adjustment. Add gasoline of a higher octane and check the timing, as soon as possible.

CAUTION: *Pinging, knocking, or dieseling can rapidly damage the engine, the problem should be cured as quickly as possible.*

Starting in 1975, all Toyota passenger cars sold in California, and all Mark II models sold nationwide are equipped with catalytic converters. Because lead ruins the catalyst, the use of unleaded fuel is mandatory. All Toyota models with catalytic converters are equipped with smaller fuel fillers, which will allow only the smaller unleaded fuel pump nozzels to be used.

1977 and later models all require the exclusive use of unleaded fuel of 87 octane or higher, and are equipped with a smaller fuel filler. All vehicles manufactured for California in 1977, and nationwide in 1978 and later use catalytic converters, making the use of unleaded fuel mandatory if damage to the catalyst is to be avoided.

Oil Changes

ENGINE

The oil should be changed at the intervals specified in the lubrication chart below. The amount of oil required for each engine and model may be found in the "Capacities" chart.

NOTE: *All models should have an oil change after the first 1,000 miles. The filter should also be changed at this time.*

To change the oil, proceed in the following manner:

1. Warm the oil by running the engine for a short period of time; this will make the oil flow more freely from the oil pan.

2. Park on a level surface and put on the parking brake. Stop the engine. Remove the oil filler cap from the top of the valve cover.

3. Place a pan of adequate capacity below the drain plug.

Engine oil drain plug location

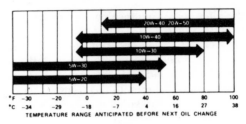

Oil viscosity recommendations for all Toyota models

NOTE: *If the crankcase holds five quarts, a two-quart milk container will not be suitable. A large flat pan makes a good container to catch oil.*

4. Use a wrench of the proper size (not pliers) to remove the drain plug. Loosen the drain plug while maintaining a slight upward force on it to keep the oil from running out around it. Allow the oil to fully drain into the container under the drain hole.

5. Remove the container used to catch the oil and wipe any excess oil from the area around the hole.

6. Install the drain plug, complete with its gasket. Be sure that the plug is tight enough that the oil does not leak out, but not tight enough to strip the threads.

NOTE: *Replace the drain plug gasket at every fourth oil change with a new one.*

7. Add clean, new oil of the proper grade and viscosity through the oil filler on the top of the valve cover. Be sure that the oil level registers near the "F" (full) mark on the dipstick.

MANUAL TRANSMISSION

The transmission oil should be replaced every 18,000 miles (1970–73), 24,000 miles (1974), 25,000 miles (1975–77), 30,000 miles (1978–81), or 24 months (all years), whichever occurs first.

To change the transmission oil, proceed as follows:

1. Park the car on a level surface and put on the parking brake.

2. Remove the oil filler (upper) plug.

3. Place a container, of a large enough capacity to catch all of the oil, under the drain (lower) plug. Use the proper size wrench to loosen the drain plug slowly, while maintaining a slight upward force to keep the oil from running out. Once the plug is removed, allow all of the oil to drain from the transmission.

4. Install the drain plug and its gasket, if so equipped.

5. Fill the transmission to capacity. (See the "Capacities" chart). Use API grade GL4 SAE 80 oil on all 1970–73 passenger cars. Use SAE 90 in 1974–77 models. Be sure that the oil level reaches the bottom of the filler plug.

6. Remember to install the filler plug when finished.

AUTOMATIC TRANSMISSION

Change the fluid in the automatic transmission every 18,000 (1970–73), 24,000 miles (1974), 25,000 miles (1975–77), 30,000 miles (1978–81), or 24 months, whichever occurs first.

To change the fluid, proceed as follows:

1. Park the car on a level surface. Set the parking brake.

2. Place a container, which is large enough to catch all of the transmission fluid, under the transmission oil pan drain plug. Unfasten the drain plug and allow all of the fluid to run out into the container.

3. Check the condition of the transmission fluid. If it is burnt, discolored, or has particles in it, the transmission needs to be overhauled. Consult your local Toyota dealer.

4. Install the drain plug in the transmission oil pan. Be sure that it is tight enough to prevent leakage, but not tight enough to strip the threads.

CAUTION: *Fill the transmission with ATF type F fluid only. Do not use DEXRON®, gear oil or engine oil supplement.*

5. Fill the transmission through the filler tube, after removing the dipstick, with ATF type F transmission fluid.

NOTE: *It may be a good idea to fill to less than the recommended capacity (see the "Capacities" chart) as some of the fluid will remain in the torque converter.*

6. Start the engine and check the transmission fluid level, as outlined under "Fluid Level Checks." Add fluid, if necessary, but do not overfill.

REAR DRIVE AXLE

All Toyota rear axles use 90 weight, API—GL-5 lubricant. Lubricant is changed every 18,000 miles (1970–73), 24,000 miles (1974), 25,000 miles (1975–77), 30,000 miles (1978–81) or 24 months, whichever comes first.

To drain and fill the rear axle, proceed as follows:

1. Park the vehicle on a level surface. Set the parking brake.

2. Remove the filler (upper) plug. Place a container which is large enough to catch all of the differential oil, under the drain plug.

3. Remove the drain (lower) plug and gasket, if so equipped. Allow all of the oil to drain into the container.

4. Install the drain plug. Tighten it so that it will not leak, but do not overtighten.

5. Refill with the proper grade and viscosity of axle lubricant (See "Fluid Level Checks.") Be sure that the level reaches the bottom of the filler plug.

6. Install the filler plug and check for leakage.

Oil Filter

All Toyota passenger cars use spin-off oil filters. These should be changed at the first 1,000 mile oil change and at the interval specified in the "Lubrication Schedule" chart. The filter should be replaced during the engine oil change procedure.

To replace the filter, proceed as follows:

1. Drain the engine oil as previously outlined. Place a container under the oil filter to catch any excess oil.

2. Use a spin-off (band) wrench to remove the filter unit. Turn the filter counterclockwise in order to remove it.

3. Wipe off the filter bracket with a clean rag.

4. Install a new filter and gasket, after first lubricating the gasket with a clean engine oil.

CAUTION: *Do not use the wrench to tighten the filter. Tighten it by hand.*

5. Add engine oil as previously outlined in the appropriate section. Check for leaks.

Removing the oil filter with a band wrench

Chassis Greasing
Corolla, Tercel, Starlet

The chassis lubrication for these models is limited to lubricating the front ball joints every 24,000 miles (1970–74), 25,000 miles (1975–77), or 30,000 miles (1978–81) or 24 months, whichever occurs first. To lubricate the ball joints, proceed as follows:

1. Remove the screw plug from the ball joint. Install a grease nipple.

2. Using a *hand-operated* grease gun, lubricate the ball joint with NGLI No. 1 molybdenum-disulphide lithium-base grease.

CAUTION: *Do not use multipurpose or chassis grease.*

3. Remove the nipple and reinstall the screw plug.

4. Repeat for the other ball joint(s).

Carina

The ball joints on these models do not normally require lubrication. If the dust boots become torn or damaged, however, the boots should be replaced and the ball joint repacked. (See Chapter 8.)

Body Lubrication

There is no set period recommended by Toyota for body lubrication. However, it is a good idea to lubricate the following body points at least once a year, especially in the fall before cold weather.

Lubricate with engine oil:
• Door lock latches
• Door lock rollers
• Station wagon tailgate hinges
• Door, hood, and hinge pivots
Lubricate with Lubriplate®:
• Trunk lid latch and hinge
• Glove box door latch

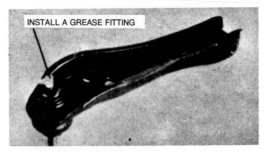

Corolla ball joint greast fitting—other models are similar

• Front seat slides
Lubricate with silicone spray:
• All rubber weather stripping
• Hood stops
When finished lubricating a body part, be sure that all the excess lubricant has been wiped off, especially in the areas of the car which may come in contact with clothing.

Wheel Bearings

Refer to the appropriate section in Chapter 9 for wheel bearing assembly and packing procedures. The front wheel bearings should be repacked every 24,000 miles on 1970–74 vehicles, 25,000 miles on 1975–77 vehicles, and 30,000 miles on 1978–81 vehicles, or every 24 months, whichever occurs first.

PUSHING, TOWING, AND JUMP STARTING

Push-start the car when the engine will not turn over; do not attempt to start the car by towing it.

Lubrication Schedule
(miles x 1,000/months)

| Model | Year | Oil Change | Oil Filter Change | Transmission Oil Change | | Rear Axle Oil Change | Lubricate Ball Joints | Chassis Lube | Repack Wheel Bearings |
				Manual	Automatic				
Corolla	1970–72	3/3	6/6	18/24	18/24	18/24	24/24	—	24/24
Carina	1972	3/3	6/6	18/24	18/24	18/24	—	①	24/24
All models	1973–74	6/6	6/6	24/24	24/24	24/24	24/24	—	24/24
All models	1975–77	6.5/6	6.5/6	25/24	25/24	25/24	25/24	—	25/24
All models	1978–81	7.5/6	7.5/6	30/24	30/24	30/24	30/24	—	30/24

① Lubricate the front shock absorber upper support bushing every 24 months or 24,000 miles.

JUMP STARTING A DEAD BATTERY

The chemical reaction in a battery produces explosive hydrogen gas. This is the safe way to jump start a dead battery, reducing the chances of an accidental spark that could cause an explosion.

Jump Starting Precautions

1. Be sure both batteries are of the same voltage.
2. Be sure both batteries are of the same polarity (have the same grounded terminal).
3. Be sure the vehicles are not touching.
4. Be sure the vent cap holes are not obstructed.
5. Do not smoke or allow sparks around the battery.
6. In cold weather, check for frozen electrolyte in the battery.
7. Do not allow electrolyte on your skin or clothing.
8. Be sure the electrolyte is not frozen.

Jump Starting Procedure

1. Determine voltages of the two batteries; they must be the same.
2. Bring the starting vehicle close (they must not touch) so that the batteries can be reached easily.
3. Turn off all accessories and both engines. Put both cars in Neutral or Park and set the handbrake.
4. Cover the cell caps with a rag—do not cover terminals.
5. If the terminals on the run-down battery are heavily corroded, clean them.
6. Identify the positive and negative posts on both batteries and connect the cables in the order shown.
7. Start the engine of the starting vehicle and run it at fast idle. Try to start the car with the dead battery. Crank it for no more than 10 seconds at a time and let it cool off for 20 seconds in between tries.
8. If it doesn't start in 3 tries, there is something else wrong.
9. Disconnect the cables in the reverse order.
10. Replace the cell covers and dispose of the rags.

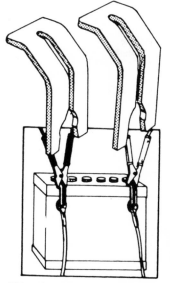

Side terminal batteries occasionally pose a problem when connecting jumper cables. There frequently isn't enough room to clamp the cables without touching sheet metal. Side terminal adaptors are available to alleviate this problem and should be removed after use

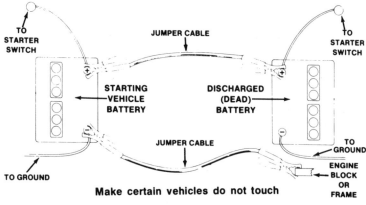

Make certain vehicles do not touch

This hook-up for negative ground cars only

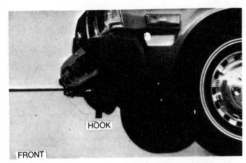

Towing a car equipped with a towing hook

Towing a car by the rear spring hanger

CAUTION: *If the car is tow-started, it may run into the back of the towing vehicle when it starts.*

To push-start the car, turn the ignition switch to "on." (On models with seat belt interlocks, fasten the seat belts first.) Fully depress the clutch pedal and shift into Second or Third gear. When the car reaches 10 mph, let the clutch pedal up slowly until the engine catches.

NOTE: *It is impossible to push-start models equipped with automatic transmission.*

The following precautions should be observed when towing the vehicle:

1. Always place the transmission in Neutral and release the parking brake.

2. Models equipped with automatic transmissions, except the Carina and 1974–77 models, may be towed with the transmission in Neutral, but only for short distances at speeds below 20 mph. On Carina and 1974–77 models, or if the transmission is inoperative, either tow the car with the rear wheels off the ground or disconnect the drive shaft at the differential end. If you are towing a 1978 or later car with an automatic transmission, you may tow the car for up to 50 miles and at speeds of up to 30 miles per hour.

3. If the rear axle is defective, the car must be towed with its rear wheels off the ground.

4. Always turn the steering column lock to "ON" and then return to "ACC." This prevents the steering column from locking.

CAUTION: *The steering column lock is not designed to hold the wheels straight while the car is being towed. Therefore, if the car is being towed with its front end down, place a dolly under the front wheels.*

JACKING

There are certain safety precautions which should be observed when jacking the vehicle. They are as follows:

1. Always jack the car on a level surface.

2. Set the parking brake if the *front* wheels are to be raised. This will keep the car from rolling backward off the jack.

3. If the rear wheels are to be raised, block the front wheels to keep the car from rolling forward.

4. Block the wheel diagonally opposite the one which is being raised.

NOTE: *The tool kit which is supplied with Toyota passenger cars includes a wheel block.*

5. If the vehicle is being raised in order to work underneath it, support it with jackstands. Do not place the jackstands against the sheet metal panels beneath the car or they will become distorted.

CAUTION: *Do not work beneath a vehicle supported only by a tire-changing jack.*

6. Do not use a bumper jack to raise the vehicle; the bumpers are not designed for this purpose.

Tune-Up

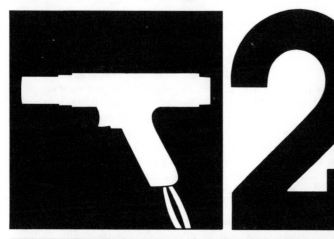

TUNE-UP PROCEDURES

This section gives specific procedures on how to tune-up your Toyota. It is intended to be as complete and as basic as possible. For generalized troubleshooting procedures see Chapter 11. However, it is felt that nothing would be lost by first reading over this section before starting your tune-up.

Spark Plugs

The job of the spark plug is to ignite the air/fuel mixture in the cylinder as the piston approaches the top of the compression stroke. The ignited mixture then expands and forces the piston down on the power stroke. This turns the crankshaft which then turns the remainder of the drive train.

The average life of a spark plug, if the engine is run on leaded fuel, is 12,000 miles, while on unleaded fuel, it may be considerably longer. Spark plug life also depends upon the mechanical condition of the engine and the type of driving you are doing. Plugs usually last longer and stay cleaner if most of your driving is done on long trips at high speeds.

The electrode end of the spark plug (the end that goes into the cylinder) is also a very good indicator of the mechanical condition of your engine. If a spark plug should foul and begin to misfire, you will have to find the condition that caused the plug to foul and correct it. It is also a good idea to occasionally give all the plugs the once-over to get an idea how the inside of your engine is doing. A small amount of deposit on a spark plug, after it has been in use for any period of time, should be considered normal. But a black liquid deposit on the plugs indicates oil fouling. You should schedule a few free Saturday afternoons to find the source of it. Because the combustion chamber is supposed to be sealed from the rest of the engine, oil on the spark plug means your engine is hemorrhaging.

Ideally, you should clean and adjust spark plugs every 6,000 miles or so, if you're using leaded fuel, or if the engine shows signs of misfire. Spark plugs should be replaced every 12,000 miles on 1970–74 vehicles, every 12,500 miles on 1975–76 vehicles, and every 15,000 miles on 1977–81 vehicles (those using unleaded fuel only).

1. If the spark plug wires are not numbered as to their cylinder, place a piece of masking tape on each wire and number it.

2. Grasp each wire by the rubber boot at the end. Pull the wires from the spark plugs. If the boots stick to the plugs, remove them with a twisting motion. Do not attempt to re-

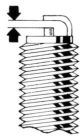

Measure the spark plug gap with a wire (round) gauge

move the spark plug wires from the plugs by pulling on the wire itself as this will damage the spark plug wires.

3. Clean any foreign material from around the spark plugs before removing them. Use the spark plug wrench supplied in the tool kit. On 2T-C engines, an extension will be necessary since the plugs are recessed in the valve cover.

Compare the condition of the spark plugs to the plugs shown in the color section. It should be remembered that any type of deposit will decrease the efficiency of the plug. If the plugs are not to be replaced, they should be thoroughly cleaned before installation. If the electrode ends of ths plugs are not worn or damaged and if they are to be reused, wipe off the porcelain insulator on each plug and check for cracks or breaks. If either condition exists, the plug must be replaced.

If the plugs are judged reusable, have them cleaned on a plug cleaning machine (found in most service stations) or remove the deposits with a stiff wire brush.

Check the plug gap on both new and used plugs before installing them in the engine. The ground electrode must be parallel to the center electrode and the specified size wire gauge should pass through the opening with a slight drag.

NOTE: *Do not use a flat gauge; an inaccurate reading will result.*

If the center or ground electrode has worn unevenly, level them off with a file. If the air gap between the two electrodes is not correct, open or close the ground electrode, with the proper tool, to bring it to specifications. Such a tool is usually provided with a gap gauge.

Install the plugs, as follows:

1. Lightly oil the spark plug threads with engine oil.

2. Insert the plugs in the engine and hand-tighten them. Do not cross-thread the plugs.

3. Torque the spark plugs to 11–14 ft. lbs. Use caution when tightening the spark plugs, since most Toyota engines have aluminum heads.

4. Install each wire on its respective plug, making sure that it is firmly connected.

Breaker Points and Condenser

The points and condenser function as a circuit breaker for the primary circuit of the ignition system. The ignition coil must boost the 12 volts (V) of electrical pressure supplied to it by the battery to about 20,000 V in order to fire the spark plugs. To do this, the coil depends on the points and condenser for assistance.

The coil has a primary and a secondary circuit. When the ignition key is turned to the "on" position, the battery supplies voltage to the primary side of the coil which passes the voltage on to the points. The points are connected to ground to complete the primary circuit. As the cam in the distributor turns, the points open and the primary circuit collapses. The magnetic force in the primary circuit. As the cam in the distributor turns, the points open and the primary circuit collapses. The magnetic force in the primary circuit of the coil cuts through the secondary circuit and increases the voltage in the secondary circuit to a level that is sufficient to fire the spark plugs. When the points open, the electrical charge contained in the primary circuit jumps the gap that is created between the two open contacts of the points. If this electrical charge was not transferred elsewhere, the material on the contacts of the points would melt and that all-important gap between the contacts would start to change. If this gap is not maintained, the points will not break the primary circuit. If the primary circuit is not broken, the secondary circuit will not have enough voltage to fire the spark plugs. Enter the condenser.

The function of the condenser is to absorb the excessive voltage from the points when they open and thus prevent the points from becoming pitted or burned.

If you have ever wondered why it is necessary to tune-up your engine occasionally, consider the fact that the ignition system must complete the above cycle each time a spark plug fires. On a four-cylinder, four-cycle engine, two of the four plugs must fire once for every engine revolution. If the idle speed of your engine is 800 revolutions per minute (800 rpm), the breaker points open

Tune-Up Specifications

Year	Engine Type	Spark Plugs Type (ND)	Gap (in.)	Distributor Point Dwell (deg)	Point Gap (in.)	Ignition Timing (deg) ③ MT	AT	Compression Press.	Fuel Pump Press.	Idle Speed (rpm) MT	AT	Valve Clearance (in.) (hot) Intake	Exhaust
1975–77	2T-C	W16EP	0.030	52 ①	0.018	10B ⑤	10B ⑤	171	2.8–4.3 ⑥	850	850	0.008	0.013
1970–77	3K-C	W20EP	0.031	52	0.018	5B	—	156	2.8–4.3	750	—	0.008	0.012
1971–74	2T-C	W20EP	0.031	52	0.018	5B	5B	170	2.8–4.3	750	650	0.007	0.013
1978–79	3K-C	BPR5EA-L	0.031	Electronic		8B	8B	156	3.0–4.5	750	750	0.008	0.012
	2T-C	BP5EA-L	0.031	Electronic		10B ⑨	10B ⑨	171	3.0–4.5	850	850	0.008	0.013
1980–81	1A-C	BP6EK-A	0.039	Electronic ②		5B	—	177	—	650	800	0.008	0.012
	3A	BPR5EA-L	0.031	52	0.018	5B	—	177	—	650	800	0.008	0.012
	3T-C	BPR5EA	0.043	Electronic		10B	10B	163	—	850 ④	850 ④	0.008	0.013
	4K-C	BPR5EA-L-11 ⑩	0.043	Electronic		8B	—	156	2.8–4.2	650 ④	—	0.008	0.012

NOTE: If the information given in this chart disagrees with the information on the emission control specification decal, use the specifications on the decal.

① Dual points—main 57°, sub. 52°
② Air gap 0.008–0.016 inch
③ With vacuum advance disconnected
④ M/T without power steering—700 rpm
   A/T without power steering—750 rpm
⑤ Dual points—main 12B, sub. 19–25B (degrees)
⑥ Electric pump (California)—2.4 to 3.8 psi
⑨ California—8B
⑩ Calif.: BPR5EA-L
M/T Manual transmission
A/T Automatic transmission
TDC Top dead center
B Before top dead center
A After top dead center

and close two times for each revolution. For every minute your engine idles, your points open and close 1,600 times (2 < 800 = 1,600). And that is just at idle. What about at 60 mph?

There are two ways to check breaker point gap: with a feeler gauge or with a dwell meter. Either way you set the points, you are adjusting the amount of time (in degrees of distributor rotation) that the points will remain open. If you adjust the points with a feeler gauge, you are setting the maximum amount the points will open when the rubbing block on the points is on a high point of the distributor cam. When you adjust the points with a dwell meter, you are measuring the number of degrees (of distributor cam rotation) that the points will remain closed before they start to open as a high point of the distributor cam approaches the rubbing block of the points.

If you still do not understand how the points function, take a friend, go outside, and remove the distributor cap from your engine. Have your friend operate the starter (make sure that the transmission is not in gear) as you look at the exposed parts of the distributor.

There are two rules that should always be followed when adjusting or replacing points. *The points and condenser are a matched set; never replace one without replacing the other. If you change the point gap or dwell of the engine, you also change the ignition timing. Therefore, if you adjust the points, you must also adjust the timing.*

INSPECTION AND CLEANING

The breaker points should be inspected and cleaned at 6,000 mile intervals. To do so, perform the following steps:

1. Disconnect the high-tension lead from the coil.

2. Unsnap the two distributor cap retaining clips and lift the cap straight up. Leave the leads connected to the cap and position it out of the way.

3. Remove the rotor and dust cover by pulling them straight up.

4. Place a screwdriver against the breaker points and pry them open. Examine their condition. If they are excessively worn, burned, or pitted, they should be replaced.

5. Polish the points with a point file. Do not use emery cloth or sandpaper; these may leave particles on the points causing them to arc.

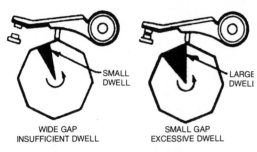

WIDE GAP
INSUFFICIENT DWELL   —SMALL DWELL

SMALL GAP
EXCESSIVE DWELL   —LARGE DWELL

Dwell as a function of point gap

6. Clean the distributor cap and rotor with alcohol. Inspect the cap terminals for looseness and corrosion. Check the rotor tip for excessive burning. Inspect both cap and rotor for cracks. Replace either if they show any of the above signs of wear or damage.

7. Check the operation of the centrifugal advance mechanism by turning the rotor clockwise. Release the rotor; it should return to its original position. If it doesn't, check for binding parts.

8. Check the vacuum advance unit, by removing the plastic cap and pressing on the octane selector. It should return to its original position. Check for binding if it doesn't.

9. If the points do not require replacement, proceed with the adjustment section below. Otherwise perform the point and condenser replacement procedures.

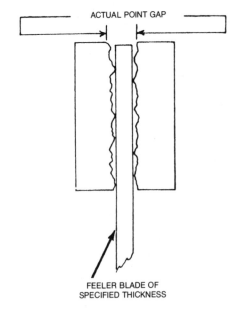

ACTUAL POINT GAP

FEELER BLADE OF
SPECIFIED THICKNESS

The feeler gauge method of checking point gap is less accurate than the dwell meter method

POINT REPLACEMENT

The points should be replaced every 12,000 miles (24,000 miles with transistorized ignition), or if they are badly pitted, worn, or burned. To replace them, proceed as follows:

1. If you have not already done so, perform Steps 1 through 3 of the preceding "inspection and Cleaning" procedure.

2. Unfasten the point lead connector.

3. Remove the point retaining clip and unfasten the point hold-down screw(s). It is a good idea to use a magnetic or locking screwdriver to remove the small screws inside the distributor, since they are almost impossible to find once they have been dropped.

4. Lift out the point set.

5. Install the new point set in the reverse order of removal. Adjust the points as detailed below, after completing installation.

CONDENSER REPLACEMENT

Replace the condenser whenever the points are replaced, or if it is suspected of being defective. On Toyota passenger cars the condenser is located on the outside of the distributor. To replace it, proceed as follows:

1. Carefully remove the nut and washer from the condenser lead terminal.

2. Use a magnetic or locking screwdriver to remove the condenser mounting screw.

3. Remove the condenser.

Installation of a new condenser is performed in the reverse order of removal.

ADJUSTMENT

Perform the gap adjustment procedure whenever new points are installed, or as part of routine maintenance. If you are adjusting an old set of points, you must check the dwell as well, since the feeler gauge is only really accurate with a new point set.

1. Rotate the engine by hand or by using

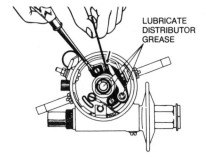

LUBRICATE
DISTRIBUTOR
GREASE

Adjustment of the points and distributor lubrication

a remote starter switch, so that the rubbing block is on the high point of the cam lobe.

2. Insert a 0.018 in. feeler gauge between the points; a slight drag should be felt.

3. If no drag is felt or if the feeler gauge cannot be inserted at all, loosen, but do not remove, the point hold-down screw.

4. Insert a screwdriver into the adjustment slot. Rotate the screwdriver until the proper point gap is attained. The point gap is increased by rotating the screwdriver counterclockwise and decreased by rotating it clockwise.

5. Tighten the point hold-down screw.

Lubricate the cam lobes, breaker arm, rubbing block, arm pivot, and distributor shaft with special high-temperature distributor grease.

Transistorized Ignition

Transistorized ignition was first used on 1974 4M engines sold in California. With the introduction of 1975 models, usage has been extended to all Toyota vehicles sold in the United States.

The transistorized ignition system employed by Toyota works very much like the conventional system previously described. Regular breaker points are used, but instead of switching primary current to the coil off-and-on, they are used to trigger a switching transistor. The transistor, in turn, switches the coil primary current on and off.

Since only a very small amount of current is needed to operate the transistor, the points will not become burned or pitted, as they would if they had full primary current passing through them. This also allows the primary current to be higher than usual because the use of a higher current would normally cause the points to fail much more rapidly.

As already stated, the condenser is used to absorb any extra high-voltage passing through the points. Since, in the transistorized system, there is no high current, no condenser is needed or used.

As a result of the lower stress placed on them, the points only have to be replaced every 24,000 miles instead of the usual 12,000 miles.

The Toyota transistorized ignition system may be quickly identified by the lack of a condenser on the outside of the distributor and by the addition of a control box, which is connected between the distributor and the primary side of the coil.

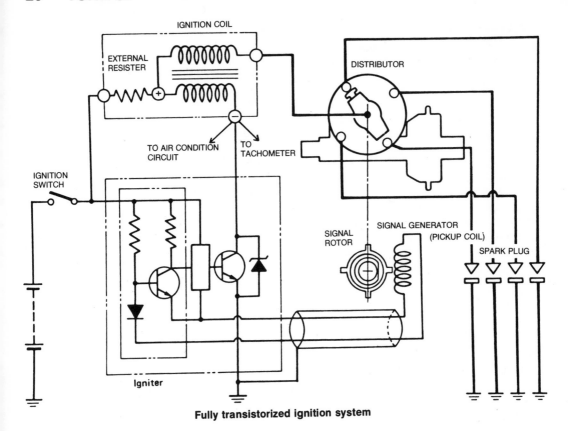

Fully transistorized ignition system

In 1975 all Toyota models are equipped with the transistorized ignition system introduced on California models a year earlier. A *fully* transistorized system, including an ignition signal generating mechanism instead of the normal contact points, was first installed on all California Celica GTs. This became the standard ignition system used on all 1978–81 models.

The mechanism consists of a timing rotor, a magnet and a pick-up coil, all mounted in place of the points inside the distributor. As the signal rotor spins, the teeth on it pass a projection leading from the pick-up coil. When this happens voltage is allowed to pass through the system, firing the sparkplugs. There is no physical contact and no electric arcing, hence no need to replace burnt or worn parts.

SERVICE PRECAUTIONS

Basically, the transistorized ignition is serviced just like its conventional counterpart. The points must be checked, adjusted, and replaced in the same manner. Point gap and dwell must be checked and set. The points should also be kept clean and should be replaced at 24,000 mile intervals. Of course,

since there is no condenser, it does not have to be replaced when the points are.

However, there are several precautions to observe when servicing the transistorized ignition system:

1. Use only pure alcohol to clean the points. Shop solvent or an oily rag will leave a film on the points which will not allow the low current to pass.

2. Hook up a tachometer, dwell meter, or a combination dwell/tachometer to the *negative* (−) side of the coil; NOT to the distributor or the positive (+) side. Damage to the switching transistor will result if the meter is connected in the usual manner.

3. See the previous section for the remaining service procedures which are identical to those for the conventional ignition system.

Dwell Angle

1. Connect a dwell meter to the ignition system, according to the manufacturer's instructions.

   a. When checking the dwell on a conventional ignition system, connect one meter lead (usually black) to a metallic part of the car to ground the meter; the other lead (usually red) is connected to the coil primary post (the one with the small lead which runs to the distributor body);

b. When checking dwell on a model with a transistorized ignition, ground one meter lead (usually black) to a metallic part of the car; hook up the other lead (usually red) to the negative (−) coil terminal. Under no circumstances should the meter be connected to the distributor or the positive (+) side of the coil. (See the preceding "Service Precautions").

2. If the dwell meter has a set line, adjust the needle until it rests on the line.

3. Start the engine. It should be warmed-up and running at the specified idle speed.

CAUTION: *Be sure to keep fingers, tools, clothes, hair, and wires clear of the engine fan. The transmission should be in Neutral (or Park), parking brake set, and running in a well-ventilated area.*

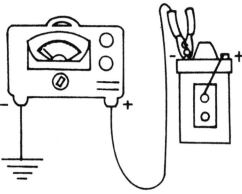

Dwell meter connections with transistorized ignition

4. Check the reading on the dwell meter. If you have a Toyota with a four-cylinder engine and your meter doesn't have a four-cylinder scale, multiply the eight-cylinder reading by two.

5. If the meter reading is within the range specified in the "Tune-Up Specifications" chart, shut the engine off and disconnect the dwell meter.

6. If the dwell is not within specifications, shut the engine off and adjust the point gap as previously outlined. Increasing the point gap decreases the dwell angle and vice versa.

7. Adjust the points until dwell is within specifications, then disconnect the dwell meter. Adjust the timing; see the following section.

Adjusting Pickup Air Gap
FULLY TRANSISTORIZED IGNITION SYSTEM

1. Remove the distributor cap, rotor, and dust shield.

2. Turn the engine over (you may use a socket wrench on the front pulley bolt to do this) until the projection on the pickup coil is *directly* opposite the signal rotor tooth.

3. Get a non-ferrous (paper, brass, or plastic) feeler gauge of .012 in., and insert it into the pickup air gap. DO NOT USE AN ORDINARY METAL FEELER GAUGE! The gauge should just touch either side of the gap (the permissible range is .008–.016 in.).

4. If the gap is either too wide or too narrow, loosen the two phillips screws mounting the pickup coil onto the distributor base plate. Then, wedge a screwdriver between the notch in the pickup coil assembly and the two dimples on the base plate, and turn the screwdriver back and forth until the pickup gap is correct.

5. Tighten the screws and recheck gap, readjusting if necessary.

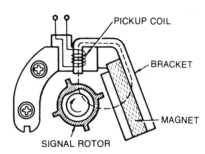

Parts of the fully transistorized ignition system signal generator

Ignition Timing

Ignition timing is the measurement in degrees of crankshaft rotation of the instant the spark plugs in the cylinders fire, in relation to the location of the piston, while the piston is on its compression stroke.

Ignition timing is adjusted by loosening the distributor locking device and turning the distributor in the engine.

Ideally, the air/fuel mixture in the cylinder will be ignited (by the spark plug) and just beginning its rapid expansion as the piston passes top dead center (TDC) of the compression stroke. If this happens, the piston will be beginning the power stroke just as the compressed (by the movement of the

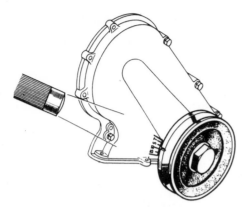

3K-C, 4K-C and 2T-C timing marks

1A-C, 3A, 3A-C timing marks

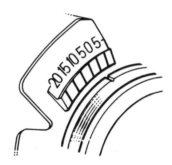

3T-C timing marks

piston) and ignited (by the spark plug) air/fuel mixture starts to expand. The expansion of the air/fuel mixture will then force the piston down on the power stroke and turn the crankshaft.

It takes a fraction of a second for the spark from the plug to completely ignite the mixture in the cylinder. Because of this, the spark plug must fire before the piston reaches TDC, if the mixture is to be completely ignited as the piston passed TDC. This measurement is given in degrees (of crankshaft rotation) *before* the piston reaches *top dead center* (BTDC). If the ignition timing setting for your engine is seven degrees

(7°) BTDC, this means that the spark plug must fire at a time when the piston for that cylinder is 7° before top dead center of its compression stroke. However, this only holds true while your engine is at idle speed.

As you accelerate from idle, the speed of your engine (rpm) increases. The increase in rpm means that the pistons are now traveling up and down much faster. Because of this, the spark plugs will have to fire even sooner if the mixture is to be completely ignited as the piston passes TDC. To accomplish this, the distributor incorporates means to advance the timing of the spark as engine speed increases.

The distributor in your Toyota has two means of advancing the ignition timing. One is called centrifugal advance and is actuated by weights in the distributor. The other is called vacuum advance and is controlled by that large circular housin6g on the side of the distributor.

In addition, some distributors have a vacuum-retard mechanism which is contained in the same housing on the side of the distributor as the vacuum advance. The function of this mechanism is to retard the timing of the ignition spark under certain engine conditions. This causes more complete burning of the air/fuel mixture in the cylinder and consequently lowers exhaust emissions.

Because these mechanisms change ignition timing, it is necessary to disconnect and plug the one or two vacuum lines from the distributor when setting the basic ignition timing.

If ignition timing is set too far advanced (BTDC), the ignition and expansion of the air/fuel mixture in the cylinder will try to force the piston down the cylinder while it is still traveling upward. This causes engine "ping," a sound which resembles marbles being dropped into an empty tin can. If the ignition timing is too far retarded (after, or ATDC), the piston will have already started down on the power stroke when the air/fuel mixture ignites and expands. This will cause the piston to be forced down only a portion of its travel. This will result in poor engine performance and lack of power.

Ignition timing adjustment is checked with a timing light. This instrument is connected to the number one (No. 1) spark plug of the engine. The timing light flashes every time an electrical current is sent from the distributor, through the No. 1 spark plug wire, to the spark plug. The crankshaft pulley and the front cover of the engine are marked with a timing pointer and a timing scale. When the timing pointer is aligned with the "0" mark on the timing scale, the piston in No. 1 cylinder is at TDC of its compression stroke. With the engine running, and the timing light aimed at the timing pointer and timing scale, the stroboscopic flashes from the timing light will allow you to check the ignition timing wetting of the engine. The timing light flashes every time the spark plug in the No. 1 cylinder of the engine fires. Since the flash from the timing light makes the crankshaft pulley seem stationary for a moment, you will be able to read the exact position of the piston in the No. 1 cylinder on the timing scale on the front of the engine.

CHECKING AND ADJUSTMENT

Single Point Distributor

1. Warm-up the engine. Connect a tachometer and check the engine idle speed to be sure that it is within the specification given in the "Tune-Up Specifications" chart at the beginning of the chapter.

2. If the timing marks are difficult to see, use a dab of paint or chalk to make them more visible.

3. Connect a timing light according to the manufacturer's instructions. If the light has three wires, one (usually blue or green) must be installed with an adapter between the No. 1 spark plug lead and the spark plug. The other leads are connected to the positive (+) battery terminal (usually a red lead) and the other to the negative (−) battery terminal (usually a black lead).

4. Disconnect the vacuum line(s) from the distributor vacuum unit. Plug it (them) with a pencil or golf tee(s).

5. Be sure that the timing light wires are clear of the fan and start the engine.

CAUTION: *Keep fingers, clothes, tools, hair, and leads clear of the spinning engine fan. Be sure that you are running the engine in a well-ventilated area.*

6. Allow the engine to run at the specified idle speed with the gearshift in Neutral with manual transmission and Drive (D) with automatic transmission.

CAUTION: *Be sure that the parking brake is set and that the front wheels are blocked to prevent the car from rolling forward, especially when Drive is selected with an automatic.*

7. Point the timing marks at the marks indicated in the chart and illustrations below.

With the engine at idle, timing should be at the specification given on the "Tune-Up Specifications" chart at the beginning of the chapter.

8. If the timing is not at the specification, loosen the pinch-bolt at the base of the distributor just enough so that the distributor can be turned. Turn the distributor to advance or retard the timing as required. Once the proper marks are seen to align with the timing light, timing is correct.

9. Stop the engine and tighten the pinch-bolt. Start the engine and recheck timing. Stop the engine; disconnect the tachometer and timing light. Connect the vacuum line(s) to the distributor vacuum unit.

Dual Point Distributor

A dual point distributor is offered as an option on some Corolla models, sold outside of California, in 1975.

To adjust the dual point system, proceed as follows:

1. Adjust the timing for the main set of points as previously outlined in the "Single Point" section.

2. Use a jumper wire to ground the terminal on the thermoswitch connector after removing the connector from the thermoswitch. The thermoswitch is threaded into the intake manifold and is connected to the dual point system relay. Be careful not to confuse it with any of the emission control system switches which are connected to the computer.

3. Check the timing with a light as described above, the timing should be 22° before top dead center (BTDC).

4. If the timing is off, connect a dwell meter to the *negative* side of the coil, and adjust the sub-points so that the dwell angle is 52°. The sub-points are adjusted in the same manner as the main points.

5. Remove the test equipment and reconnect the thermoswitch.

Fully Transistorized Ignition Troubleshooting

Troubleshooting this system is easy, but you must have an accurate ohmmeter and voltmeter. The numbers in the diagram correspond to the numbers of the following troubleshooting steps. Be sure to perform each step in order.

1. Check for a spark at the spark plugs by hooking up a timing light in the usual man-

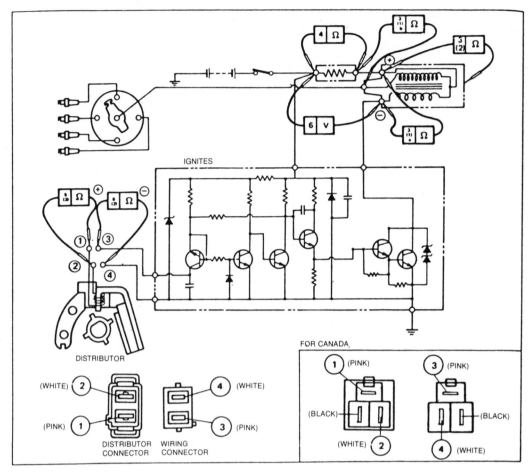

Fully transistorized ignition troubleshooting

ner. If the light flashes, it can be assumed that voltage is reaching the plugs, which should then be inspected, along with the fuel system. If no flash is generated, go on to the following ignition checks.

2. Check all wiring and plastic connectors for tight and proper connections.

3. (1) With an ohmmeter, check between the positive (+) and negative (−) primary terminals of the ignition coil. The resistance (cold) should be 1.3–1.7 ohms. Between the (+) primary terminal and the high tension terminal, the resistance (cold) should be 12–16 kilo-ohms.

(2) The insulation resistance between the (+) primary terminal and the ignition coil case should be infinite.

4. The resistor wire (brown and yellow) resistance should be 1.2 ohms (cold). To measure, disconnect the plastic connector at the igniter and connect one wire of the ohmmeter to the yellow wire and one to the brown.

5. Remove the distributor cap and ignition rotor . (1) Check the air gap between the tim-

ing rotor spoke and the pick-up coil. When aligned, the air gap should be 0.008–0.016 in. You will probably have to bump the engine around with the starter to line up the timing rotor.

(2) Unplug the distributor connector at the distributor. Connect one wire of the ohmmeter to the white wire, and one wire to the pink wire. The resistance of the signal generator should be 130–190 ohms.

6. (1) Checking the igniter last, connect the (−) voltmeter wire to the (−) ignition coil primary terminal, and the (+) voltmeter wire to the yellow resistor wire at the connector unplugged in Step 4. With the ignition switch turned to "On" (not "Start") the voltage should measure 12 volts.

(2) Check the voltage between the (−) ignition coil primary terminal and the yellow resistor wire again, but this time use the ohmmeter as resistance. Using the igniter end of the distributor connector unplugged in Step 5, connect the positive (+) ohmmeter wire to the pink distributor wire, and the

negative (−) ohmmeter wire to the white wire.

CAUTION: *Do not intermix the (+) and (−) terminals of the ohmmeter.*

Select either the 1 ohm or 10 ohm range of the ohmmeter. With the voltmeter connected as in Step 6 (1), and the ignition switch turned to "On" (not "Start"), the voltage should measure nearly zero.

Octane Selector

The octane selector is used as a fine adjustment to match the vehicle's ignition timing to the grade of gasoline being used. It is located near the distributor vacuum unit, beneath a plastic dust cover. Normally the octane slector should not require adjustment, however, adjustment is as follows:

1. Align the setting line with the threaded end of the housing and then align the center line with the setting mark on the housing.

2. Drive the car to the speed specified in the "Octane Selector Test Speeds" chart in High gear on a level road.

3. Depress the accelerator pedal all the way to the floor. A slight "pinging" sound should be heard. As the car accelerates, the sound should gradually go away.

4. If the pinging sound is low or if it fails to disappear as the vehicle speed increases, retard the timing by turning the knob toward "R" (Retard).

5. If there is no pinging sound at all, advance the timing by turning the knob toward "A" (Advance).

NOTE: *On 1973–79 models, do not turn the octane selector more than ½ turn toward "R." Do not turn it toward "A" at all.*

6. When the adjustment is completed, replace the plastic dust cover.

NOTE: *One graduation of the octane selector is equal to about ten degrees of crankshaft angle.*

Valve Adjustment

Since all Toyota models are equipped with mechanical valve lifters, they should be ad-

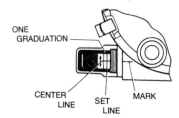

ONE GRADUATION

CENTER LINE   SET LINE   MARK

Octane selector

Octane Selector Test Speeds

Engine Type	Test Speed (mph)
3K-C	19–21
2T-C	16–22

justed at the factory-recommended intervals (every 12,000 miles).

Valve adjustment is one factor which determines how far the intake and exhaust valves will open into the cylinder.

If the valve clearance is too large, part of the lift of the camshaft will be used up in removing the excessive clearance, thus the valves will not be opened far enough. This condition has two effects, the valve train components will emit a tapping noise as they take up the excessive clearance and the engine will perform poorly, since the less the intake valves open, the smaller the amount of air/fuel mixture that will be admitted to the cylinders. The less the exhaust valves open, the greater the back-pressure in the cylinder which prevents the proper air/fuel mixture from entering the cylinder.

If the valve clearance is too small, the intake and exhaust valves will not fully seat on the cylinder head when they close. When a valve seats on the cylinder head it does two things; it seals the combustion chamber so none of the gases in the cylinder can escape and it cools itself by transferring some of the heat it absorbed from the combustion process through the cylinder head and into the engine cooling system. Therefore, if the valve clearance is too small, the engine will run poorly (due to gases escaping from the combustion chamber), and the valves will overheat and warp (since they cannot transfer heat unless they are touching the seat in the cylinder head).

While all valve adjustments must be as accurate as possible, it is better to have the valve adjustment slightly loose than slightly tight, as burnt valves may result from overly tight adjustments.

ADJUSTMENT PROCEDURES
3K-C and 2T-C Engines

1. Start the engine and allow it to reach normal operating temperature (165–185° F). Once the engine is warmed-up, be careful when touching any metal parts under the hood, particularly the exhaust manifold, as things get hot.

2. Stop the engine. Remove the air

Special oil splash tray for 3K-C

cleaner assembly, its hoses, and its bracket. Remove any other hoses, cables, etc., attached to the valve cover. On 2T-C engines, temporarily remove the spark plug leads after marking them for correct installation. Remove the valve cover. Reinstall the spark plug leads.

3. On 3K-C engines, tighten the cylinder head bolts, in the proper sequence (see Chapter 3) to the following values:

3K-C—35–48 ft. lbs.

4. Next, on the 3K-C engine only, tighten the valve rocker support bolts to 13–17 ft. lbs.

CAUTION: *Tighten all of the above bolts in the proper sequence (see Chapter 3) and in three stages.*

5. Install a suitable oil tray on the 3K-C engine, to prevent hot engine oil from being splashed out.

NOTE: *The tray may be ordered from a dealer or fabricated from sheet metal. (See the illustration.)*

6. Start the engine. Check the clearance between the rocker arm and the valve stem with a feeler gauge, for each valve. The clearance specifications are given in the "Tune-Up Specifications" chart at the beginning of this chapter.

7. If the valves require adjustment, loosen the locknut and turn the adjustment screw to obtain the proper clearance.

8. Tighten the locknut. Check the valve clearance to be sure that it was not disturbed when the locknut was tightened.

9. When the valve inspection and adjustment are completed, replace the valve cover and all of the other components which are removed.

1A-C, 2A, 3A, 4K-C

1. Run the engine to normal operating temperature.

2. Stop the engine. Remove the air cleaner and any other components that are in the way.

3. Turn the crankshaft to align the timing marks 2T TDC. Check that the rocker arms on #1 cylinder are loose and those on #4 are

tight. If not, turn the crankshaft 1 complete revolution.

4. Adjust #1 int. and exh.; #2 int.; #3 exh.

5. Check the clearance between the rocker arm and the valve stem. This measurement is listed in the tune-up chart.

6. If the clearance is not correct loosen the nut and turn the adjusting screw to the correct gap.

NOTE: *For this measurement you will need a set of feeler gauges.*

7. Once you have the proper clearance tighten the nut, and at the same time hold onto the adjusting screw. This is accomplished by using a box type wrench and a screwdriver.

8. Turn the crankshaft 1 complete revolution and adjust the remaining valves.

9. Reinstall the valve cover.

NOTE: *Make sure that you install a new valve cover gasket.*

Carburetor

This section contains only carburetor adjustments as they normally apply to engine tuneup. Descriptions of the carburetor and complete adjustment procedures can be found in Chapter 4.

When the engine in your Toyota is running, air/fuel mixture from the carburetor is being drawn into the engine by a partial vacuum which is created by the downward movement of the pistons on the intake stroke of the four-stroke cycle of the engine. The amount of air/fuel mixture that enters the engine is controlled by throttle plates in the bottom of the carburetor. When the engine is not running, the throttle plates are closed, completely blocking off the bottom of the carburetor from the inside of the engine. The throttle plates are connected, through the throttle linkage, to the gas pedal in the passenger compartment of the car. After you start the engine and put the transmission in gear, you depress the gas pedal to start the car moving. What you actually are doing when you depress the gas pedal is opening the throttle plate in the carburetor to admit more of the air/fuel mixture to the engine. The further you open the throttle plates in the carburetor, the higher the engine speed becomes.

As previously stated, when the engine is not running, the throttle plates in the carburetor are closed. When the engine is idling, it is necessary to open the throttle plates slightly. To prevent having to keep your foot on the gas pedal when the engine is idling, an idle speed adjusting screw was added to the carburetor. This screw has the same effect as keeping your foot slightly depressed on the gas pedal. The idle speed adjusting screw contacts a lever (the throttle lever) on the outside of the carburetor. When the screw is turned in, it opens the throttle plate on the carburetor, raising the idle speed of the engine. This screw is called the curb idle adjusting screw, and the procedures in this section will tell you how to adjust it.

Since it is difficult for the engine to draw the air/fuel mixture from the carburetor with the small amount of throttle plate opening that is present when the engine is idling, an idle mixture passage is provided in the carburetor. This passage delivers air/fuel mixture to the engine from a hole which is located in the bottom of the carburetor below the throttle plates. This idle mixture passage contains an adjusting screw which restricts the amount of air/fuel mixture that enters the engine at idle. The procedures given in this section will tell how to set the idle mixture adjusting screw.

IDLE SPEED AND MIXTURE

1970–74

NOTE: *Perform the following adjustments with the air cleaner in place. When adjusting the idle speed and mixture, the gear selector should be placed in Drive (D) on 1970–73 models equipped with an automatic transmission. Be sure to set the parking brake and block the front wheels. On all cars equipped with manual transmissions and all 1974 automatics, adjust the idle speed with the gearshift in Neutral (N).*

1. Run the engine until it reaches normal operating temperature. Stop the engine.
2. Connect a tachometer to the engine as detailed in the manufacturer's instructions.

   a. On models having a conventional ignition system, one lead (usually black) goes to a good chassis ground. The other lead (usually red) goes to the distributor primary side of the coil (the terminal with small wire running to the distributor body);

   b. On models with transistorized ignition, connect one lead (usually black) of the tachometer to a good chassis ground. Connect the other lead (usually red) to the negative (−) coil terminal; NOT to the distributor or positive (+) side. Connecting the

Vacuum at Idle
(in. Hg)

Year	Engine	Transmission	Minimum Vacuum Gauge Reading
1970–72	3K-C	All	16.9
	2T-C	All	16.9
1973	3K-C	MT	16.5
	2T-C	MT AT	16.9 14.1
1974	3K-C	MT	16.5
	2T-C ①	All	16.9
	2T-C ②	All	15.7

MT—Manual transmission
AT—Automatic transmission
① All US cars except California
② California only

tach to the wrong side will damage the switching transistor.

3. Remove the plug and install a vacuum gauge in the manifold vacuum port by using a suitable metric adapter.
4. Start the engine and allow it to stabilize at idle.
5. Turn the idle speed screw until the engine runs smoothly at the lowest possible engine speed without stalling.
6. Turn the idle speed screw until the vacuum gauge indicates the highest specified reading (see the "Vacuum At Idle" chart) at the specified idle speed. (See the "Tune-Up Specifications" chart at the beginning of the chapter.)
7. Tighten the idle speed screw to the point just before the engine rpm and vacuum readings drop off.
8. Remove the tachometer and the vacuum gauge. Install the plug back in the manifold vacuum port. Road-test the vehicle.
9. In some states, emission inspection is required. In such cases, you should take your car to a diagnostic center which has an HC/CO meter, and have the idle emission level checked to be sure that it is in accordance with state regulations. Starting 1974, CO levels at idle are given on the engine tune-up decal under the hood.

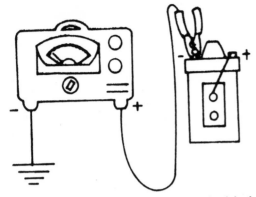

Tachometer connection with transistorized ignition

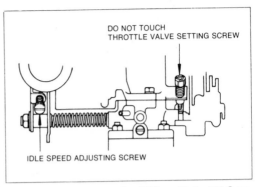

Carburetor adjustment for 1978 and later 3K-C engine

1975–77

The idle speed and mixture should be adjusted under the following conditions: the air cleaner must be installed, the choke fully opened, the transmission should be in Neutral (N), all accessories should be turned off, all vacuum lines should be connected, and the ignition timing should be set to specification.

1. Start the engine and allow it to reach normal operating temperature (180°F).

2. Check the float setting; the fuel level should be just about even with the spot on the sight glass. If the fuel level is too high or low, adjust the float level. (See Chapter 4).

3. Connect a tachometer in accordance with the manufacturer's instructions. However, connect the tachometer positive (+) lead to the coil Negative (−) terminal. Do NOT hook it up to the distributor or positive (+) side; damage to the transistorized ignition will result.

4. Adjust the speed to the highest rpm it will attain with the idle mixture adjusting screw.

5. Set the rpm to the idle mixture speed of 930 rpm. by turning the idle speed adjusting screw. You may have to repeat Steps 4 and 5 a few times until the highest idle reached in Step 4 will go no further.

6. Now set the speed to the initial idle speed of 850 rpm ±50 by turning the idle mixture adjusting screw in (clockwise).

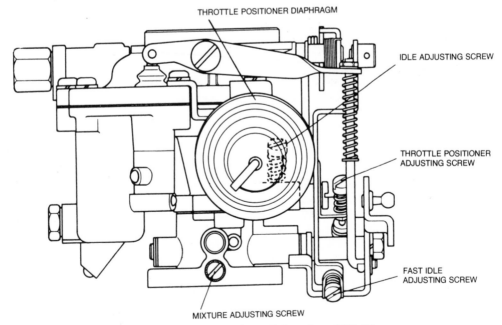

Carburetor adjustments for 3K-C engine—1971–77

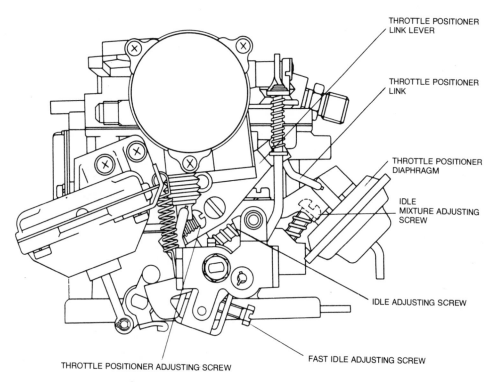

Carburetor adjustments for 2T-C engines—1971–74

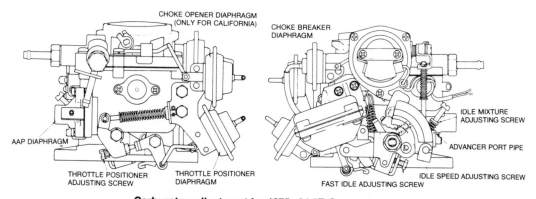

Carburetor adjustment for 1975–81 2T-C engine

7. Disconnect the tachometer.

1978–81

Use the same procedure for 1975–77 models, described above. However, substitute different idle mixture and idle speeds as specified below:

a. For idle mixture speeds (Step 5), use the following specifications:

1978–81 2T-C—920 Federal Engines, 910 California and High Altitude engines

1978–81 3K-C	830
1979–81 3K-C	830
1981 4K-C	650

b. For idle speed (Step 6), use the following figures:

1978–81 2T-C	850
1978–81 3K-C	750
1980–81 1A-C, 3A, 3A-C	750
1981 4K-C	680

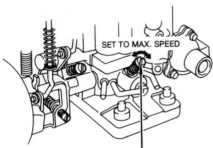

SET TO MAX. SPEED

IDLE MIXTURE ADJUSTING SCREW

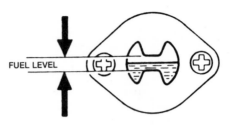

FUEL LEVEL

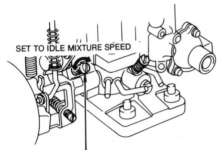

SET TO IDLE MIXTURE SPEED

IDLE SPEED ADJUSTING SCREW

SET TO MAXIMUM SPEED

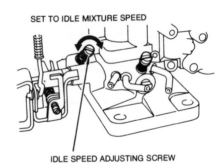

IDLE MIXTURE ADJUSTING SCREW

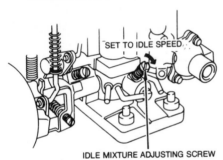

SET TO IDLE SPEED

IDLE MIXTURE ADJUSTING SCREW

3T-C carburetor adjustment points

SET TO IDLE MIXTURE SPEED

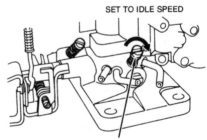

IDLE SPEED ADJUSTING SCREW

IDLE SPEED ADJUSTING SCREW

SET TO IDLE SPEED

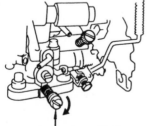

IDLE MIXTURE ADJUSTING SCREW

IDLE MIXTURE ADJUSTING SCREW

1A-C, 3A, 3A-C carburetor adjustment points

4K-C carburetor adjustment points

Engine and Engine Rebuilding

ENGINE ELECTRICAL

Distributor

REMOVAL

To remove the distributor, proceed in the following order:

1. Unfasten the retaining clips and lift the distributor cap straight up. It will be easier to install the distributor if the wiring is left connected to the cap. If the wires must be removed from the cap, mark their positions to aid in installation.

2. Remove the dust cover and mark the position of the rotor relative to the distributor body; then mark the position of the body relative to the block.

3. Disconnect the coil primary wire and the vacuum line(s). If the distributor vacuum unit has two vacuum lines, mark which is which for installation.

4. Remove the pinch-bolt and lift the distributor straight up, away from the engine. The rotor and body are marked so that they can be returned to the position from which they were removed. Do not turn or disturb the engine (unless absolutely necessary, such as for engine rebuilding), after the distributor has been removed.

INSTALLATION—TIMING NOT DISTURBED

1. Insert the distributor in the block and align the matchmarks made during removal.

2. Engage the distributor driven gear with the distributor drive.

3. Install the distributor clamp and secure it with the pinch-bolt.

4. Install the cap, primary wire, and vacuum line(s).

5. Install the spark plug leads. Consult the marks made during removal to be sure that the proper lead goes to each plug. Install the high-tension wire if it was removed.

6. Start the engine. Check the timing and adjust it and the octane selector, as outlined in chapter 2.

INSTALLATION—TIMING LOST

If the engine has been cranked, dismantled, or the timing otherwise lost, proceed as follows:

1. Determine top dead center (TDC) of the No. 1 cylinder's compression stroke by removing the spark plug from the No. 1 cylinder and placing your finger on a vacuum gauge over the spark plug hole. This is important because the timing marks will also line up with the last cylinder in the firing order in its exhaust stroke.

CAUTION: *On engines which have the spark plugs buried in the exhaust manifold, use a compression gauge or a screwdriver handle, not your finger, if the manifold is still hot.*

Crank the engine until compression pressure starts to build up. Continue cranking the engine until the timing marks indicate TDC (or "0").

2. Next align the timing marks to the specifications given in the "Ignition Timing" column of the "Tune-Up Specifications" chart at the beginning of Chapter 2.

3. Temporarily install the rotor in the distributor without the dust cover. Turn the distributor shaft so that the rotor is pointing toward the No. 1 terminal in the distributor cap. The points should just be about to open.

4. Use a small screwdriver to align the slot on the distributor drive (oil pump driveshaft) with the key on the bottom of the distributor shaft.

5. Align the matchmarks on the distributor body and the block which were made during the removal. Install the distributor in the block by rotating it slightly (no more than one gear tooth in either direction) until the driven gear meshes with the drive.

NOTE: *Oil the distributor spiral gear and the oil pump driveshaft end before distributor installation.*

6. Rotate the distributor, once it is installed, so that the points are just about to open or the projection on the pickup coil is almost opposite the signal rotor tooth. Temporarily tighten the pinchbolt.

7. Remove the rotor and install the dust cover. Replace the rotor and the distributor cap.

8. Install the primary wire and the vacuum line(s).

9. Install the No. 1 spark plug. Connect the cables to the spark plugs in the proper order by using the marks made during removal. Install the high-tension lead if it was removed.

10. Start the engine. Adjust the ignition timing and the octane selector, as outlined in Chapter 2.

Firing Order

To avoid confusion, spark plug wires should be replaced one at a time.

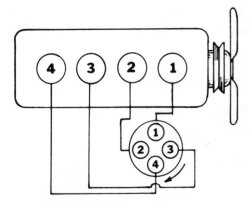

All four cylinder engines

Alternator

ALTERNATOR PRECAUTIONS

1. Always observe proper polarity of the battery connections; be especially careful when jump-starting the car.

2. Never ground or short out any alternator or alternator regulator terminals.

3. Never operate the alternator with any of its or the battery's leads disconnected.

4. Always remove the battery or disconnect its output lead while charging it.

5. Always disconnect the ground cable when replacing any electrical components.

6. Never subject the alternator to excessive heat or dampness if the engine is being steam-cleaned.

7. Never use arc-welding equipment with the alternator connected.

REMOVAL AND INSTALLATION

NOTE: *On some models the alternator is mounted very low on the engine. On these models it may be necessary to remove the gravel shield and work from underneath the car in order to gain access to the alternator.*

1. Unfasten the starter-to-battery cable at the battery end.

2. Remove the air cleaner, if necessary, to gain access to the alternator.

3. Unfasten the bolts which attach the adjusting link to the alternator. Remove the alternator drive belt.

4. Unfasten the alternator wiring connections.

5. Remove the alternator attaching bolt and then withdraw the alternator from its bracket.

6. Installation is performed in the reverse

order of removal. After installing the alternator, adjust the belt tension as detailed in Chapter 1.

Regulator

REMOVAL AND INSTALLATION

1. Remove the cable from the negative (−) battery terminal and then remove the cable from the positive (+) battery terminal.
2. Disconnect the wiring harness connector at the regulator.
3. Unfasten the bolts which secure the regulator. Remove the regulator and its condenser.
4. Installation is the reverse of removal.

VOLTAGE ADJUSTMENT

1. Connect a voltmeter up to the battery terminals. Negative (black) lead to the negative (−) terminal; positive (red) lead to positive (+) terminal.
2. Start the engine and gradually increase its speed to about 1,500 rpm.
3. At this speed, the voltage reading should fall within the range specified in the "Alternator and Regulator Specifications" chart.
4. If the voltage does not fall within the specifications, remove the cover from the regulator and adjust it by bending the adjusting arm.
5. Repeat Steps 2 and 3 if the voltage cannot be brought to specification, proceed with the mechanical adjustments which follow.

MECHANICAL ADJUSTMENTS

NOTE: *Perform the voltage adjustment outlined above, before beginning the mechanical adjustments.*

Field Relay

1. Remove the cover from the regulator assembly.
2. Use a feeler gauge to check the amount that the contact spring is deflected while the armature is being depressed.
3. If the measurement is not within specifications (see the "Alternator and Regulator Specifications" chart), adjust the regulator by bending point holder P_2. (See the illustration.)
4. Check the point gap with a feeler gauge against the specifications in the chart.
5. Adjust the point gap, as required, by

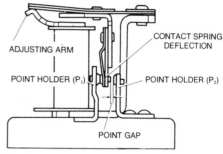

Field-relay components

bending the point holder P_1. (See the illustration.)
6. Clean off the points with emery cloth if they are dirty and wash them with solvent.

Voltage Regulator

1. Use a feeler gauge to measure the air (armature) gap. If it is not within the specifications (see the "Alternator and Regulator Specifications chart), adjust it by bending the *low*-speed point holder. (See the illustration.)
2. Check the point gap with a feeler gauge. If it is not within specifications, adjust it by bending the *high*-speed point holder. (See the illustration.) Clean the points with emery cloth and wash them off with solvent.

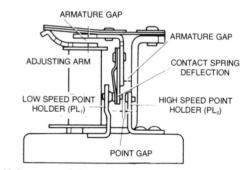

Voltage regulator components

3. Check the amount of contact spring deflection while depressing the armature. The specification should be the same as that for the contact spring on the field relay. If the amount of deflection is not within specification, replace, do not adjust, the voltage regulator.

Go back and perform the steps outlined under "Voltage Adjustment." If the voltage cannot be brought within specifications, replace the voltage regulator. If the voltage still fails to come within specifications, the alter-

Alternator and Regulator Specifications

| Engine Type | Alternator | | Regulator | | | | | |
| | Manufacturer | Output (amps) | Manufacturer | Field Relay | | | Regulator | |
				Contact Spring Deflection (in.)	Point Gap (in.)	Volts to Close	Air Gap (in.)	Point Gap (in.)	Volts
3K-C	Nippondenso	25 ①	Nippondenso	0.008– 0.024	0.016– 0.047	4.5– 5.8	0.012	0.010– 0.018	13.8– 14.8 ②
2T-C	Nippondenso	40 ③	Nippondenso	0.008– 0.024	0.016– 0.047	4.5– 5.8	0.012	0.010– 0.018	13.8– 14.8 ②
1A-C, 3A, 3A-C, 4K-C	Nippondenso	30, 40, 50, 55	Nippondenso	—————————Not Adjustable—————————					13.8– 14.7 ④

① 1976–79: 50 and 55
② w/55 amp alt.: 14.0–14.7
③ Optional: 55
④ 55 amp: 14.0–14.7

nator is probably defective and should be replaced.

Starter

REMOVAL AND INSTALLATION

1. Disconnect the cable which runs from starter to the battery at the battery end.

2. Remove the air cleaner assembly, if necessary, to gain access to the starter.

NOTE: *On some models with automatic transmissions, it may be necessary to unfasten the throttle linkage connecting rod.*

3. On Corolla 1200 models, perform the following:

   a. Disconnect the manual choke cable and the accelerator cable from the carburetor;

   b. Unfasten the front exhaust pipe flange from the manifold and then remove the complete manifold assembly. (See the appropriate section below for details.)

4. Disconnect all of the wiring at the starter.

5. Unfasten the starter securing nuts and withdraw the starter assembly toward the front of the car.

6. Installation is in the reverse order of removal.

STARTER SOLENOID AND BRUSH REPLACEMENT

Direct Drive Type

NOTE: *The starter must be removed from the car in order to perform this operation.*

1. Remove the field coil lead from the solenoid terminal.

2. Unfasten the solenoid retaining screws. Remove the solenoid by tilting it upward and withdrawing it.

3. Unfasten the end frame bearing cover screws and remove the cover.

4. Unfasten and withdraw the thrubolts. Remove the commutator endframe.

5. Withdraw the brushes from their holder if they are to be replaced.

6. Check the brush length against the specification in the "Battery and Starter Specifications" chart. Replace the brushes with new ones if required.

7. Dress the new brushes with emery cloth so that they will make proper contact.

8. Use a spring scale to check the brush spring tensions against the specification in the chart. Replace the springs if they do not meet specification.

Remove direct-drive starter solenoid in direction of arrow

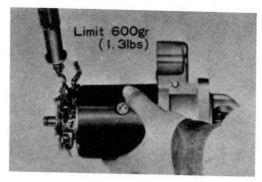

Checking the brush spring tension—direct-drive starter

Assembly is the reverse order of disassembly. Remember to pack the end bearing cover with multipurpose grease before installing it.

Gear Reduction Type

NOTE: *The starter must be removed from the car in order to perform this operation.*

1. Disconnect the solenoid lead.

2. Loosen the two bolts on the starter housing and separate the field frame from the solenoid. Remove the O-ring and felt dust seal.

3. Unfasten the two screws and separate the starter drive from the solenoid.

4. Withdraw the clutch and gears. Remove the ball from the clutch shaft bore or solenoid.

5. Remove the brushes from the holder.

6. Measure the brush length and compare it to the figure in the "Battery and Starter Specifications" chart. Replace the brushes with new ones if they are too short.

7. Replace any worn or chipped gears.

Assembly is performed in the reverse or-

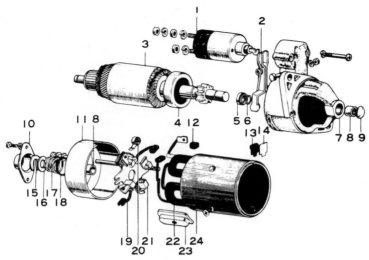

1. Solenoid	9. Bearing cover	17. Brake spring
2. Engagement lever	10. Bearing cover	18. Gasket
3. Armature	11. Commutator end frame	19. Brush
4. Overrunning clutch	12. Rubber bushing	20. Brush spring
5. Clutch stop	13. Rubber grommet	21. Brush holder
6. Snap-ring	14. Plate	22. Field coil
7. Drive housing	15. Lockplate	23. Pole shoes
8. Bushing	16. Washer	24. Field yoke

Components of the direct-drive starter motor

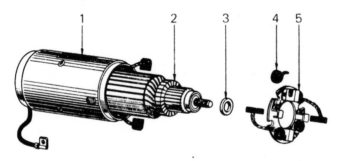

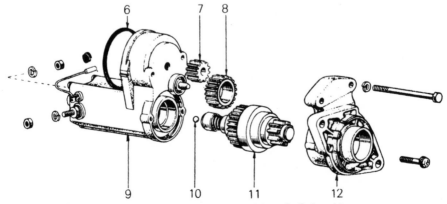

1. Field frame assembly	5. Brush holder	9. Solenoid
2. Armature	6. O-ring	10. Steel ball
3. Felt seal	7. Pinion gear	11. Clutch assembly
4. Brush spring	8. Idler gear	12. Starter housing

Components of the gear reduction starter motor

der of disassembly. Lubricate all gears and bearings with high temperature grease. Grease the ball before inserting it in the clutch shaft bore. Align the tab on the brush holder with the notch on the field frame. Check the positive (+) brush leads to ensure that they aren't grounded. Align the solenoid marks with the field frame bolt anchors.

Battery

REMOVAL AND INSTALLATION

1. Unfasten the battery ground cable at the negative (−) battery terminal, *first*.
2. Next, unfasten the "hot" cable at the starter.
3. Loosen the hold-down clamps and remove the battery.

CAUTION: *Use care in handling the battery; remember, it is filled with a highly corrosive acid.*

4. Installation is the *exact* reverse of removal.

ENGINE MECHANICAL

Understanding the Engine

The basic piston engine is a metal block containing a series of chambers. The upper engine block is usually an iron or aluminum alloy casting, consisting of outer walls, which form hollow jackets around the cylinder walls. The lower block provides a number of rigid mounting points for the bearings which hold the crankshaft in place, and is known as the crankcase. The hollow jackets of the upper block add to the rigidity of the engine and contain the liquid coolant which carries the heat away from the cylinders and other engine parts. The block of an air cooled engine consists of a crankcase which provides for the rigid mounting of the crankshaft and for studs which hold the cylinders in place. The cylinders are individual, single-wall castings, finned for cooling, and are usually bolted to the crankcase, rather than cast integrally with the block. In a water-cooled engine, only the cylinder head is bolted to the top of the block. The water pump is mounted directly to the block.

The crankshaft is a long, iron or steel shaft mounted rigidly in the bottom of the crankcase, at a number of points (usually 4–7). The crankshaft is free to turn and contains a number of counterweighted crankpins (one for each cylinder) that are offset several inches from the center of the crankshaft and turn in a circle as the crankshaft turns. The crankpins are centered under each cylinder. Pistons with circular rings to seal the small space between the pistons and wall of the cylinders are connected to the crankpins by steel connecting rods. The rods connect the pistons at their upper ends with the crankpins at their lower ends.

When the crankshaft spins, the pistons move up and down in the cylinder, depending on the position of the piston. Two openings in each cylinder head (above the cylinders) allow the intake of the air/fuel mixture and the exhaust of burned gasses. The volume of the combustion chamber must be variable for the engine to compress the fuel charge before combustion, to make use of the expansion of the burning gasses and to exhaust the burned gasses and take in a fresh fuel mixture. As the pistons are forced downward by the expansion of burning fuel, the connecting rods convert the reciprocating (up and down) motion of the pistons into rotary (turning) motion of the crankshaft. A round flywheel at the rear of the crankshaft provides a large, stable mass to smooth out the rotation.

The cylinder heads form tight covers for the tops of the cylinders and contain machined chambers into which the fuel mixture is forced as it is compressed by the pistons reaching the upper limit of their travel. Each combustion chamber contains one intake valve, one exhaust valve and one spark plug per cylinder. The spark plugs are screwed into holes in the cylinder head so that the tips protrude into the combustion chambers. The valve in each opening in the cylinder head is opened and closed by the action of the camshaft. The camshaft is driven by the crankshaft through a chain or belt at ½ crankshaft speed (the camshaft gear is twice the size of the crankshaft gear). The valves are operated either through rocker arms and pushrods (overhead valve engine) or directly by the camshaft (overhead cam engine).

Lubricating oil is stored in a pan at the bottom of the engine and is force fed to all parts of the engine by a gear type pump, driven from the crankshaft. The oil lubricates the entire engine and also seals the piston rings, giving good compression.

Battery and Starter Specifications—1970–77

Engine Type	Battery			Starters							
	Ampere Hour Capacity	Volts	Terminal Grounded	Lock Test			No-Load Test			Minimum Brush Tension (oz)	Minimum Brush Length (in.)
				Amps	Volts	Torque (ft. lbs.)	Amps	Volts	RPM		
3K-C	48	12	Neg	450	8.5	8	55	11	3,500	21	0.51
2T-C	50	12	Neg	Not Recommended			①	11.5	3,500	52.8	0.55
1977 3K-C	50	12	Neg	600	7.0	13	50	11	5,000	21	0.47
2T-C	60	12	Neg	Not Recommended			90	11.5	4,000	21	0.33

① Less than 90 amps

Battery and Starter Specifications—1978–81

Engine Type	Battery			Starters								
	Ampere Hour Capacity	Volts	Terminal Grounded	Lock Test			No-Load Test			Minimum Brush Tension (oz)	Minimum Brush Length (in.)	
				Amps	Volts	Torque (ft. lbs.)	Amps	Volts	RPM			
3K-C, 4K-C	110 ①	12	N	Not Recommended			50	11	5,000	—	.6	
2T-C, 1A-C 3A-C	50, 60, 110	12	N	Not Recommended			90	11.5	3,500	31.6	.57	

Design

Toyota passenger car engines are divided into four families (K, T, R, and M). The smallest engine, used from 1971–74, was a 1166 cc four used in the Corolla 1200.

Engine Removal and Installation

3K-C, 4K-C ENGINE

1. Drain the entire cooling system. Remove any emissions systems hoses which are in the way, but mark them beforehand so that you'll know where to put them back.

2. Unfasten the cable which runs from the battery to the starter at the battery terminal; first disconnect the ground (−) cable.

3. Scribe marks on the hood and hinges to aid in hood alignment during assembly. Remove the hood.

4. Unfasten the headlight bezel retaining screws and remove the bezels. Remove the radiator grille attachment screws and remove the grille.

5. Remove the hood lock assembly after detaching the release cable.

6. Unfasten the nuts from the horn retainers and disconnect the wiring. Withdraw the horn assembly.

7. Remove the air cleaner from its bracket after unfastening the hoses from it.

8. Remove the windshield washer tank from its bracket but first drain its contents into a clean container.

9. Remove both the upper and lower radiator hoses from the engine after loosening the hose clamps.

NOTE: *On models with automatic transmissions, disconnect and plug the oil lines from the oil cooler.*

10. Detach the radiator mounting bolts and remove the radiator.

11. Remove the accelerator cable from its

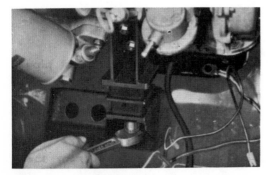

Removing the 3K-C right-hand engine mount

support on the cylinder head cover. Unfasten the cable at the carburetor throttle arm. Unfasten the choke cable from the carburetor.

12. Detach the water hose retainer from the cylinder head.

13. Disconnect the by-pass and heater hoses at the water pump. Disconnect the other end of the heater hose from the water valve. Remove the heater control cable from the wiring harness multiconnectors.

14. Detach the exhaust pipe from the exhaust manifold.

15. Detach the wires from the water temperature and oil pressure sending units.

16. Remove the nut from the front left-hand engine mount.

17. Remove the fuel line from the fuel pump.

18. Detach the battery ground cable from the cylinder block.

19. Remove the nut from the front right-hand engine mount.

20. Remove the clip and detach the cable from the clutch release lever.

21. Remove the primary and high-tension wires from the coil.

22. Detach the back-up light switch wire at its connector on the right-side of the extension housing.

The following steps apply to Corolla models with manual transmissions and Starlet:

23. Remove the carpet from the transmission tunnel. Remove the boots from the shift lever.

24. Remove the snap-ring from the gearshift selector lever base. Withdraw the selector lever assembly.

The following steps apply to Corolla models with automatic transmissions:

25. Disconnect the accelerator linkage torque rod at the carburetor.

26. Disconnect the throttle linkage connecting rod from the bellcrank lever.

27. Drain the oil from the transmission oil pan. (See Chapter 1.)

28. Detach the transmission gear selector shift rod from the control shaft.

The following steps apply to Corollas with both manual and automatic transmissions and Starlet:

29. Raise the rear wheels of the car. Support the car with jackstands.

CAUTION: *Be sure that the car is supported securely; remember, you will be working underneath it.*

30. Disconnect the driveshaft from the transmission.

General Engine Specifications

Year	Engine Type	Engine Cu In. Displacement (cm³/cu in.)	Carburetor Type	Horsepower @ rpm▲	Torque @ rpm (ft. lbs.)▲	Bore x Stroke (in.)	Compression Ratio
1970–71	3K-C	1,166/71	2-bbl	73 @ 6,000	69.4 @ 4.200	2.95 x 2.60	9.0:1
	2T-C ①	1,588/96.9	2-bbl	102 @ 6,000	101 @ 3,800	3.35 x 2.76	8.5:1
1972–74	3K-C	1,166/71.8	2-bbl	65 @ 6,000	67 @ 3,800	2.95 x 2.60	9.0:1
	2T-C	1,588/96.9	2-bbl	88 @ 6,000	97.3 @ 3,800	3.35 x 2.76	8.5:1
1975–77	2T-C	1,588/96.9	2-bbl	75 @ 5,800	83 @ 3,800	3.35 x 2.76	9.0:1
	3K-C	1,166/71.8	2-bbl	65 @ 6,000	67 @ 3,800	2.95 x 2.60	9.0:1
1978–79	2T-C	1,588/96.9	2-bbl	75 @ 5,400	85 @ 2,800	3.35 x 2.76	9.0:1
	3K-C	1,166/71.2	2-bbl	58 @ 5,800	63 @ 3,800	2.95 x 2.60	9.0:1
1980–81	1A-C	1,452/88.6	2-bbl	60 @ 4,800	72 @ 2,800	3.05 x 3.03	8.7:1
	3A	1,452/88.6	2-bbl	60 @ 4,800	72 @ 2,800	3.05 x 3.03	8.7:1
	3T-C	1,800/108.0	2-bbl	75 @ 5,000 ②	95 @ 2,600 ②	3.35 x 3.07	9.0:1
1981	3A-C	1,452/88.6	2-bbl	62 @ 4,800	75 @ 2,800	3.05 x 3.03	9.0:1
1981	4K-C	1,290/78.7	2-bbl	58 @ 5,200	67 @ 3,600	2.95 x 2.87	9.0:1

EFI Electronic fuel injection
▲ Horsepower and torque ratings given in SAE net figures
① 2T-C engine was introduced in 1971
② Calif.: 73 hp @ 5,000; 90 ft. lb. @ 2,600

NOTE: *Drain the oil from the manual transmission, first, to prevent it from leaking out. (See Chapter 1.)*

31. Detach the exhaust pipe support bracket from the extension housing.

32. Remove the insulator bolt from the rear engine mount.

33. Place a jack under the transmission and remove the four bolts from the rear (engine support) crossmember.

34. Install lifting hooks on the engine lifting brackets. Attach a suitable hoist.

35. Lift the engine slightly; then move it toward the front of the car. Bring the engine the rest of the way out at an angle.

CAUTION: *Use care not to damage other parts of the automobile.*

Engine installation is the reverse order of removal. Adjust all transmission and carburetor linkages, as detailed in the appropriate chapter. Install and adjust the hood as outlined in Chapter 10. Refill the engine, radiator, and transmission to capacity, as detailed in Chapter 1.

2T-C 3T-C ENGINE

1. Drain the radiator, cooling system, transmission, and engine oil.

2. Disconnect the battery-to-starter cable at the positive battery terminal, after first disconnecting the negative cable.

3. Scribe marks on the hood and its hinges to aid in alignment during installation.

4. Remove the hood supports from the body. Remove the hood.

Valve Specifications

Engine Type	Seat Angle (deg)	Face Angle (deg)	Spring Pressure (lbs.)		Spring Installed Height (in.)		Stem To Guide Clearance (in.)		Stem Diameter (in.)	
			Inner	Outer	Inner	Outer	Intake	Exhaust	Intake	Exhaust
3K-C	45	44.5	—	70.1	—	1.512	0.0010–0.0020 ①	0.0020–0.0030 ②	0.3140	0.3140
4K-C	45	44.5	—	70.1	—	1.512	0.0012–0.0026	0.0014–0.0028	0.3139	0.3137
2T-C	45	44.5	—	58.4 ③	—	1.484	0.0012–0.0020	0.0012–0.0024	0.3140	0.3140
1A-C, 3A, 3A-C	45	44.5	—	52.0	—	1.520	0.0010–0.0024	0.0012–0.0026	0.2747	0.2745
3T-C	45	44.5	—	57.9	—	1.484	0.0010–0.0024	0.0012–0.0026	0.3139	0.3139

① 1978 and later: 0.0012–0.0026
② 1978 and later: 0.0014–0.0028
③ 1978 and later: 57.9

Crankshaft and Connecting Rod Specifications
All measurements in inches

Engine Type	Crankshaft				Connecting Rod		
	Main Brg. Journal Dia.	Main Brg. Oil Clearance	Shaft End-Play	Thrust on No.	Journal Diameter	Oil Clearance	Side Clearance
3K-C	1.9675–1.9685	0.0005–0.0015	0.0020–0.0090 ①	3	1.6525–1.6535	0.0006–0.0015 ②	0.0040–0.0080 ③
2-TC	2.2827–2.2834	0.0012–0.0024 ②	0.0030–0.0070 ④	3	1.8889–1.8897	0.0008–0.0020	0.0063–0.0102
1A-C, 3A, 3A-C	1.8892–1.8898	0.0005–0.0019	0.0008–0.0073	3	1.5742–1.5748	0.0008–0.0020	0.0059–0.0098
3T-C	2.2825–2.2835	0.0009–0.0019	0.0008–0.0087	3	1.8889–1.8897	0.0009–0.0019	0.0063–0.0012
4K-C	1.9676–1.9685	0.0006–0.0016	0.0016–0.0095	3	1.6526–1.6535	0.0006–0.0016	0.0079–0.0150

① 1978 and later: 0.0016–0.0087
② 1978 and later: 0.0009–0.0019
③ 1978 and later: 0.0043–0.0084
④ 1978 and later: 0.0010–0.0090

Piston and Ring Specifications

All measurements in inches

Engine Type	Piston Clearance	Ring Gap			Ring Side Clearance		
		Top Compression	Bottom Compression	Oil Control	Top Compression	Bottom Compression	Oil Control
3K-C	0.0010–0.0020	0.0006–0.0014 ①	0.0006–0.0014 ①	0.0006–0.0014 ②	0.0011–0.0027	0.0007–0.0023 ③	0.0006–0.0023
2T-C	0.0024–0.0031	0.0008–0.0016 ④	0.0004–0.0012 ⑤	0.0004–0.0012 ⑥	0.0008–0.0024	0.0008–0.0024 ⑦	0.0008–0.0024 ⑧
1A-C, 3A, 3A-C	0.0039–0.0047	0.0079–0.0157	0.0059–0.0138	0.0039–0.0236	0.0016–0.0031	0.0012–0.0028	—
3T-C	0.0020–0.0028	0.0039–0.0098	0.0059–0.0118	0.0079–0.0276	0.0008–0.0024	0.0006–0.0022	—
4K-C	0.0012–0.0020	0.0039–0.0110	0.0039–0.0018	0.0080–0.0350	0.0012–0.0028	0.0008–0.0024	—

① 1978 and later: 0.004–0.011 inch
② 1978 and later: 0.008–0.035 inch
③ 1978 and later: 0.001–0.003 inch
④ 1978 and later: 0.006–0.011 inch
⑤ 1978 and later: 0.008–0.013 inch
⑥ 1978 and later: 0.008–0.028 inch
⑦ 1978 and later: 0.0006–0.0022 inch
⑧ 1978–79: 0.008–0.035
⑨ 1978–79: 0.0020–0.0030 inch

Torque Specifications
All readings in ft. lbs.

Engine Type	Cylinder Head Bolts	Rod Bearing Bolts	Main Bearing Bolts	Crankshaft Pulley Bolt	Flywheel to Crankshaft Bolts	Manifold	
						Intake	Exhaust
3K-C	39.0–47.7	28.9–37.6	39.0–47.7	29–43 ④	39–48		14–22 ①
2T-C	52.0–63.5 ⑤	28.9–36.1	52.0–63.5	28.9–43.3 ②	41.9–47.7 ③	7.2–11.6 ⑥	7.2–11.6 ⑦
1A-C, 3A, 3A-C	40–47	26–32	40–47	55–61	55–61	15–21	15–21
3T-C	62–68	29–36	53–63	47–61	42–47	14–18	22–32
4K-C	40–47	29–37	40–47	55–75	40–47	15–21	15–21

① Intake and exhaust manifolds combined
② 1975: 43–51 ft. lbs.; 1976: 116–145 ft. lbs.
③ 1975–76: 58–64 ft. lbs.
④ 1977: 32.5–39.8
⑤ 1977–79: 61.5–68.7
⑥ 1978–79: 14–18
⑦ 1978–79: 22–32

NOTE: *Do not remove the supports from the hood.*

5. On Carina models, remove the headlight bezels. Disconnect the hood release cable then remove the grille, lower grille molding, hood lock base, and base support.

6. On Corolla models, perform Steps 4–6 as previously detailed in the "3K-C Engine Removal" section.

7. Detach both the upper and lower hoses from the radiator. On cars with automatic transmissions, disconnect and plug the lines from the oil cooler. Remove the radiator.

8. Unfasten the clamps and remove the heater and by-pass hoses from the engine. Remove the heater control cable from the water valve.

9. Remove the wiring from the coolant temperature and oil pressure sending units.

10. Remove the air cleaner from its bracket, complete with its attendant hoses.

11. Unfasten the accelerator torque rod from the carburetor. On models equipped with automatic transmissions, remove the transmission linkage as well.

12. Remove the emission control system hoses and wiring, as necessary. (Mark them to aid in installation.)

13. Remove the clutch hydraulic line support bracket.

14. Unfasten the high-tension and primary wires from the coil.

15. Mark the spark plug cables and remove them from the distributor.

16. Detach the right-hand front engine mount.

17. Remove the fuel line at the pump (filter on 1975–76 models with electric pumps).

18. Detach the downpipe from the exhaust manifold.

19. Detach the left-hand front engine mount.

20. Disconnect all of the wiring harness multiconnectors.

21. On cars equipped with manual transmissions, remove the shift lever boot and the shift lever cap boot.

22. Unfasten the four gear selector lever cap retaining screws, remove the gasket and withdraw the gear selector lever assembly from the top of the transmission.

NOTE: *On all Carina models and on Corolla five-speed models, the floor console must be removed first.*

23. Lift the rear wheels of the car off the ground and support the car with jackstands.

CAUTION: *Be sure that the car is securely supported.*

24. On cars equipped with automatic transmissions, disconnect the gear selector control rod.

25. Detach the exhaust pipe support bracket.

26. Disconnect the driveshaft from the rear of the transmission.

27. Unfasten the speedometer cable from the transmission. Disconnect the wiring from the back-up light switch and the neutral safety switch (automatic only).

28. Detach the clutch release cylinder assembly, complete with hydraulic lines. Do not disconnect the lines.

29. Unbolt the rear support member mounting insulators.

30. Support the transmission and detach the rear support member retaining bolts. Withdraw the support member from under the car.

31. Install lifting hooks on the engine lifting brackets. Attach a suitable hoist to the engine.

32. Remove the jack from under the transmission.

33. Raise the engine and move it toward the front of the car. Use care to avoid damaging the components which remain on the car.

34. Support the engine on a workstand.

Install the engine in the reverse order of removal. Adjust all of the linkages as detailed in the appropriate chapter. Install the hood and adjust it as outlined in Chapter 10. Replenish the fluid levels in the engine, radia-

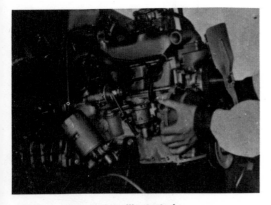

Lift the engine out as illustrated

tor, and transmission as detailed in Chapter 1.

1A-C, 2A AND 3A

1. Disconnect the negative battery terminal.

2. Remove the hood.

3. Remove the air cleaner and all necessary lines attached to it.

4. Drain the radiator.

5. Cover both driveshaft boots with a shop towel.

6. Remove the solenoid valve connector, water temperature switch connector, and the electric fan connector.

7. Remove the exhaust support plate bolts, and the exhaust pipe.

8. Remove the top radiator support.

9. Remove the top and bottom radiator hoses and remove the radiator with the fan.

NOTE: *On cars equipped with automatic transmissions remove the cooling lines before removing the radiator.*

10. Remove the windshield washer tank.

11. Remove the heater hoses and the lines to the fuel pump.

NOTE: *Plug the gas line to prevent gas from leaking out.*

12. Remove the accelarator cable, choke cable, and the ground strap.

13. Remove the brake booster vacuum line.

14. Remove the coil wire and unplug the alternator.

15. Remove the clutch release cable.

16. Remove the wires on the starter.

17. Remove the temperature sending and oil pressure switch connectors.

18. Remove the battery ground strap from the block.

19. Jack up your vehicle and support it with jack stands.

20. Remove the engine mounting bolts and the engine shock absorbers.

21. Support the differential with a jack.

22. Remove the transaxle mounting bolts.

NOTE: *It is probably easier to remove these bolts from underneath the car.*

23. Remove the engine.

24. Tie the bell housing to the cowl to keep support on the transaxle.

NOTE: *The Grill may be removed if necessary to give better leverage when removing the engine.*

25. Installation is the reverse of removal.

Adjust all linkages as covered in the appropriate section. Refill all fluids to the proper levels. Tighten the transaxle bolts 37–57 ft. lbs.

On cars with automatic transmissions, the following procedures are necessary.

1. Remove the starter.

2. Remove the cooling lines from the transmission.

3. Support the transmission with a jack.

4. Remove the transaxle mounting bolts.

5. Remove the torque converter bolts (4).

NOTE: *In order to turn the converter, place a wrench on the crankshaft pulley and turn it until you see a bolt appear in the area where the starter was.*

6. While the engine is suspended from your hoist, pull it forward about 2 inches.

7. Insert a pry bar in this opening and gently separate the torque converter from the engine.

8. Installation is the reverse of removal.

The following are necessary before the cylinder head can be installed. Confirm that the converter contact surface is 1.02 inches from the housing. Install a guide bolt in one of the mounting bolt holes. Remove the engine mounting insulator (left side) and the mounting bracket (right side). To secure the transaxle to the engine temporarily install the top two mounting bolts. This will facilitate easier engine installation.

Cylinder Head

REMOVAL AND INSTALLATION

3K-C 4K-C Engine

CAUTION: *Do not perform this operation on a warm engine.*

1. Disconnect the battery and drain the cooling system.

2. Remove the air cleaner assembly from its bracket, complete with its attendant hoses.

3. Disconnect the hoses from the air injection system (1970–71) or the vacuum switching valve lines (1972–74).

4. Detach the accelerator cable from its support on the cylinder head cover and also from the carburetor throttle arm.

5. Remove the choke cable and fuel lines from the carburetor.

6. Remove the water hose bracket from the cylinder head cover.

7. Unfasten the water hose clamps and

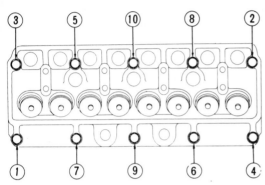

3K-C, 4K-C engine head bolt removal sequence

remove the hoses from the water pump and the water valve. Detach the heater temperature control cable from the water valve.

8. Disconnect the PCV line from the cylinder head cover.

9. Unbolt and remove the valve cover.

10. Remove the valve rocker support securing bolts and nuts. Lift out the valve rocker assembly.

11. Withdraw the pushrods from their bores.

CAUTION: *Keep the pushrods in their original order.*

12. Unfasten the hose clamps and remove the upper radiator hose from the water outlet.

13. Remove the wires from the spark plugs.

14. Disconnect the wiring and the fluid line from the windshield washer assembly. Remove the assembly.

NOTE: *Use a clean container to catch the fluid from the windshield washer reservoir when disconnecting its fluid line.*

15. Unfasten the exhaust pipe flange from the exhaust manifold.

16. Remove the head assembly retaining bolts and remove the head from the engine.

CAUTION: *Remove the head bolts in the sequence illustrated and in two or three stages.*

17. Place the cylinder head on *wooden* blocks to prevent damage to it.

Installation is essentially the reverse order of removal. Clean both the cylinder head and block gasket mounting surfaces. Always use a new head gasket.

NOTE: *Be sure that the top side of the gasket is facing upward. (See the illustration.)*

When installing the head on the block, be sure to tighten the bolts in the sequence shown (see "Torque Sequences"), in several stages, to the torque specified in the "Torque Specifications" chart.

The valve rocker assembly nuts and bolts should be tightened to 13–16 ft. lbs.

NOTE: *The valve clearance should be adjusted to specification with each piston at top dead center (TDC) of its compression stroke.*

2T-C 3T-C Engine

CAUTION: *Do not perform this operation on a warm engine.*

1. Perform Steps 1–2 of the "3K-C Head Removal" procedure.

2. Disconnect the vacuum lines which run from the vacuum switching valve to the various emission control devices mounted on the cylinder head. Disconnect the air injection system lines on engines so equipped.

3. Disconnect the mixture control valve hose which runs to the intake manifold and remove the valve from its mounting bracket (1971–74).

4. Perform Step 7 of the "3K-C Engine Removal" procedure.

5. Detach the water temperature sender wiring.

6. Remove the choke stove pipe and its intake pipe.

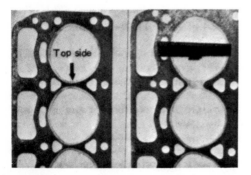

Identification of the 3K-C, 4K-C head gasket top side

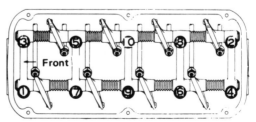

2T-C and 3T-C engine head bolt removal sequence

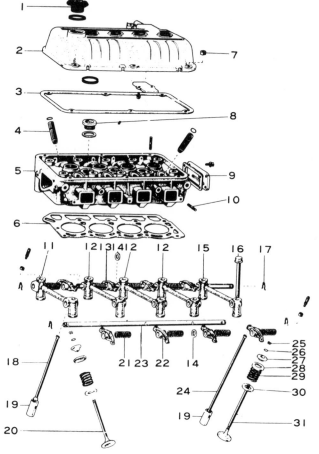

1. Oil filler cap
2. Valve cover
3. Valve cover gasket
4. Valve guide (intake)
5. Cylinder head
6. Cylinder head gasket
7. Nut
8. Screw plug
9. Cylinder head rear cover
10. Stud
11. Valve rocker support
12. Valve rocker support
13. Valve rocker arm
14. Washer
15. Valve rocker support
16. Bolt
17. Retainer spring
18. Pushrod
19. Valve lifter
20. Intake valve
21. Compression spring
22. Valve rocker arm
23. Valve rocker shaft
24. Pushrod
25. Lock spring
26. O-ring
27. Valve spring retainer
28. Oil splash shield
29. Compression spring
30. Plate washer
31. Exhaust valve

2T-C cylinder head components

7. Remove the PCV hose from the intake manifold.

8. Disconnect the fuel and vacuum lines from the carburetor.

9. Remove the clutch hydraulic line bracket from the cylinder head.

10. Raise the car and support it with jackstands. Unfasten the exhaust pipe clamp. Remove the exhaust manifold from the cylinder head. (See below.)

11. Label and disconnect the spark plug leads. Remove the valve cover.

12. Remove the cylinder head bolts in the sequence illustrated.

CAUTION: *Remove the bolts in stages; not one at a time.*

13. Perform Steps 10–11 of the "3K-C, 4K-C Engine Removal" procedure.

14. Remove the cylinder head, complete with the intake manifold.

15. Separate the intake manifold from the cylinder head.

Install the cylinder head in the following order:

1. Clean the gasket mounting surfaces of the cylinder head and the block completely.

NOTE: *Remove oil from the cylinder head bolt holes, if present.*

2. Place a *new* gasket on the block and install the head assembly.

CAUTION: *Do not slide the cylinder head across the block, as there are locating pins on the block.*

3. Install the pushrods and the valve rocker assembly.

4. Tighten the cylinder head bolts *evenly*, in stages, as illustrated in the "Torque Sequence" diagrams. See the "Torque Specifications" chart for the proper tightening torque.

5. Install the intake manifold, using a new gasket and tighten it to specifications.

6. The rest of the installation procedure is

the reverse of removal. Remember to adjust the valve clearances. (See Chapter 2.)

1A-C, 3A and 3A-C

1. Disconnect the negative battery terminal.

2. Remove the exhaust pipe from the manifold.

3. Drain the cooling system. Save the coolant as it can be reused.

4. Remove the air cleaner and all necessary hoses.

5. Mark all vacuum lines for easy installation and then remove them.

6. Remove all linkage from the carburetor, fuel lines, etc. from the head and manifold.

7. Remove the fuel pump.

NOTE: *Before removing the carburetor cover it with a clean rag to prevent dirt from entering it.*

8. Remove the carburetor.

9. Remove the manifold.

10. Remove the valve cover.

11. Note the position of the spark plug wires and remove them.

12. Remove the spark plugs.

13. Set the engine on No. 1 cylinder—top dead center. This is accomplished by removing the No. 1 spark plug, placing our finger over the hole and then turning the crankshaft pulley until you feel pressure exerted against your finger.

CAUTION: *Do not put your finger into the spark plug hole.*

14. Remove the crankshaft pulley with an appropriate puller.

15. Remove the water pump pulley.

16. Remove the top and bottom timing chain cover.

17. matchmark the camshaft pulley and timing belt for reassembly.

18. Loosen the belt tensioner.

19. Remove the water pump.

20. Remove the timing belt. Do not bend, twist, or turn the belt inside out.

NOTE: *Check the belt for wear, cracks, or glazing. Once the belt is removed it is a good idea to replace it with a new one even though it is not necessary.*

21. Remove the rocker arm bolts and remove the rocker arms.

22. Remove the camshaft pulley by holding the camshaft with a pair of channel lock pliers and removing the belt in the pulley end of the shaft.

NOTE: *Do not hold the cam on the lobes, as damage will result.*

23. Remove the camshaft seal.

24. Remove the camshaft bearing caps and set them down in the order they appear on the engine.

25. Remove the camshaft.

26. Loosen the head bolts in the proper order to prevent warping of the head.

27. Lift the head directly up. Do not attempt to slide it off.

28. Installation is the reverse of removal.

NOTE: *When replacing the head always use a new gasket. Also replace the camshaft seal, making sure to grease the lip before installation.*

The following torques are needed for installation: cam bearing caps 8–10 ft. lbs., cam sprocket 29–39 ft. lbs., crankshaft pulley 55–61 ft. lbs., manifold bolts 15–21 ft. lbs., rocker arm bolts 17–19 ft. lbs., timing gear idler bolt 22–32 ft. lbs., belt tension 0.24–0.28 in. Adjust the valves to the proper clearances.

Cylinder Head

Installation Torque Sequences

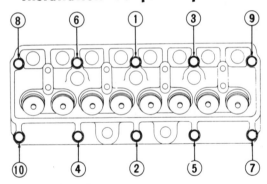

3K-C, 4K-C engine

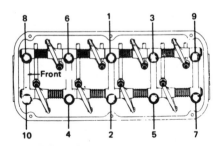

2T-C and 3T-C engine

OVERHAUL

General cylinder head overhaul procedures are given in the "Engine Rebuilding" section at the end of this chapter. Those operations which differ greatly from the ones at the end of the chapter are detailed below.

Valve Guide Replacement—All Except 2T-C, 3T-C

1. Heat the cylinder head to 176–212°F, evenly, before beginning the replacement procedure.

2. Use a brass rod to break the valve guide off above its snap-ring. (See the illustration.)

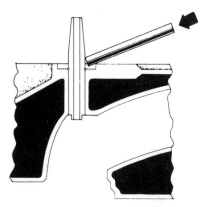

Use a brass drift to break the valve guide off

3. Drive out the valve guide, toward the combustion chamber. Use a tool fabricated as described in the "Engine Rebuilding" section.

4. Install a snap-ring on the new valve guide. Apply liquid sealer. Drive in the valve guide until the snap-ring contacts the head. Use the tool previously described.

5. Measure the guide bore; if the stem-to-guide clearance is below specification, ream it out, using a valve guide reamer.

Valve Rocker Shafts

REMOVAL AND INSTALLATION

Valve rocker shaft removal and installation is given as part of the various "Cylinder Head Removal and Installation" procedures.

Perform only the steps of the appropriate "Cylinder Head Removal and Installation" procedures necessary to remove and install the rocker shafts.

Intake Manifold

REMOVAL AND INSTALLATION

2T-C, 3T-C Engine

1. Drain the cooling system.

2. Remove the air cleaner assembly, complete with hoses, from its bracket.

3. Remove the choke stove hoses, fuel lines, and vacuum lines from the carburetor. Unfasten the emission control system wiring, hoses, and the accelerator linkage from it.

4. Unfasten the four nuts which secure the carburetor to the manifold and remove the carburetor.

5. Remove the mixture control valve line from its intake manifold fitting (1971–74).

6. Disconnect the PCV hose.

7. Disconnect the water by-pass hose from the intake manifold.

8. Unbolt and remove the manifold.

Installation is performed in the reverse order of removal. Remember to use *new* gaskets. Tighten the intake manifold bolts to the specifications given in the "Torque Specification" chart.

NOTE: *Tighten the bolts, in several stages, working from the inside out.*

Exhaust Manifold

REMOVAL AND INSTALLATION

CAUTION: *Do not perform this operation on a warm or hot engine.*

2T-C, 3T-C Engine

1. Detach the manifold heat stove intake pipe.

2. Unfasten the nut on the stove outlet pipe union.

3. Remove the wiring from the emission control system thermosensor.

4. Unfasten the U-bolt from the downpipe bracket.

5. Unfasten the downpipe flange from the manifold.

6. In order to remove the manifold, unfasten the manifold retaining bolts.

CAUTION: *Remove the bolts in two or three stages and starting from the inside working out.*

Installation of the manifold is performed in the reverse order of removal. Remember to use a *new* gasket. See the "Torque Specifications" chart for the proper tightening torque.

Combination Manifold

REMOVAL AND INSTALLATION

CAUTION: *Do not perform this procedure on a warm engine.*

3K-C, 4K-C

1. Remove the air cleaner assembly, complete with hoses.

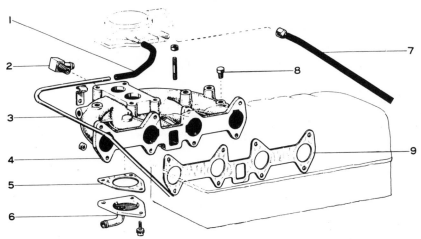

1. Choke stove intake hose
2. Elbow
3. Choke stove intake
4. Intake manifold
5. Gasket
6. Water by-pass outlet
7. Choke stove outlet
8. Plug
9. Intake manifold gasket

2T-C and 3T-C intake manifold assembly

2. Disconnect the accelerator and choke linkages from the carburetor, as well as the fuel and vacuum lines.

3. Remove, or move aside, any of the emission control system components which are in the way.

4. Unfasten the retaining bolts and remove the carburetor from the manifold.

5. Loosen the manifold retaining nuts, working from the inside out, in two or three stages.

6. Remove the intake/exhaust manifold assembly from the cylinder head as a complete unit.

Installation is performed in the reverse order of removal. Always use *new* gaskets.

Tighten the bolts, working from the inside out, to the specifications given in the "Torque Specifications" chart.

NOTE: *Tighten the bolts in two or three stages.*

1A-C, 3A, and 3A-C

1. Disconnect the negative battery terminal.

2. Remove the air cleaner and all necessary hoses.

3. Remove all the carburetor linkages.

4. Remove the carburetor.

NOTE: *Cover the carburetor with a clean towel to prevent dirt from entering it.*

5. Remove the exhaust manifold pipe.

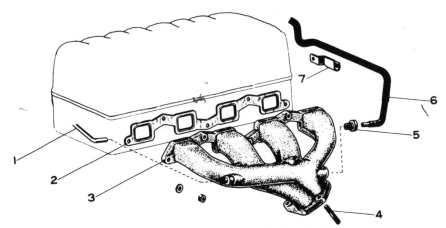

1. Automatic choke stove intake pipe
2. Exhaust manifold gasket
3. Exhaust manifold
4. Stud
5. Union
6. Automatic choke stove outlet
7. Clamp

2T-C and 3T-C exhaust manifold assembly

6. Remove the exhaust manifold.

7. Installation is the reverse of removal. Tighten the manifold bolts to 15–21 ft. lbs.

Timing Gear Cover
REMOVAL AND INSTALLATION
3K-C, 4K-C, 2T-C and 3T-C Engines

1. Drain the cooling system and the crankcase.

2. Disconnect the battery.

3. Remove the air cleaner assembly, complete with hoses, from its bracket.

4. Remove the hood latch as well as its brace and support.

5. Remove the headlight bezels and grille assembly.

6. Unfasten the upper and lower radiator hose clamps and remove both of the hoses from the engine.

7. Unfasten the radiator securing bolts and remove the radiator.

NOTE: *Take off the shroud first, if so equipped.*

8. Loosen the drive belt adjusting link and remove the drive belt. Unfasten the alternator multiconnector, withdraw the retaining bolts, and remove the alternator.

9. Perform Step 8 to the air injection pump, if so equipped. Disconnect the hoses from the pump before removing it.

10. Unfasten the crankshaft pulley retaining bolt. Remove the crankshaft pulley with a gear puller.

12. Remove the gravel shield from underneath the engine.

13. The following steps apply to the 3K-C engine only:

    a. Remove the nuts and washers from both the right and left front engine mounts;

    b. Detach the exhaust pipe flange from the exhaust manifold;

    c. Slightly raise the front of the engine.

14. On 2T-C engines, remove the right-hand brace plate.

15. Remove the front oil pan bolts, to gain access to the bottom of the timing chain cover.

NOTE: *It may be necessary to insert a thin knife between the pan and the gasket in order to break the pan loose. Use care not to damage the gasket.*

Installation is basically the reverse order of removal. There are, however, several points to remember:

1. Apply sealer to the two front corners of the 2T-C engine's oil pan gasket.

2. Tighten the crankshaft pulley to the figure given in the "Torque Specifications" chart.

3. Adjust the drive belts as outlined in Chapter 1.

1A-C, 2A and 3A

1. Disconnect the negative battery terminal.

2. Remove all the drive belts.

3. Bring the engine to the top dead center timing position. See the cylinder head removal section.

4. Remove the crankshaft pulley with a suitable puller.

5. Remove the water pump pulley.

6. Remove the upper and lower timing case covers.

7. Installation is the reverse of removal. Tighten the timing belt cover to 61–99 in. lbs.

Timing Chain Cover Oil Seal Replacement
All Engines Exc. 1A-C, 3A, 3A-C

1. Remove the timing chain cover, as previously detailed in the appropriate section.

2. Inspect the oil seal for signs of wear, leakage, or damage.

3. If worn, pry, the old oil seal out, using a large flat-bladed screwdriver. Remove it toward the *front* of the cover.

NOTE: *Once the oil seal has been removed, it must be replaced with a new one.*

4. Use a socket, pipe, or block of wood and a hammer to drift the oil seal into place. Work from the *front* of the cover.

CAUTION: *Be extremely careful not to damage the seal or else it will leak.*

5. Install the timing chain cover as previously outlined.

Timing Chain and Tensioner
REMOVAL AND INSTALLATION
3K-C, 4K-C Engine

1. Remove the timing chain cover as previously detailed in the appropriate section.

2. Unbolt and remove the chain tensioner.

3. Remove the crankshaft chain sprocket and then the chain itself.

4. Check the timing chain for wear, cracks, or loose links.

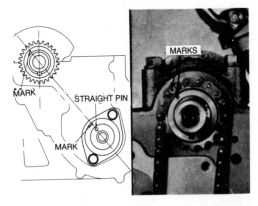

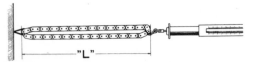

Aligning the marks on the timing chain and sprockets—3K-C, 4K-C engine

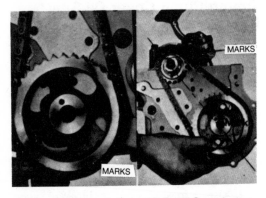

Measure the timing chain stretch along "L"—3K-C and 2T-C engines

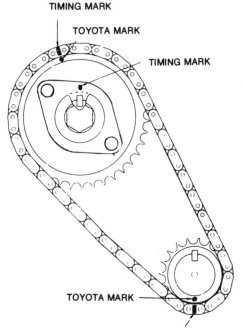

Timing chain installation—3K-C, 4K-C engine

5. Secure one end of the chain to a fixed hook and pull on the other end with a spring scale. When the scale indicates 11 lbs., the chain should be no longer than 10.7 in. Replace the chain if it exceeds this specification.

Installation is performed in the following order:

1. Install the crankshaft chain sprocket. Align the sprocket "0" mark with the straight pin on the crankshaft as illustrated.

2. Fit the timing chain on the crankshaft sprocket.

3. Align the mating marks on the timing chain with the "0" marks on both sprockets as illustrated.

4. Align the camshaft sprocket "0" mark with the one on the crankshaft as illustrated.

5. Tighten the camshaft timing sprocket securing bolt to 16–22 ft. lbs.

6. Install the chain tensioner assembly and chain vibration damper. Tighten their bolts to 4–6 ft. lbs.

7. Install the timing chain cover as previously detailed.

2T-C, 3T-C Engine

1. Perform Steps 1–3 of the "3K-C 4K-C Timing Chain Removal" procedure.

2. Perform Steps 4–5 of the "3K-C 4K-C Timing Chain Removal" procedure (chain inspection). The chain should stretch no more than 11.472 in. at 11 lbs. on the spring scale.

Installation is performed in the following order:

1. Rotate the crankshaft so that its key points straight up.

NOTE: *The Nos. 1 and 4 pistons should be at TDC.*

2. Rotate the camshaft so that its key is aligned with the timing mark on the thrust plate.

3. Fit the chain on the camshaft and crankshaft timing sprockets so that the marks on the timing chain align with the "Toyota" trademarks on each of the sprockets.

NOTE: *The above step is performed with the sprockets off the engine.*

Aligning the timing marks on the 2T-C and 3T-C timing chain and sprocket

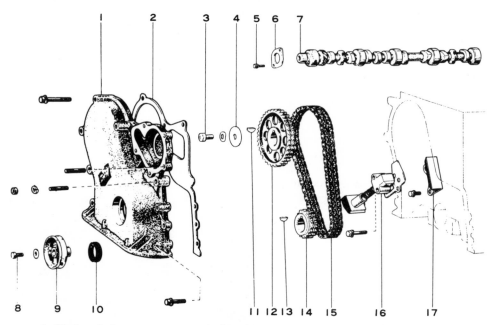

1. Timing chain cover
2. Timing chain cover gasket
3. Bolt
4. Plate washer
5. Bolt
6. Plate
7. Camshaft
8. Bolt
9. Crankshaft pulley
10. Front oil seal
11. Woodruff key
12. Camshaft sprocket
13. Woodruff key
14. Crankshaft sprocket
15. Timing chain
16. Chain tensioner
17. Chain vibration damper

Timing chain cover and seal components, and camshaft assembly—2T-C and 3T-C engines

4. Being careful to keep all of the parts in proper alignment, fit the timing chain/sprocket assembly to the engine. When assembled, the marks should align as in the illustration.

5. Torque the camshaft timing gear bolt to 50.6–79.6 ft. lbs.

6. Fill the chain tensioner with engine oil and install it. Install the chain damper.

7. Install the timing chain cover as previously outlined.

1A-C, 2A and 3A

1. Remove the crankshaft and water pump pulleys.

2. Remove the top and bottom timing covers.

3. Remove the belt tensioner.

4. Matchmark the belt and camshaft gear for easy reinstallation.

5. Remove the timing belt.
NOTE: *Do not bend, twist, or turn the belt inside out. Do not allow grease or water to come in contact with it.*

6. Check for damaged teeth, cracks, or excessive wear. If the belt shows any of the problems it should be replaced.

7. Installation is the reverse of removal.

The following torque specifications are needed: crankshaft pulley 55–61 ft. lbs., camshaft pulley 29–39 ft. lbs., timing belt tension 0.24–0.28 in.

Timing Gears
REMOVAL AND INSTALLATION
1A-C, 2A and 3A

1. Remove the air cleaner.

2. Remove the throttle linkage.

3. Remove the valve cover.

4. Remove the crankshaft and water pump pulleys.

5. Remove the top and bottom timing belt cover.

6. Remove the belt tensioner.

7. Matchmark the belt and camshaft gear for easy reinstallation.

8. Remove the timing belt.

9. Remove the bolt from the camshaft gear and remove the gear.
NOTE: *In order to remove this gear use a pair of channelock pliers to hold the cam*

from turning. Do not hold the cam by the lobes as damage may result.

10. Installation is the reverse of removal.

Camshaft

REMOVAL AND INSTALLATION

3K-C 4K-C Engine

1. Perform the "Timing Chain Cover" and "Timing Chain Removal" procedures.

2. Perform Steps 1–11 of the "3K-C, 4K-C Engine Cylinder Head Removal" procedure.

NOTE: *It is unnecessary to remove the cylinder head.*

3. Unfasten the spark plug wires and remove the spark plugs.

4. Remove the valve lifters in sequence.

NOTE: *Keep the valve lifters in their proper sequence, so that they go back into their original bores.*

5. If you have not already done so, disconnect the vacuum line and the primary wire from the distributor, loosen its clamping bolts, and remove it.

6. Detach the fuel lines from the fuel pump and remove the pump.

7. Remove the bolts securing the camshaft thrust plate and then remove the thrust plate, itself.

8. Carefully remove the camshaft from the cylinder block.

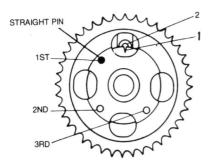

Camshaft sprocket—normal valve timing

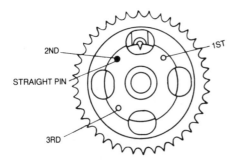

Camshaft sprocket—valve timing retarded 3 to 9°

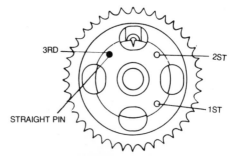

Camshaft sprocket—valve timing retarded 9 to 12°

Removing the camshaft from the 3K-C 4K-C engine

CAUTION: *Use care not to damage the camshaft lobes, journals, or bearings.*

Installation of the camshaft is performed in the reverse order of removal. Coat the camshaft bearings and journals lightly with engine oil. The camshaft thrust plate attaching bolt should be tightened to 4–6 ft. lbs.

2T-C 3T-C Engine

1. Perform the "Cylinder Head," "Timing Chain Cover," and "Timing Chain Removal" procedures.

2. Unfasten the primary wire and vacuum lines from the distributor. Loosen its clamping bolt and withdraw it from the engine block.

3. Unfasten the lines from the fuel pump and remove the pump.

4. Remove the gearshifter shaft lever.

5. Use a jack to *lightly* support the transmission.

6. Remove the engine rear supporting crossmember.

7. Carefully lower the jack from beneath the transmission.

8. Unbolt and remove the camshaft thrust plate.

9. Ease out the camshaft, being careful not to damage the camshaft lobes or bearings.

Installation is performed in the reverse order of removal. Lubricate the camshaft journals and bearings lightly with engine oil prior to camshaft installation. Tighten the camshaft thrust plate attaching bolts to 7.2–11.6 ft. lbs.

1A-C, 2A and 3A

1. Perform the timing gear removal from the previous section.

2. Pry out the camshaft seal with a screwdriver.

3. Remove the camshaft bearing caps. Keep them in the order in which they were removed.

4. Remove the camshaft.

5. Installation is the reverse of removal.

NOTE: *When reinstalling the camshaft seal place some multipurpose grease on the lip of the seal before installation.*

Torque the cam to its proper specifications.

Pistons and Connecting Rods

REMOVAL AND INSTALLATION

All Engines

1. Remove the cylinder head as outlined in the appropriate preceding section.

2. Remove the oil pan and pump; see "Engine Lubrication."

3. Ream the ridges from the top of the cylinder bores, as detailed in "Engine Rebuilding," at the end of this chapter. Remove the oil strainer if it is in the way.

4. Unbolt the connecting rod caps. Mark the caps with the number of the cylinder from which they were removed.

5. Remove the connecting rod and piston through the top of the cylinder bore. CAUTION: *Use care not to scratch the journals or the cylinder walls.*

6. Mark the pistons and connecting rods with the numbers of the cylinders from which they were removed.

Installation is performed in the following order:

1. Apply a light coating of engine oil to the pistons, rings, and wrist pins.

2. Examine the piston to ensure that it has been assembled with its parts positioned correctly. (See the illustrations.) Be sure that the ring gaps are not pointed toward the thrust face of the piston and that they do not overlap.

3. Install the pistons, using a ring compressor, into the cylinder bore. Be sure that the appropriate marks on the piston are facing the front of the cylinder.

Piston and Ring Positioning

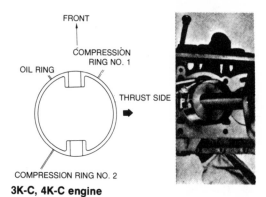

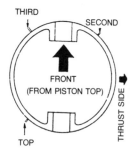

3K-C, 4K-C engine

2T-C and 3T-C engines

CAUTION: *It is important that the pistons, rods, bearings, etc., be returned to the same cylinder bore from which they were removed.*

4. Install the connecting rod bearing caps and tighten them to the torque figures given in the "Torque Specifications" chart.

CAUTION: *Be sure that the mating marks on the connecting rods and rod bearing caps are aligned.*

Piston and Connecting Rod Positioning

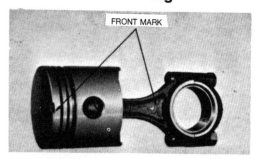

3K-C, 4K-C engine

2T-C and 3T-C engines

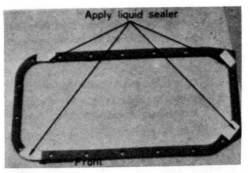

Applying sealer to the corners of the 2T-C and 3T-C oil pan

5. The rest of the removal procedure is performed in the reverse order of installation.

ENGINE LUBRICATION

Oil Pan

REMOVAL AND INSTALLATION

Corolla, Starlet

1. Open the engine compartment hood.
NOTE: *Leave it open for the duration of this procedure.*
2. Raise the front end of the car and support it with jackstands.
CAUTION: *Be sure that the car is securely supported. Remember, you will be working underneath it.*
3. Remove the splash shield from underneath the engine.
4. Place a jack under the transmission to support it.
5. Unfasten the bolts which secure the engine rear supporting crossmember to the chassis.
6. Raise the jack under the transmission, *slightly.*
7. Unbolt the oil pan and work it out from underneath the engine.
NOTE: *If the oil pan does not come out easily, it may be necessary to unfasten the rear engine mounts from the crossmember.*
Installation is performed in the reverse order of removal. On Corolla models equipped with the 2T-C (1600 cm³) engine, apply liquid sealer to the four corners of the oil pan. Tighten the oil pan securing bolts to the following specifications:
• 3K-C, 4K-C engine:
    1.8–2.5 ft. lbs.
• 2T-C engine:
    3.6–5.8 ft. lbs.

Carina

1. Drain the oil.
2. Raise the front end of the car with jacks and support it with jackstands.
CAUTION: *Be sure that the car is supported securely. Remember, you will be working underneath it.*
3. Detach the steering relay rod and the tie rods from the idler arm, pitman arm, and steering knuckles, as detailed in Chapter 8.
4. Remove the engine stiffening plates.
5. Remove the splash shields from underneath the engine.
6. Support the front of the engine with a jack and remove the front engine mount attaching bolts.
7. Raise the front of the engine *slightly* with the jack.
CAUTION: *Be sure that the hood is open before raising the front of the engine.*
8. Unbolt and withdraw the oil pan.
Installation is performed in the reverse order of removal. Apply liquid sealer to the four corners of the oil pan gasket used on 2T-C or 20R engines. Torque the oil pan securing bolts to the following specifications:
• 2T-C engine:
    3.6–5.8 ft. lbs.

Tercel

1. Disconnect the negative battery terminal.
2. Jack up the vehicle and support it with jack stands.
3. Drain the oil.
4. Remove the sway bar and any other necessary steering linkage parts.
5. Disconnect the exhaust pipe from the manifold.
6. Jack up the engine enough to take the weight off it.

7. Remove the engine mounts and engine shock absorber.

8. Continue to jack up the engine enough to remove the pan.

9. Remove the pan bolts and remove the pan.

10. Installation is the reverse of removal.

Always use a new pan gasket when reinstalling the pan.

Rear Main Oil Seal
REPLACEMENT
All Engines

NOTE: *This procedure applies only to those models with manual transmissions. If your car has an automatic transmission, leave removal of the oil seal to your dealer.*

1. Remove the transmission as detailed in Chapter 6.

2. Remove the clutch cover assembly and flywheel. See Chapter 6 also.

3. Remove the oil seal retaining plate, complete with the oil seal.

4. Use a screwdriver to pry the old seal from the retaining plate. Be careful not to damage the plate.

5. Install the new seal, carefully, by using a block of wood to drift it into place.

CAUTION: *Do not damage the seal; a leak will result.*

6. Lubricate the lips of the seal with multipurpose grease.

Installation is performed in the reverse order from removal.

Oil Pump
REMOVAL AND INSTALLATION
All engines

1. Remove the oil pan, as outlined in the appropriate preceding section.

2. Unbolt the oil pump securing bolts and remove it as an assembly.

Installation is the reverse of removal.

ENGINE COOLING

Radiator
REMOVAL AND INSTALLATION
All Models

1. Drain the cooling system.

2. Unfasten the clamps and remove the radiator upper and lower hoses. If equipped

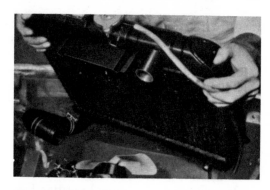
Removing the radiator

with an automatic transmission, remove the oil cooler lines.

3. Detach the hood lock cable and remove the hood lock from the radiator upper support.

NOTE: *It may be necessary to remove the grille in order to gain access to the hood lock/radiator support assembly.*

4. Remove the fan shroud, if so equipped.

5. On models equipped with a coolant recovery system, disconnect the hose from the thermal expansion tank from its bracket.

6. Unbolt and remove the radiator upper support.

7. Unfasten the bolts and remove the radiator.

CAUTION: *Use care not to damage the radiator fins on the cooling fan.*

Installation is performed in the reverse order of removal. Remember to check the transmission fluid level on cars with automatic transmissions. (See Chapter 1.)

Fill the radiator to the specified level, as detailed under "Fluid Level Checks," in Chapter 1.

The re-introduced 3K-C engine for 1977 is equipped with an electric, rather than a belt-driven, cooling fan. Using a radiator-mounted thermo-switch, the fan operates when the coolant temperatures reach 203°F and stops when it lowers to 190°F. It is at-

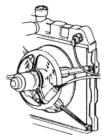
Radiator-mounted cooling fan for 1977 3K-C engine

tached to the radiator by the four radiator retaining bolts. Radiator removal is the same for this engine as all others, except for disconnecting the wiring harness and thermo switch connector.

Water Pump
REMOVAL AND INSTALLATION
All Engines exc. 1A-C, 3A, 3A-C

1. Drain the cooling system.
2. Unfasten the fan shroud securing bolts and remove the fan shroud, if so equipped.
3. Loosen the alternator adjusting link bolt and remove the drive belt.
4. Repeat Step 3 for the air and/or power steering pump drive belt, if so eqiupped.
5. Detach the by-pass hose from the water pump.
6. Unfasten the water pump retaining bolts and remove the water pump and fan assembly, using care not to damage the radiator with the fan.

CAUTION: *If the fan is equipped with a fluid coupling, do not tip the fan/pump assembly on its side, as the fluid will run out.*

Installation is performed in the reverse order of removal. Always use a new gasket between the pump body and its mounting. Remember to check for leaks after installation is completed.

1A-C, 2A and 3A only

1. Drain the radiator. Save the coolant as it can be reused.
2. Loosen all necessary drive belts.
3. Remove the top timing belt cover.
4. Remove the bottom radiator hose from the water pump.
5. Remove the pump bolts and remove the pump.
NOTE: *Always use a new gasket when replacing the pump.*
6. Installation is the reverse of removal.

THERMOSTAT

Removal and Installation
ALL ENGINES

1. Drain the cooling system.
2. Unfasten the clamp and remove the upper radiator hose from the water outlet elbow.
3. Unbolt and remove the water outlet (thermostat housing).
4. Withdraw the thermostat.
Installation is performed in the reverse order of the removal procedure. Use a new gasket on the water outlet.

CAUTION: *Be sure that the thermostat is installed with the spring pointing down.*

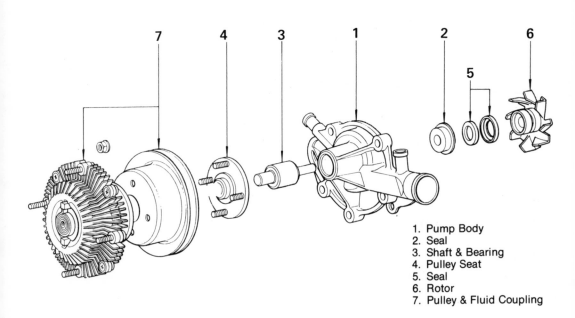

1. Pump Body
2. Seal
3. Shaft & Bearing
4. Pulley Seat
5. Seal
6. Rotor
7. Pulley & Fluid Coupling

Typical water pump components

ENGINE REBUILDING

Most procedures involved in rebuilding an engine are fairly standard, regardless of the type of engine involved. This section is a guide to accepted rebuilding procedures. Examples of standard rebuilding practices are illustrated and should be used along with specific details concerning your particular engine, found earlier in this chapter.

The procedures given here are those used by any competent rebuilder. Obviously some of the procedures cannot be performed by the do-it-yourself mechanic, but are provided so that you will be familiar with the services that should be offered by rebuilding or machine shops. As an example, in most instances, it is more profitable for the home mechanic to remove the cylinder heads, buy the necessary parts (new valves, seals, keepers, keys, etc.) and deliver these to a machine shop for the necessary work. In this way you will save the money to remove and install the cylinder head and the mark-up on parts.

On the other hand, most of the work involved in rebuilding the lower end is well within the scope of the do-it-yourself mechanic. Only work such as hot-tanking, actually boring the block or Magnafluxing (invisible crack detection) need be sent to a machine shop.

Tools

The tools required for basic engine rebuilding should, with a few exceptions, be those included in a mechanic's tool kit. An accurate torque wrench, and a dial indicator (reading in thousandths) mounted on a universal base should be available. Special tools, where required, are available from the major tool suppliers. The services of a competent automotive machine shop must also be readily available.

Precautions

Aluminum has become increasingly popular for use in engines, due to its low weight and excellent heat transfer characteristics. The following precautions must be observed when handling aluminum (or any other) engine parts:
—Never hot-tank aluminum parts.
—Remove all aluminum parts (identification tags, etc.) from engine parts before hot-tanking (otherwise they will be removed during the process).

—Always coat threads lightly with engine oil or anti-seize compounds before installation, to prevent seizure.
—Never over-torque bolts or spark plugs in aluminum threads. Should stripping occur, threads can be restored using any of a number of thread repair kits available (see next section).

Inspection Techniques

Magnaflux and Zyglo are inspection techniques used to locate material flaws, such as stress cracks. Magnaflux is a magnetic process, applicable only to ferrous materials. The Zyglo process coats the matrial with a fluorescent dye penetrant, and any material may be tested using Zyglo. Specific checks of suspected surface cracks may be made at lower cost and more readily using spot check dye. The dye is sprayed onto the suspected area, wiped off, and the area is then sprayed with a developer. Cracks then will show up brightly.

Overhaul

The section is divided into two parts. The first, Cylinder Head Reconditioning, assumes that the cylinder head is removed from the engine, all manifolds are removed, and the cylinder head is on a workbench. The camshaft should be removed from overhead cam cylinder heads. The second section, Cylinder Block Reconditioning, covers the block, pistons, connecting rods and crankshaft. It is assumed that the engine is mounted on a work stand, and the cylinder head and all accessories are removed.

Procedures are identified as follows:
Unmarked—Basic procedures that must be performed in order to successfully complete the rebuilding process.
Starred (*)—Procedures that should be performed to ensure maximum performance and engine life.
Double starred (**)—Procedures that may be performed to increase engine performance and reliability.

When assembling the engine, any parts that will be in frictional contact must be pre-lubricated, to provide protection on initial start-up. Any product specifically formulated for this purpose may be used. NOTE: *Do not use engine oil. Where semi-permanent* (locked but removable) installation of bolts or nuts is desired, threads should be cleaned and located with Loctite ® or a similar product (non-hardening).

Repairing Damaged Threads

Several methods of repairing damaged threads are available. Heli-Coil® (shown here), Keenserts® and Microdot® are among the most widely used. All involve basically the same principle—drilling out stripped threads, tapping the hole and installing a pre-wound insert—making welding, plugging and oversize fasteners unnecessary.

Two types of thread repair inserts are usually supplied—a standard type for most Inch Coarse, Inch Fine, Metric Coarse and Metric Fine thread sizes and a spark plug type to fit most spark plug port sizes. Consult the individual manufacturer's catalog to determine exact applications. Typical thread repair kits will contain a selection of pre-wound threaded inserts, a tap (corresponding to the outside diameter threads of the insert) and an installation tool. Spark plug inserts usually differ because they require a tap equipped with pilot threads and a combined reamer/tap section. Most manufacturers also supply blister-packed thread repair inserts separately in addition to a master kit containing a variety of taps and inserts plus installation tools.

Before effecting a repair to a threaded hole, remove any snapped, broken or damaged bolts or studs. Penetrating oil can be used to free frozen threads; the offending item can be removed with locking pliers or with a screw or stud extractor. After the hole is clear, the thread can be repaired, as follows:

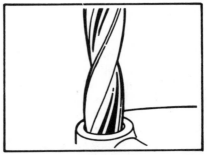

Drill out the damaged threads with specified drill. Drill completely through the hole or to the bottom of a blind hole

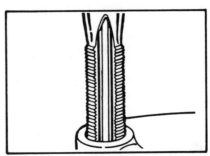

With the tap supplied, tap the hole to receive the thread insert. Keep the tap well oiled and back it out frequently to avoid clogging the threads

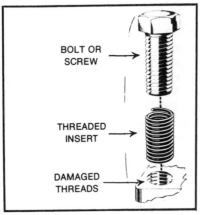

BOLT OR SCREW

THREADED INSERT

DAMAGED THREADS

Damaged bolt holes can be repaired with thread repair inserts

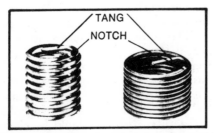

TANG

NOTCH

Standard thread repair insert (left) and spark plug thread insert (right)

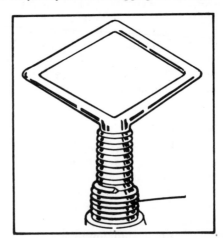

Screw the threaded insert onto the installation tool until the tang engages the slot. Screw the insert into the tapped hole until it is ¼–½ turn below the top surface. After installation break off the tang with a hammer and punch

Standard Torque Specifications and Fastener Markings

The Newton-metre has been designated the world standard for measuring torque and will gradually replace the foot-pound and kilogram-meter. In the absence of specific torques, the following chart can be used as a guide to the maximum safe torque of a particular size/grade of fastener.

- There is no torque difference for fine or coarse threads.
- Torque values are based on clean, dry threads. Reduce the value by 10% if threads are oiled prior to assembly.
- The torque required for aluminum components or fasteners is considerably less.

U. S. BOLTS

SAE Grade Number	1 or 2			5			6 or 7		
Bolt Markings									
Manufacturer's marks may vary—number of lines always 2 less than the grade number.									
Usage	*Frequent*			*Frequent*			*Infrequent*		
Bolt Size (inches)—(Thread)	*Maximum Torque*			*Maximum Torque*			*Maximum Torque*		
	Ft-Lb	*kgm*	*Nm*	*Ft-Lb*	*kgm*	*Nm*	*Ft-Lb*	*kgm*	*Nm*
¼—20	5	0.7	6.8	8	1.1	10.8	10	1.4	13.5
—28	6	0.8	8.1	10	1.4	13.6			
⁵⁄₁₆—18	11	1.5	14.9	17	2.3	23.0	19	2.6	25.8
—24	13	1.8	17.6	19	2.6	25.7			
⅜—16	18	2.5	24.4	31	4.3	42.0	34	4.7	46.0
—24	20	2.75	27.1	35	4.8	47.5			
⁷⁄₁₆—14	28	3.8	37.0	49	6.8	66.4	55	7.6	74.5
—20	30	4.2	40.7	55	7.6	74.5			
½—13	39	5.4	52.8	75	10.4	101.7	85	11.75	115.2
—20	41	5.7	55.6	85	11.7	115.2			
⁹⁄₁₆—12	51	7.0	69.2	110	15.2	149.1	120	16.6	162.7
—18	55	7.6	74.5	120	16.6	162.7			
⅝—11	83	11.5	112.5	150	20.7	203.3	167	23.0	226.5
—18	95	13.1	128.8	170	23.5	230.5			
¾—10	105	14.5	142.3	270	37.3	366.0	280	38.7	379.6
—16	115	15.9	155.9	295	40.8	400.0			
⅞— 9	160	22.1	216.9	395	54.6	535.5	440	60.9	596.5
—14	175	24.2	237.2	435	60.1	589.7			
1— 8	236	32.5	318.6	590	81.6	799.9	660	91.3	894.8
—14	250	34.6	338.9	660	91.3	849.8			

METRIC BOLTS

NOTE: *Metric bolts are marked with a number indicating the relative strength of the bolt. These numbers have nothing to do with size.*

Description	Torque ft-lbs (Nm)			
Thread size x pitch (mm)	Head mark—4		Head mark—7	
6 x 1.0	2.2–2.9	(3.0–3.9)	3.6–5.8	(4.9–7.8)
8 x 1.25	5.8–8.7	(7.9–12)	9.4–14	(13–19)
10 x 1.25	12–17	(16–23)	20–29	(27–39)
12 x 1.25	21–32	(29–43)	35–53	(47–72)
14 x 1.5	35–52	(48–70)	57–85	(77–110)
16 x 1.5	51–77	(67–100)	90–120	(130–160)
18 x 1.5	74–110	(100–150)	130–170	(180–230)
20 x 1.5	110–140	(150–190)	190–240	(160–320)
22 x 1.5	150–190	(200–260)	250–320	(340–430)
24 x 1.5	190–240	(260–320)	310–410	(420–550)

NOTE: *This engine rebuilding section is a guide to accepted rebuilding procedures. Typical examples of standard rebuilding procedures are illustrated. Use these procedures along with the detailed instructions earlier in this chapter, concerning your particular engine.*

Cylinder Head Reconditioning

Procedure	Method
Remove the cylinder head:	See the engine service procedures earlier in this chapter for details concerning specific engines.
Identify the valves:	Invert the cylinder head, and number the valve faces front to rear, using a permanent felt-tip marker.
Remove the rocker arms (OHV engines only):	Remove the rocker arms with shaft(s) or balls and nuts. Wire the sets of rockers, balls and nuts together, and identify according to the corresponding valve.
Remove the camshaft (OHC engines only):	See the engine service procedures earlier in this chapter for details concerning specific engines.
Remove the valves and springs:	Using an appropriate valve spring compressor (depending on the configuration of the cylinder head), compress the valve springs. Lift out the keepers with needlenose pliers, release the compressor, and remove the valve, spring, and spring retainer. See the engine service procedures earlier in this chapter for details concerning specific engines.

Cylinder Head Reconditioning

Procedure	Method

Check the valve stem-to-guide clearance:

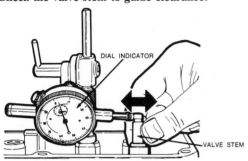

Check the valve stem-to-guide clearance

Clean the valve stem with lacquer thinner or a similar solvent to remove all gum and varnish. Clean the valve guides using solvent and an expanding wire-type valve guide cleaner. Mount a dial indicator so that the stem is at 90° to the valve stem, as close to the valve guide as possible. Move the valve off its seat, and measure the valve guide-to-stem clearance by rocking the stem back and forth to actuate the dial indicator. Measure the valve stems using a micrometer, and compare to specifications, to determine whether stem or guide wear is responsible for excessive clearance.

NOTE: *Consult the Specifications tables earlier in this chapter.*

De-carbon the cylinder head and valves:

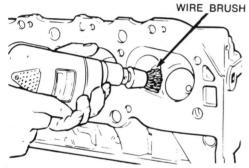

Remove the carbon from the cylinder head with a wire brush and electric drill

Chip carbon away from the valve heads, combustion chambers, and ports, using a chisel made of hardwood. Remove the remaining deposits with a stiff wire brush.

NOTE: *Be sure that the deposits are actually removed, rather than burnished.*

Hot-tank the cylinder head (cast iron heads only):
CAUTION: *Do not hot-tank aluminum parts.*

Have the cylinder head hot-tanked to remove grease, corrosion, and scale from the water passages.

NOTE: *In the case of overhead cam cylinder heads, consult the operator to determine whether the camshaft bearings will be damaged by the caustic solution.*

Degrease the remaining cylinder head parts:

Clean the remaining cylinder head parts in an engine cleaning solvent. Do not remove the protective coating from the springs.

Check the cylinder head for warpage:

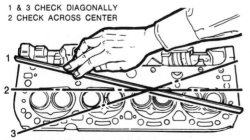

Check the cylinder head for warpage

Place a straight-edge across the gasket surface of the cylinder head. Using feeler gauges, determine the clearance at the center of the straight-edge. If warpage exceeds .003″ in a 6″ span, or .006″ over the total length, the cylinder head must be resurfaced.

NOTE: *If warpage exceeds the manufacturer's maximum tolerance for material removal, the cylinder head must be replaced.* When milling the cylinder heads of V-type engines, the intake manifold mounting position is altered, and must be corrected by milling the manifold flange a proportionate amount.

Cylinder Head Reconditioning

Procedure	Method

*Knurl the valve guides:

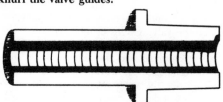

Cut-away view of a knurled valve guide

*Valve guides which are not excessively worn or distorted may, in some cases, be knurled rather than replaced. Knurling is a process in which metal is displaced and raised, thereby reducing clearance. Knurling also provides excellent oil control. The possibility of knurling rather than replacing valve guides should be discussed with a machinist.

Replace the valve guides:
NOTE: *Valve guides should only be replaced if damaged or if an oversize valve stem is not available.*

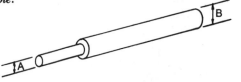

A—VALVE GUIDE I.D.   B—LARGER THAN THE VALVE GUIDE O.D.

A—VALVE GUIDE I.D.   B—LARGER THAN THE VALVE GUIDE O.D.
Valve guide installation tool using washers for installation

See the engine service procedures earlier in this chapter for details concerning specific engines. Depending on the type of cylinder head, valve guides may be pressed, hammered, or shrunk in. In cases where the guides are shrunk into the head, replacement should be left to an equipped machine shop. In other cases, the guides are replaced using a stepped drift (see illustration). Determine the height above the boss that the guide must extend, and obtain a stack of washers, their I.D. similar to the guide's O.D., of that height. Place the stack of washers on the guide, and insert the guide into the boss.
NOTE: *Valve guides are often tapered or beveled for installation.* Using the stepped installation tool (see illustration), press or tap the guides into position. Ream the guides according to the size of the valve stem.

Replace valve seat inserts:

Replacement of valve seat inserts which are worn beyond resurfacing or broken, if feasible, must be done by a machine shop.

Resurface (grind) the valve face:

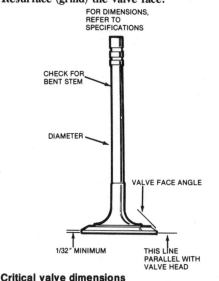

Critical valve dimensions

Using a valve grinder, resurface the valves according to specifications given earlier in this chapter.
CAUTION: *Valve face angle is not always identical to valve seat angle.* A minimum margin of

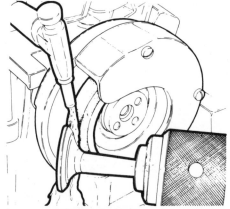

Valve grinding by machine

Cylinder Head Reconditioning

Procedure	Method
	$^1/_{32}$" should remain after grinding the valve. The valve stem top should also be squared and resurfaced, by placing the stem in the V-block of the grinder, and turning it while pressing lightly against the grinding wheel. NOTE: *Do not grind sodium filled exhaust valves on a machine. These should be hand lapped.*
Resurface the valve seats using reamers or grinder: 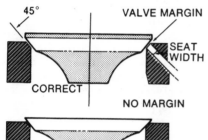 **Valve seat width and centering** 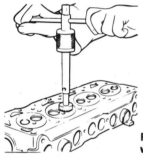 **Reaming the valve seat with a hand reamer**	Select a reamer of the correct seat angle, slightly larger than the diameter of the valve seat, and assemble it with a pilot of the correct size. Install the pilot into the valve guide, and using steady pressure, turn the reamer clockwise. CAUTION: *Do not turn the reamer counterclockwise.* Remove only as much material as necessary to clean the seat. Check the concentricity of the seat (following). If the dye method is not used, coat the valve face with Prussian blue dye, install and rotate it on the valve seat. Using the dye marked area as a centering guide, center and narrow the valve seat to specifications with correction cutters. NOTE: *When no specifications are available, minimum seat width for exhaust valves should be $^5/_{64}$", intake valves $^1/_{16}$".* After making correction cuts, check the position of the valve seat on the valve face using Prussian blue dye. To resurface the seat with a power grinder, select a pilot of the correct size and coarse stone of the proper angle. Lubricate the pilot and move the stone on and off the valve seat at 2 cycles per second, until all flaws are gone. Finish the seat with a fine stone. If necessary the seat can be corrected or narrowed using correction stones.
Check the valve seat concentricity:  **Check the valve seat concentricity with a dial gauge**	Coat the valve face with Prussian blue dye, install the valve, and rotate it on the valve seat. If the entire seat becomes coated, and the valve is known to be concentric, the seat is concentric. *Install the dial gauge pilot into the guide, and rest of the arm on the valve seat. Zero the gauge, and rotate the arm around the seat. Run-out should not exceed .002".

Cylinder Head Reconditioning

Procedure	*Method*
*Lap the valves: NOTE: *Valve lapping is done to ensure efficient sealing of resurfaced valves and seats.*	*Invert the cylinder head, lightly lubricate the valve stems, and install the valves in the head as numbered. Coat valve seats with fine grinding compound, and attach the lapping tool suction cup to a valve head. NOTE: *Moisten the suction cup.* Rotate the tool between the palms, changing position and lifting the tool often to prevent grooving. Lap the valve until a smooth, polished seat is evident. Remove the valve and tool, and rinse away all traces of grinding compound.

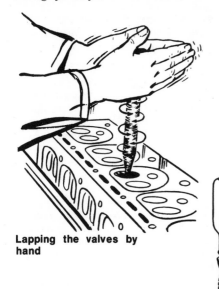

Lapping the valves by hand

Home-made valve lapping tool

HAND DRILL

ROD

SUCTION CUP

**Fasten a suction cup to a piece of drill rod, and mount the rod in a hand drill. Proceed as above, using the hand drill as a lapping tool.
CAUTION: *Due to the higher speeds involved when using the hand drill, care must be exercised to avoid grooving the seat.* Lift the tool and change direction of rotation often.

Check the valve springs:

NOT MORE THAN 5/64"

CLOSED COIL END DOWNWARD

Check the valve spring free length and squareness

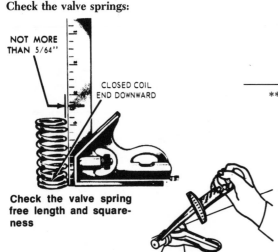

Check the valve spring test pressure

Place the spring on a flat surface next to a square. Measure the height of the spring, and rotate it against the edge of the square to measure distortion. If spring height varies (by comparison) by more than $1/16''$ or if distortion exceeds $1/16''$, replace the spring.

**In addition to evaluating the spring as above, test the spring pressure at the installed and compressed (installed height minus valve lift) height using a valve spring tester. Springs used on small displacement engines (up to 3 liters) should be ∓ 1 lb of all other springs in either position. A tolerance of ∓ 5 lbs is permissible on larger engines.

Cylinder Head Reconditioning

Procedure	Method

*Install valve stem seals:

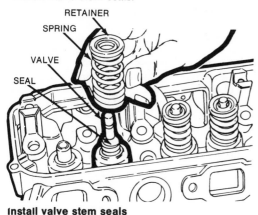

RETAINER
SPRING
VALVE
SEAL

Install valve stem seals

* Due to the pressure differential that exists at the ends of the intake valve guides (atmospheric pressure above, manifold vacuum below), oil is drawn through the valve guides into the intake port. This has been alleviated somewhat since the addition of positive crankcase ventilation, which lowers the pressure above the guides. Several types of valve stem seals are available to rocker arms and balls, and install them on the the stem and guide boss, while others require that the boss be machined. Recently, Teflon guide seals have become popular. Consult a parts supplier or machinist concerning availability and suggested usages.

NOTE: *When installing seals, ensure that a small amount of oil is able to pass the seal to lubricate the valve guides; otherwise, excessive wear may result.*

Install the valves:

See the engine service procedures earlier in this chapter for details concerning specific engines.

Lubricate the valve stems, and install the valves in the cylinder head as numbered. Lubricate and position the seals (if used) and the valve springs. Install the spring retainers, compress the springs, and insert the keys using needle-nose pliers or a tool designed for this purpose.

NOTE: *Retain the keys with wheel bearing grease during installation.*

Check valve spring installed height:

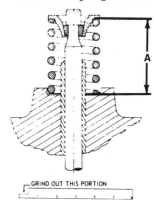

A

GRIND OUT THIS PORTION

Measure the valve spring installed height (A) with a modified steel rule

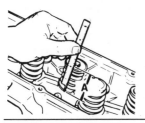

A

Valve spring installed height (A)

Measure the distance between the spring pad and the lower edge of the spring retainer, and compare to specifications. If the installed height is incorrect, add shim washers between the spring pad and the spring.

CAUTION: *Use only washers designed for this purpose.*

Install the camshaft (OHC engines only) and check end-play:

See the engine service procedures earlier in this chapter for details concerning specific engines.

Cylinder Head Reconditioning

Procedure	Method

Inspect the rocker arms, balls, studs, and nuts (OHV engines only):

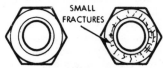

Stress cracks in the rocker nuts

Visually inspect the rocker arms, balls, studs, and nuts for cracks, galling, burning, scoring, or wear. If all parts are intact, liberally lubricate the rocker arms and balls, and install them on the cylinder head. If wear is noted on a rocker arm at the point of valve contact, grind it smooth and square, removing as little material as possible. Replace the rocker arm if excessively worn. If a rocker stud shows signs of wear, it must be replaced (see below). If a rocker nut shows stress cracks, replace it. If an exhaust ball is galled or burned, substitute the intake ball from the same cylinder (if it is intact), and install a new intake ball.

NOTE: *Avoid using new rocker balls on exhaust valves.*

Replacing rocker studs (OHV engines only):

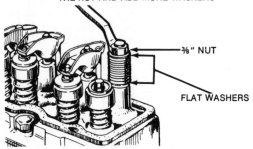

Extracting a pressed-in rocker stud

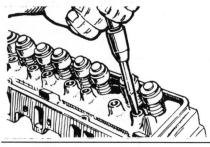

Ream the stud bore for oversize rocker studs

In order to remove a threaded stud, lock two nuts on the stud, and unscrew the stud using the lower nut. Coat the lower threads of the new stud with Loctite, and install.

Two alternative methods are available for replacing pressed in studs. Remove the damaged stud using a stack of washers and a nut (see illustration). In the first, the boss is reamed .005–.006″ oversize, and an oversize stud pressed in. Control the stud extension over the boss using washers, in the same manner as valve guides. Before installing the stud, coat it with white lead and grease. To retain the stud more positively drill a hole through the stud and boss, and install a roll pin. In the second method, the boss is tapped, and a threaded stud installed.

Inspect the rocker shaft(s) and rocker arms (OHV engines only)

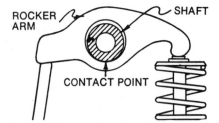

Check the rocker arm-to-rocker shaft contact area

Remove rocker arms, springs and washers from rocker shaft.

NOTE: *Lay out parts in the order as they are removed.* Inspect rocker arms for pitting or wear on the valve contact point, or excessive bushing wear. Bushings need only be replaced if wear is excessive, because the rocker arm normally contacts the shaft at one point only. Grind the valve contact point of rocker arm smooth if necessary, removing as little material as possible. If excessive material must be removed to smooth and square the arm, it should be replaced. Clean out all oil holes and passages in rocker shaft. If shaft is grooved or worn, replace it. Lubricate and assemble the rocker shaft.

Cylinder Head Reconditioning

Procedure	Method
Inspect the pushrods (OHV engines only):	Remove the pushrods, and, if hollow, clean out the oil passages using fine wire. Roll each pushrod over a piece of clean glass. If a distinct clicking sound is heard as the pushrod rolls, the rod is bent, and must be replaced.
	*The length of all pushrods must be equal. Measure the length of the pushrods, compare to specifications, and replace as necessary.
Inspect the valve lifters (OHV engines only): 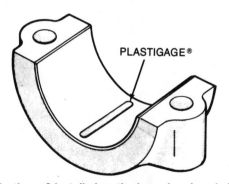 CHECK FOR CONCAVE WEAR ON FACE OF TAPPET USING TAPPET FOR STRAIGHT EDGE **Check the lifter face for squareness**	Remove lifters from their bores, and remove gum and varnish, using solvent. Clean walls of lifter bores. Check lifters for concave wear as illustrated. If face is worn concave, replace lifter, and carefully inspect the camshaft. Lightly lubricate lifter and insert it into its bore. If play is excessive, an oversize lifter must be installed (where possible). Consult a machinist concerning feasibility. If play is satisfactory, remove, lubricate, and reinstall the lifter.
*Testing hydraulic lifter leak down (OHV engines only):	Submerge lifter in a container of kerosene. Chuck a used pushrod or its equivalent into a drill press. Position container of kerosene so pushrod acts on the lifter plunger. Pump lifter with the drill press, until resistance increases. Pump several more times to bleed any air out of lifter. Apply very firm, constant pressure to the lifter, and observe rate at which fluid bleeds out of lifter. If the fluid bleeds very quickly (less than 15 seconds), lifter is defective. If the time exceeds 60 seconds, lifter is sticking. In either case, recondition or replace lifter. If lifter is operating properly (leak down time 15–60 seconds), lubricate and install it.

Cylinder Block Reconditioning

Procedure	Method
Checking the main bearing clearance: PLASTIGAGE® **Plastigage® installed on the lower bearing shell**	Invert engine, and remove cap from the bearing to be checked. Using a clean, dry rag, thoroughly clean all oil from crankshaft journal and bearing insert. NOTE: *Plastigage® is soluble in oil; therefore, oil on the journal or bearing could result in erroneous readings.* Place a piece of Plastigage along the full length of journal, reinstall cap, and torque to specifications. NOTE: *Specifications are given in the engine specifications earlier in this chapter.* Remove bearing cap, and determine bearing clearance by comparing width of Plastigage to the scale on Plastigage envelope. Journal taper is determined by comparing width of the Plastigage strip near its ends. Rotate crankshaft 90° and retest, to determine journal eccentricity. NOTE: *Do not rotate crankshaft with Plastigage*

Cylinder Block Reconditioning

Procedure	Method

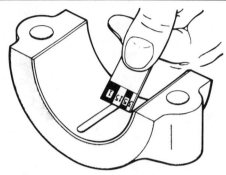

Measure Plastigage® to determine main bearing clearance

installed. If bearing insert and journal appear intact, and are within tolerances, no further main bearing service is required. If bearing or journal appear defective, cause of failure should be determined before replacement.

*Remove crankshaft from block (see below). Measure the main bearing journals at each end tiwce (90° apart) using a micrometer, to determine diameter, journal taper and eccentricity. If journals are within tolerances, reinstall bearing caps at their specified torque. Using a telescope gauge and micrometer, measure bearing I.D. parallel to piston axis and at 30° on each side of piston axis. Subtract journal O.D. from bearing I.D. to determine oil clearance. If crankshaft journals appear defective, or do not meet tolerances, there is no need to measure bearings; for the crankshaft will require grinding and/or undersize bearings will be required. If bearing appears defective, cause for failure should be determined prior to replacement.

Check the connecting rod bearing clearance:

Connecting rod bearing clearance is checked in the same manner as main bearing clearance, using Plastigage. Before removing the crankshaft, connecting rod side clearance also should be measured and recorded.

*Checking connecting rod bearing clearance, using a micrometer, is identical to checking main bearing clearance. If no other service is required, the piston and rod assemblies need not be removed.

Remove the crankshaft:

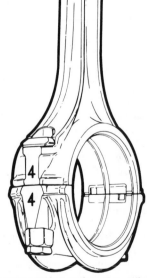

Using a punch, mark the corresponding main bearing caps and saddles according to position (i.e., one punch on the front main cap and saddle, two on the second, three on the third, etc.). Using number stamps, identify the corresponding connecting rods and caps, according to cylinder (if no numbers are present). Remove the main and connecting rod caps, and place sleeves of plastic tubing or vacuum hose over the connecting rod bolts, to protect the journals as the crankshaft is removed. Lift the crankshaft out of the block.

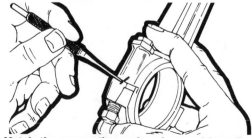

Match the connecting rod to the cylinder with a number stamp

Match the connecting rod and cap with scribe marks

Cylinder Block Reconditioning

Procedure	Method
Remove the ridge from the top of the cylinder: 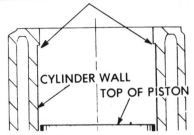 **Cylinder bore ridge**	In order to facilitate removal of the piston and connecting rod, the ridge at the top of the cylinder (unworn area; see illustration) must be removed. Place the piston at the bottom of the bore, and cover it with a rag. Cut the ridge away using a ridge reamer, exercising extreme care to avoid cutting too deeply. Remove the rag, and remove cuttings that remain on the piston. **CAUTION:** *If the ridge is not removed, and new rings are installed, damage to rings will result.*
Remove the piston and connecting rod: 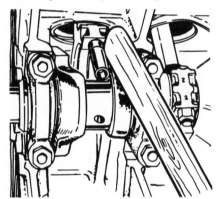 **Push the piston out with a hammer handle**	Invert the engine, and push the pistons and connecting rods out of the cylinders. If necessary, tap the connecting rod boss with a wooden hammer handle, to force the piston out. **CAUTION:** *Do not attempt to force the piston past the cylinder ridge* (see above).
Service the crankshaft:	Ensure that all oil holes and passages in the crankshaft are open and free of sludge. If necessary, have the crankshaft ground to the largest possible undersize.
	**Have the crankshaft Magnafluxed, to locate stress cracks. Consult a machinist concerning additional service procedures, such as surface hardening (e.g., nitriding, Tuftriding) to improve wear characteristics, cross drilling and chamfering the oil holes to improve lubrication, and balancing.
Removing freeze plugs:	Drill a small hole in the middle of the freeze plugs. Thread a large sheet metal screw into the hole and remove the plug with a slide hammer.
Remove the oil gallery plugs:	Threaded plugs should be removed using an appropriate (usually square) wrench. To remove soft, pressed in plugs, drill a hole in the plug, and thread in a sheet metal screw. Pull the plug out by the screw using pliers.
Hot-tank the block: NOTE: *Do not hot-tank aluminum parts.*	Have the block hot-tanked to remove grease, corrosion, and scale from the water jackets. **NOTE:** *Consult the operator to determine whether the camshaft bearings will be damaged during the hot-tank process.*

The RIDGE CAUSED BY CYLINDER WEAR, CYLINDER WALL, TOP OF PISTON (labels in illustration 1)

Cylinder Block Reconditioning

Procedure	Method

Check the block for cracks:	Visually inspect the block for cracks or chips. The most common locations are as follows:
	    Adjacent to freeze plugs.
	    Between the cylinders and water jackets.
	    Adjacent to the main bearing saddles.
	    At the extreme bottom of the cylinders.
	Check only suspected cracks using spot check dye (see introduction). If a crack is located, consult a machinist concerning possible repairs.

	** Magnaflux the block to locate hidden cracks. If cracks are located, consult a machinist about feasibility of repair.
Install the oil gallery plugs and freeze plugs:	Coat freeze plugs with sealer and tap into position using a piece of pipe, slightly smaller than the plug, as a driver. To ensure retention, stake the edges of the plugs. Coat threaded oil gallery plugs with sealer and install. Drive replacement soft plugs into block using a large drift as driver.
	* Rather than reinstalling lead plugs, drill and tap the holes, and install threaded plugs.
Check the bore diameter and surface: 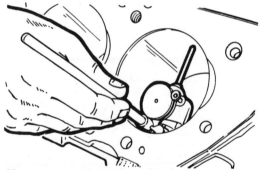 **Measure the cylinder bore with a dial gauge**	Visually inspect the cylinder bores for roughness, scoring, or scuffing. If evident, the cylinder bore must be bored or honed oversize to eliminate imperfections, and the smallest possible oversize piston used. The new pistons should be given to the machinist with the block, so that the cylinders can be bored or honed exactly to the piston size (plus clearance). If no flaws are evident, measure the bore diameter using a telescope gauge and micrometer, or dial gauge, parallel and perpendicular to the engine centerline, at the top (below the ridge) and bottom of the bore. Subtract the bottom measurements from the top to determine taper, and the parallel to the centerline measurements from the perpendicular measurements to determine eccentricity. If the measurements are not within specifications, the cylinder must be bored or honed, and an oversize piston installed. If the measurements are within specifications the cylinder may be used as is, with only finish honing (see below).

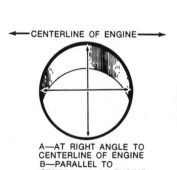

A—AT RIGHT ANGLE TO CENTERLINE OF ENGINE
B—PARALLEL TO CENTERLINE OF ENGINE

Cylinder bore measuring points

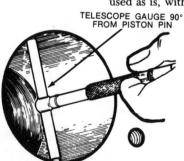

Measure the cylinder bore with a telescope gauge

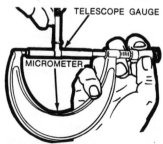

Measure the telescope gauge with a micrometer to determine the cylinder bore

Cylinder Block Reconditioning

Procedure	Method
	NOTE: *Prior to submitting the block for boring, perform the following operation(s).*
Check the cylinder block bearing alignment: 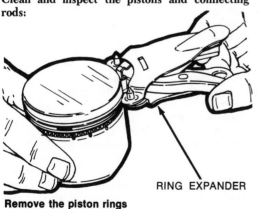 **Check the main bearing saddle alignment**	Remove the upper bearing inserts. Place a straightedge in the bearing saddles along the centerline of the crankshaft. If clearance exists between the straightedge and the center saddle, the block must be alignbored.
*Check the deck height:	The deck height is the distance from the crankshaft centerline to the block deck. To measure, invert the engine, and install the crankshaft, retaining it with the center main cap. Measure the distance from the crankshaft journal to the block deck, parallel to the cylinder centerline. Measure the diameter of the end (front and rear) main journals, parallel to the centerline of the cylinders, divide the diameter in half, and subtract it from the previous measurement. The results of the front and rear measurements should be identical. If the difference exceeds .005″, the deck height should be corrected. NOTE: *Block deck height and warpage should be corrected at the same time.*
Check the block deck for warpage:	Using a straightedge and feeler gauges, check the block deck for warpage in the same manner that the cylinder head is checked (see Cylinder Head Reconditioning). If warpage exceeds specifications, have the deck resurfaced. NOTE: *In certain cases a specification for total material removal (Cylinder head and block deck) is provided. This specification must not be exceeded.*
Clean and inspect the pistons and connecting rods:	Using a ring expander, remove the rings from the piston. Remove the retaining rings (if so equipped) and remove piston pin. NOTE: *If the piston pin must be pressed out, determine the proper method and use the proper tools; otherwise the piston will distort.* Clean the ring grooves using an appropriate tool, exercising care to avoid cutting too deeply. Thoroughly clean all carbon and varnish from the piston with solvent. CAUTION: *Do not use a wire brush or caustic solvent on pistons.* Inspect the pistons for scuffing, scoring, cracks, pitting, or excessive ring groove wear. If wear is evident, the piston must be replaced. Check the connecting rod length by measuring the rod from the inside of the large end to the

RING EXPANDER

Remove the piston rings

Cylinder Block Reconditioning

Procedure	Method

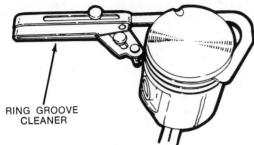

RING GROOVE
CLEANER

Clean the piston ring grooves

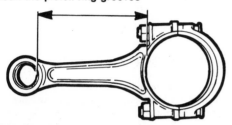

Check the connecting rod length (arrow)

inside of the small end using calipers (see illustration). All connecting rods should be equal length. Replace any rod that differs from the others in the engine.

* Have the connecting rod alignment checked in an alignment fixture by a machinist. Replace any twisted or bent rods.

* Magnaflux the connecting rods to locate stress cracks. If cracks are found, replace the connecting rod.

Fit the pistons to the cylinders:

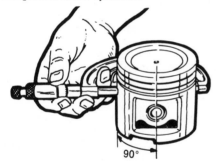

90°
Measure the piston prior to fitting

Using a telescope gauge and micrometer, or a dial gauge, measure the cylinder bore diameter perpendicular to the piston pin, 2½" below the deck. Measure the piston perpendicular to its pin on the skirt. The difference between the two measurements is the piston clearance. If the clearance is within specifications or slightly below (after boring or honing), finish honing is all that is required. If the clearance is excessive, try to obtain a slightly larger piston to bring clearance within specifications. Where this is not possible, obtain the first oversize piston, and hone (or if necessary, bore) the cylinder to size.

Assemble the pistons and connecting rods:

Install the piston pin lock-rings (if used)

Inspect piston pin, connecting rod small end bushing, and piston bore for galling, scoring, or excessive wear. If evident, replace defective part(s). Measure the I.D. of the piston boss and connecting rod small end, and the O.D. of the piston pin. If within specifications, assemble piston pin and rod.
CAUTION: *If piston pin must be pressed in, determine the proper method and use the proper tools; otherwise the piston will distort.*
Install the lock rings; ensure that they seat properly. If the parts are not within specifications, determine the service method for the type of engine. In some cases, piston and pin are serviced as an assembly when either is defective. Others specify reaming the piston and connecting rods for an oversize pin. If the connecting rod bushing is worn, it may in many cases be replaced. Reaming the piston and replacing the rod bushing are machine shop operations.

Cylinder Block Reconditioning

Procedure	Method

Clean and inspect the camshaft:

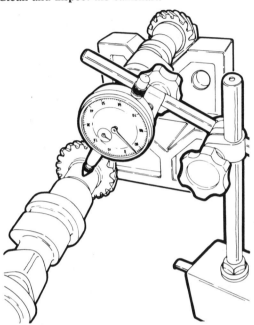

Degrease the camshaft, using solvent, and clean out all oil holes. Visually inspect cam lobes and bearing journals for excessive wear. If a lobe is questionable, check all lobes as indicated below. If a journal or lobe is worn, the camshaft must be reground or replaced.

NOTE: *If a journal is worn, there is a good chance that the bushings are worn.* If lobes and journals appear intact, place the front and rear journals in V-blocks, and rest a dial indicator on the center journal. Rotate the camshaft to check straightness. If deviation exceeds .001″, replace the camshaft.

* Check the camshaft lobes with a micrometer, by measuring the lobes from the nose to base and again at 90° (see illustration). The lift is determined by subtracting the second measurement from the first. If all exhaust lobes and all intake lobes are not identical, the camshaft must be reground or replaced.

Check the camshaft for straightness

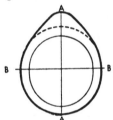

Camshaft lobe measurement

Replace the camshaft bearings (OHV engines only):

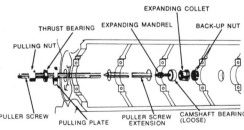

Camshaft bearing removal and installation tool (OHV engines only)

If excessive wear is indicated, or if the engine is being completely rebuilt, camshaft bearings should be replaced as follows: Drive the camshaft rear plug from the block. Assemble the removal puller with its shoulder on the bearing to be removed. Gradually tighten the puller nut until bearing is removed. Remove remaining bearings, leaving the front and rear for last. To remove front and rear bearings, reverse position of the tool, so as to pull the bearings in toward the center of the block. Leave the tool in this position, pilot the new front and rear bearings on the installer, and pull them into position: Return the tool to its original position and pull remaining bearings into position.

NOTE: *Ensure that oil holes align when installing bearings.* Replace camshaft rear plug, and stake it into position to aid retention.

Finish hone the cylinders:

Chuck a flexible drive hone into a power drill, and insert it into the cylinder. Start the hone, and move it up and down in the cylinder at a rate which will produce approximately a 60° crosshatch pattern.

NOTE: *Do not extend the hone below the cylin-*

Cylinder Block Reconditioning

Procedure	Method

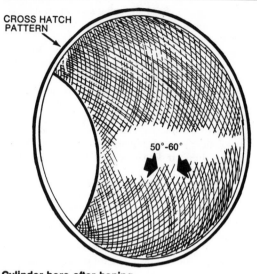

CROSS HATCH PATTERN

50°-60°

Cylinder bore after honing

der bore. After developing the pattern, remove the hone and recheck piston fit. Wash the cylinders with a detergent and water solution to remove abrasive dust, dry, and wipe several times with a rag soaked in engine oil.

Check piston ring end-gap:

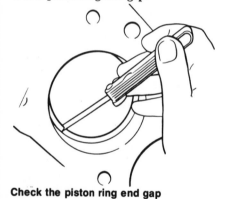

Check the piston ring end gap

Compress the piston rings to be used in a cylinder, one at a time, into that cylinder, and press them approximately 1″ below the deck with an inverted piston. Using feeler gauges, measure the ring end-gap, and compare to specifications. Pull the ring out of the cylinder and file the ends with a fine file to obtain proper clearance.
CAUTION: *If inadequate ring end-gap is utilized, ring breakage will result.*

Install the piston rings:

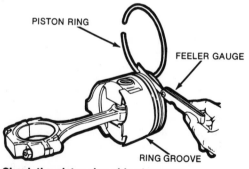

PISTON RING

FEELER GAUGE

RING GROOVE

Check the piston ring side clearance

Inspect the ring grooves in the piston for excessive wear or taper. If necessary, recut the grooves(s) for use with an overwidth ring or a standard ring and spacer. If the groove is worn uniformly, overwidth rings, or standard rings and spacers may be installed without recutting. Roll the outside of the ring around the groove to check for burrs or deposits. If any are found, remove with a fine file. Hold the ring in the groove, and measure side clearance. If necessary, correct as indicated above.
NOTE: *Always install any additional spacers above the piston ring.*
The ring groove must be deep enough to allow the ring to seat below the lands (see illustration). In many cases, a "go-no-go" depth gauge will be provided with the piston rings. Shallow grooves may be corrected by recutting, while deep grooves require some type of filler or expander behind the piston. Consult the piston ring sup-

Cylinder Block Reconditioning

Procedure	Method

	plier concerning the suggested method. Install the rings on the piston, lowest ring first, using a ring expander.

NOTE: *Position the ring as specified by the manufacturer.* Consult the engine service procedures earlier in this chapter for details concerning specific engines.

Install the camshaft (OHV engines only):

Liberally lubricate the camshaft lobes and journals, and install the camshaft.

CAUTION: *Exercise extreme care to avoid damaging the bearings when inserting the camshaft.*

Install and tighten the camshaft thrust plate retaining bolts.

See the engine service procedures earlier in this chapter for details concerning specific engines.

Check camshaft end-play (OHV engines only):

Using feeler gauges, determine whether the clearance between the camshaft boss (or gear) and backing plate is within specifications. Install shims behind the thrust plate, or reposition the camshaft gear and retest endplay. In some cases, adjustment is by replacing the thrust plate.

See the engine service procedures earlier in this chapter for details concerning specific engines.

Check the camshaft end-play with a feeler gauge

* Mount a dial indicator stand so that the stem of the dial indicator rests on the nose of the camshaft, parallel to the camshaft axis. Push the camshaft as far in as possible and zero the gauge. Move the camshaft outward to determine the amount of camshaft endplay. If the endplay is not within tolerance, install shims behind the thrust plate, or reposition the camshaft gear and retest.

See the engine service procedures earlier in this chapter for details concerning specific engines.

DIAL INDICATOR

CAMSHAFT

Check the camshaft end-play with a dial indicator

Install the rear main seal:

See the engine service procedures earlier in this chapter for details concerning specific engines.

Install the crankshaft:

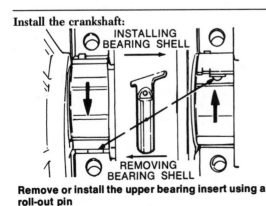

INSTALLING BEARING SHELL

REMOVING BEARING SHELL

Remove or install the upper bearing insert using a roll-out pin

Thoroughly clean the main bearing saddles and caps. Place the upper halves of the bearing inserts on the saddles and press into position.

NOTE: *Ensure that the oil holes align.* Press the corresponding bearing inserts into the main bearing caps. Lubricate the upper main bearings, and lay the crankshaft in position. Place a strip of Plastigage on each of the crankshaft journals, install the main caps, and torque to specifications. Remove the main caps, and compare the Plastigage to the scale on the Plastigage envelope. If clearances are within tolerances, remove the Plastigage, turn the crankshaft 90°, wipe off all oil and retest. If all clearances are correct, re-

Cylinder Block Reconditioning

Procedure	Method

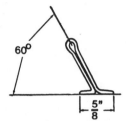

Home-made bearing roll-out pin

move all Plastigage, thoroughly lubricate the main caps and bearing journals, and install the main caps. If clearances are not within tolerance, the upper bearing inserts may be removed, without removing the crankshaft, using a bearing roll out pin (see illustration). Roll in a bearing that will provide proper clearance, and retest. Torque all main caps, excluding the thrust bearing cap, to specifications. Tighten the thrust bearing cap finger tight. To properly align the thrust bearing, pry the crankshaft the extent of its axial travel several times, the last movement held toward the front of the engine, and torque the thrust bearing cap to specifications. Determine the crankshaft end-play (see below), and bring within tolerance with thrust washers.

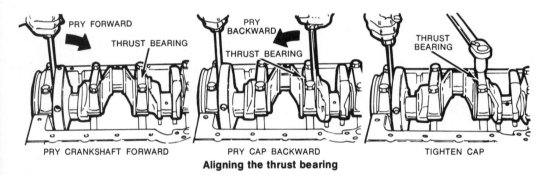

Aligning the thrust bearing

Measure crankshaft end-play:

Mount a dial indicator stand on the front of the block, with the dial indicator stem resting on the nose of the crankshaft, parallel to the crankshaft axis. Pry the crankshaft the extent of its travel rearward, and zero the indicator. Pry the crankshaft forward and record crankshaft end-play.

NOTE: *Crankshaft end-play also may be measured at the thrust bearing, using feeler gauges (see illustration).*

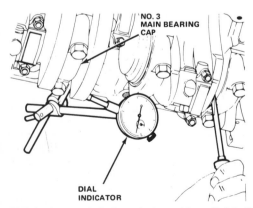

Check the crankshaft end-play with a dial indicator

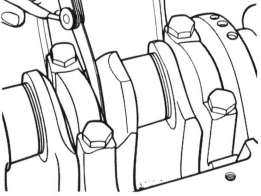

Check the crankshaft end-play with a feeler gauge

Cylinder Block Reconditioning

Procedure	Method
Install the pistons:	Press the upper connecting rod bearing halves into the connecting rods, and the lower halves into the connecting rod caps. Position the piston ring gaps according to specifications (see car section), and lubricate the pistons. Install a ring compresser on a piston, and press two long (8″) pieces of plastic tubing over the rod bolts. Using the tubes as a guide, press the pistons into the bores and onto the crankshaft with a wooden hammer handle. After seating the rod on the crankshaft journal, remove the tubes and install the cap finger tight. Install the remaining pistons in the same manner. Invert the engine and check the bearing clearance at two points (90° apart) on each journal with Plastigage.

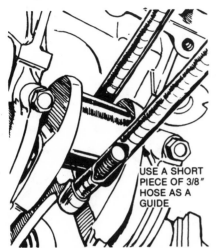

USE A SHORT PIECE OF 3/8″ HOSE AS A GUIDE

Use lengths of vacuum hose or rubber tubing to protect the crankshaft journals and cylinder walls during piston installation

NOTE: *Do not turn the crankshaft with Plastigage installed.* If clearance is within tolerances, remove *all* Plastigage, thoroughly lubricate the journals, and torque the rod caps to specifications. If clearance is not within specifications, install different thickness bearing inserts and recheck.

CAUTION: *Never shim or file the connecting rods or caps.* Always install plastic tube sleeves over the rod bolts when the caps are not installed, to protect the crankshaft journals.

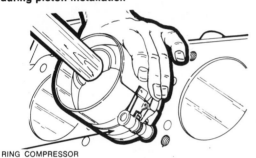

RING COMPRESSOR

Install the piston using a ring compressor

Procedure	Method
Check connecting rod side clearance:	Determine the clearance between the sides of the connecting rods and the crankshaft, using feeler gauges. If clearance is below the minimum tolerance, the rod may be machined to provide adequate clearance. If clearance is excessive, substitute an unworn rod, and recheck. If clearance is still outside specifications, the crankshaft must be welded and reground, or replaced.

Check the connecting rod side clearance with a feeler gauge

Procedure	Method
Inspect the timing chain (or belt):	Visually inspect the timing chain for broken or loose links, and replace the chain if any are found. If the chain will flex sideways, it must be replaced. Install the timing chain as specified. Be sure the timing belt is not stretched, frayed or broken. NOTE: *If the original timing chain is to be reused, install it in its original position.*

Cylinder Block Reconditioning

Procedure	Method
Check timing gear backlash and runout (OHV engines):  Check the camshaft gear backlash	Mount a dial indicator with its stem resting on a tooth of the camshaft gear (as illustrated). Rotate the gear until all slack is removed, and zero the indicator. Rotate the gear in the opposite direction until slack is removed, and record gear backlash. Mount the indicator with its stem resting on the edge of the camshaft gear, parallel to the axis of the camshaft. Zero the indicator, and turn the camshaft gear one full turn, recording the runout. If either backlash or runout exceed specifications, replace the worn gear(s). 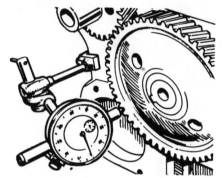 Check the camshaft gear run-out

Completing the Rebuilding Process

Following the above procedures, complete the rebuilding process as follows:

Fill the oil pump with oil, to prevent cavitating (sucking air) on initial engine start up. Install the oil pump and the pickup tube on the engine. Coat the oil pan gasket as necessary, and install the gasket and the oil pan. Mount the flywheel and the crankshaft vibration damper or pulley on the crankshaft. NOTE: *Always use new bolts when installing the flywheel.* Inspect the clutch shaft pilot bushing in the crankshaft. If the bushing is excessively worn, remove it with an expanding puller and a slide hammer, and tap a new bushing into place.

Position the engine, cylinder head side up. Lubricate the lifters, and install them into their bores. Install the cylinder head, and torque it as specified. Insert the pushrods (where applicable), and install the rocker shaft(s) (if so equipped) or position the rocker arms on the pushrods. Adjust the valves.

Install the intake and exhaust manifolds, the carburetor(s), the distributor and spark plugs. Adjust the point gap and the static ignition timing. Mount all accessories and install the engine in the car. Fill the radiator with coolant, and the crankcase with high quality engine oil.

Break-in Procedure

Start the engine, and allow it to run at low speed for a few minutes, while checking for leaks. Stop the engine, check the oil level, and fill as necessary. Restart the engine, and fill the cooling system to capacity. Check the point dwell angle and adjust the ignition timing and the valves. Run the engine at low to medium speed (800–2500 rpm) for approximately ½ hour, and retorque the cylinder head bolts. Road test the car, and check again for leaks.

Follow the manufacturer's recommended engine break-in procedure and maintenance schedule for new engines.

Emission Controls and Fuel System

EMISSION CONTROLS

Positive Crankcase Ventilation (PCV) System

A positive crankcase ventilation (PCV) system is used on all Toyotas sold in the United States. Blow-by gases are routed from the crankcase to the carburetor, where they are combined with the fuel/air mixture and burned during combustion.

A valve (PCV) is used in the line to prevent the gases in the crankcase from being ignited in case of a backfire. The amount of blow-by gases entering the mixture is also regulated by the PCV valve, which is spring-loaded and has a variable orifice.

On Toyotas, the valve is either mounted on the valve cover (3K-C, 4K-C) or in the line which runs from the intake manifold to the crankcase.

The valve should be replaced at the following intervals:
- 1970–71 models—12,000mi/12mo
- 1972–74 models—24,000mi/24mo
- 1975–77 models—25,000mi/24mo
- 1978–81 models—30,000mi/24mo

REMOVAL AND INSTALLATION

Remove the PCV valve from the cylinder head cover on 3K-C, and 4K-C engines. Remove the hose from the valve.

On the remainder of the engines, remove the valve from the manifold-to-crankcase hose.

Installation is the reverse of removal.

TESTING

Check the PCV system hoses and connections, to ensure that there are no leaks; then replace or tighten, as necessary.

To check the valve, remove it and blow through both of its ends. When blowing from the side which goes toward the intake manifold, very little air should pass through it. When blowing from the crankcase (valve cover) side, air should pass through freely.

Replace the valve with a new one, if the valve fails to function as outlined.

NOTE: *Do not attempt to clean or adjust the valve; replace it with a new one.*

Air Injection System

A belt-drive air pump supplies air to an injection manifold which has nozzles in each exhaust port. Injection of air at this point causes combustion of unburned hydrocarbons in the exhaust manifold rather than allowing them to escape into the atmosphere. An anti-back-fire valve controls the flow of air from the pump to prevent backfiring which results

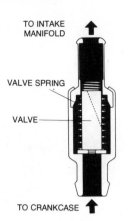

IDLE SPEED OR DECELERATION
(HIGH MANIFOLD VACUUM)

TO INTAKE MANIFOLD

VALVE SPRING

VALVE

TO CRANKCASE

NOT RUNNING
OR BACKFIRE

PCV valve operation

from an overly rich mixture under closed throttle conditions. There are two types of antibackfire valve used on Toyota models: 1970–71 models use "gulp" valves; 1972–81 models "air by-pass" valves.

A check valve prevents hot exhaust gas backflow into the pump and hoses, in case of a pump failure, or when the antibackfire valve is not working.

In addition all 1975–81 engines have an air switching valve (ASV). On engines without catalytic converters, the ASV is used to stop air injection under a constant heavy engine load condition.

On engines with catalytic converters, the ASV is also used to protect the catalyst from overheating, by blocking the injected air necessary for the operation of the converter.

On all 1975–81 passenger car engines, the pump relief valve is built into the ASV.

The following engines use air injection:
- 3K-C—1970–71
- 2T-C—1974 California; 1975–81 All
- 3T-C-All
- 1A-C, 3A, 3A-C-All

REMOVAL AND INSTALLATION
Air Pump

1. Disconnect the air hoses from the pump.

2. Loosen the bolt on the adjusting link and remove the drive belt.

3. Remove the mounting bolts and withdraw the pump.

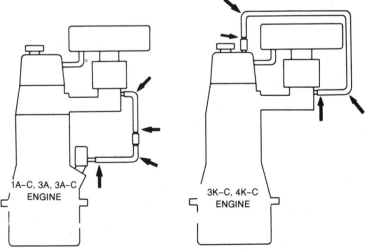

1A–C, 3A, 3A–C ENGINE

3K–C, 4K–C ENGINE

Hose routing for PCV system—arrows indicate inspection points

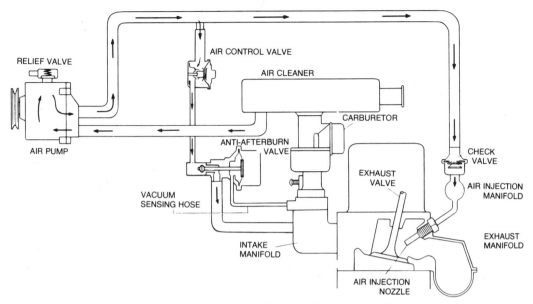

Air injection system (without catalytic converter)

CAUTION: *Do not pry on the pump housing; it may be distorted.*

Installation is in the reverse order of removal. Adjust the drive belt tension after installation. Belt deflection should be ½–¾ in. with 22 lbs. pressure.

Anti-backfire Valve and Air Switching Valve

1. Detach the air hoses from the valve, and electrical leads (4M, ASV 1975).
2. Remove the valve securing bolt.
3. Withdraw the valve.

Installation is performed in the reverse order of removal.

Check Valve

1. Detach the intake hose from the valve.
2. Use an open-end wrench to remove the valve from its mounting.

Installation is the reverse of removal.

Relief Valve—1970–74

1. Remove the air pump from the car.
2. Support the pump so that it cannot rotate.

CAUTION: *Never clamp the pump in a vise; the aluminum case will be distorted.*

3. Use a bridge to remove the relief valve from the top of the pump.
4. Position the new relief valve over the opening in the pump.

NOTE: *The air outlet should be pointing toward the left.*

5. Gently tap the relief valve home, using a block of wood and a hammer.
6. Install the pump on the engine, as outlined above.

NOTE: *For 1975–77 models with ASV-mounted relief valves, replace the entire ASV/relief valve as an assembly.*

Removing the check valve

Removing the pump-mounted relief valve

Air Injection Manifold

1. Remove the check valve, as previously outlined.

2. Loosen the air injection manifold attachment nuts and withdraw the manifold.

Installation is in the reverse order of removal.

Air Injection Nozzles

1. Remove the air injection manifold as previously outlined.

2. Remove the cylinder head, as detailed in Chapter 3.

3. Place a new nozzle on the cylinder head.

4. Install the air injection manifold over it.

5. Install the cylinder head on the engine block.

Air Control Valve—3K-C 4K-C Engine

The air control valve is used only on the 3K-C and 4K-C engines. It is removed by simply unfastening the hoses from it.

TESTING

Air Pump

> CAUTION: *Do not hammer, pry, or bend the pump housing while tightening the drive belt or testing the pump.*

BELT TENSION AND AIR LEAKS

1. Before proceeding with the tests, check the pump drive belt tension to ensure that it is within specifications.

2. Turn the pump by hand. If it has seized, the belt will slip, making a noise. Disregard any chirping, squealing, or rolling sounds from inside the pump; these are normal when it is turned by hand.

3. Check the hoses and connections for leaks. Hissing or a blast of air is indicative of a leak. Soapy water, applied lightly around the area in question, is a good method for detecting leaks.

AIR OUTPUT

1. Disconnect the air supply hose at the antibackfire valve.

2. Connect a vacuum gauge, using a suitable adaptor, to the air supply hose.
NOTE: *If there are two hoses, plug the second one.*

3. With the engine at normal operating temperature, increase the idle speed and watch the vacuum gauge.

4. The airflow from the pump should be steady and fall between 2 and 6 psi. If it is unsteady or falls below this, the pump is defective and must be replaced.

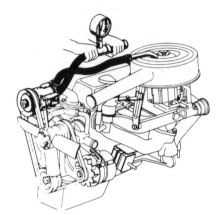

Checking the air pump output

PUMP NOISE DIAGNOSIS

The air pump is normally noisy; as engine speed increases, the noise of the pump will rise in pitch. The rolling sound the pump bearings make is normal. But if this sound becomes objectionable at certain speeds, the pump is defective and will have to be replaced.

A continual hissing sound from the air pump pressure relief valve at idle, indicates a defective valve. Replace the relief valve.

If the pump rear bearing fails, a continual knocking sound will be heard. Since the rear bearing is not separately replaceable, the pump will have to be replaced as an assembly.

Anti-backfire Valve Tests

There are two different types of anti-backfire valve used with air injection systems. A bypass valve is used on 1972 and later engines, while 1970–71 engines use a gulp type of anti-backfire valve. Test procedures for both types are given below.

GULP VALVE

1. Detach the air supply hose which runs between the pump and the gulp valve.

2. Connect a tachometer and run the engine to 1,500–2,000 rpm.

3. Allow the throttle to snap shut. This should produce a loud sucking sound from the gulp valve.

4. Repeat this operation several times. If

no sound is present, the valve is not working or else the vacuum connections are loose.

5. Check the vacuum connections. If they are secure, replace the gulp valve.

BY-PASS VALVE

1. Detach the hose, which runs from the by-pass valve to the check valve, at the by-pass valve hose connection.

2. Connect a tachometer to the engine. With the engine running at normal idle speed, check to see that air is flowing from the by-pass valve hose connection.

3. Speed up the engine so that it is running at 1,500–2,000 rpm. Allow the throttle to snap shut. The flow of air from the by-pass valve at the check valve hose connection should stop momentarily and air should then flow from the exhaust port on the valve body or the silencer assembly.

4. Repeat Step 3 several times. If the flow of air is not diverted into the atmosphere from the valve exhaust port or if it fails to stop flowing from the hose connection, check the vacuum lines and connections. If these are tight, the valve is defective and requires replacement.

5. A leaking diaphragm will cause the air to flow out both the hose connection and the exhaust port at the same time. If this happens, replace the valve.

Check Valve Test

1. Before starting the test, check all of the hoses and connections for leaks.

2. Detach the air supply hose from the check valve.

3. Insert a suitable probe into the check valve and depress the plate. Release it; the plate should return to its original position against the valve seat. If binding is evident, replace the valve.

4. With the engine running at normal operating temperature, gradually increase its speed to 1,500 rpm. Check for exhaust gas leakage. If any is present, replace the valve assembly.

NOTE: *Vibration and flutter of the check valve at idle speed is a normal condition and does not mean that the valve should be replaced.*

Air Switching Valve (ASV) Tests

1975–81 2T-C ENGINES

1. Start the engine and allow it to reach normal operating temperature and speed.

2. At curb idle, the air from the by-pass

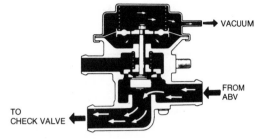

Checking the 2T-C ASV

valve should be discharged through the hose which runs to the ASV.

3. When the vacuum line to the ASV is disconnected, the air from the by-pass valve should be diverted out through the ASV-to-air cleaner hose. Reconnect the vacuum line.

4. Disconnect the ASV-to-check valve hose and connect a pressure gauge to it.

5. Increase the engine speed. The relief valve should open when the pressure gauge registers 2.7–6.5 psi.

6. If the ASV fails any of the above tests, replace it. Reconnect all hoses.

Vacuum Delay Valve Test

1975–81 2T-C ENGINES

The vacuum delay valve is located in the line which runs from the intake manifold to either the vacuum surge tank (20R) or to the ASV (2T-C). To check it, proceed as follows:

1. Remove the vacuum delay valve from the vacuum line. Be sure to note which end points toward the intake manifold.

2. When air is blown in from the ASV (surge tank) side, it should pass through the valve freely.

3. When air is blown in from the intake manifold side, a resistance should be felt.

4. Replace the valve if it fails either of the above tests.

5. Install the valve in the vacuum line, being careful not to install it backward.

Evaporative Emission Control System

To prevent hydrocarbon emissions from entering the atmosphere, Toyota vehicles use evaporative emission control (EEC) systems. Models produced between 1970 and 1971 use a "case" storage system, while 1972–81 models use a "charcoal canister" storage system.

The major components of the case storage system are a purge control or vacuum switch-

Air Injection System Diagnosis Chart

Problem	Cause	Cure
1. Noisy drive belt	1a Loose belt 1b Seized pump	1a Tighten belt 1b Replace
2. Noisy pump	2a Leaking hose 2b Loose hose 2c Hose contacting other parts 2d Diverter or check valve failure 2e Pump mounting loose 2f Defective pump	2a Trace and fix leak 2b Tighten hose clamp 2c Reposition hose 2d Replace 2e Tighten securing bolts 2f Replace
3. No air supply	3a Loose belt 3b Leak in hose or at fitting 3c Defective antibackfire valve 3d Defective check valve 3e Defective pump 3f Defective ASV	3a Tighten belt 3b Trace and fix leak 3c Replace 3d Replace 3e Replace 3f Replace
4. Exhaust backfire	4a Vacuum or air leaks 4b Defective antibackfire valve 4c Sticking choke 4d Choke setting rich	4a Trace and fix leak 4b Replace 4c Service choke 4d Adjust choke

ing valve, a fuel vapor storage case, an air filter, a thermal expansion tank, and a special fuel tank.

When the vehicle is stopped or the engine is running at a low speed, the purge control or vacuum switching valve is closed; fuel vapor travels only as far as the case where it is stored.

When the engine is running at a high speed (cruising speed), the purge control valve is opened by pressure from the air pump or else the vacuum switching valve

opens—depending upon the type of emission control system used (see the "Evaporative Emission Control System Usage" chart). This allows the vapor stored in the case to be drawn into the intake manifold along with fresh air which is drawn in from the filter.

The charcoal canister storage system functions in a similar manner to the case system, except that the fuel vapors are stored in a canister filled with activated charcoal, rather than in a case, and that all models use a vacuum switching valve to purge the system.

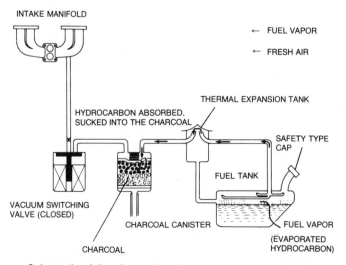

Schematic of the charcoal canister vapor storage system

The air filter is not external as it is on the case system; rather it is an integral part of the charcoal canister.

REMOVAL AND INSTALLATION

Removal and installation of the various evaporative emission control system components consists of unfastening hoses, loosening securing screws, and removing the part which is to be replaced from its mounting bracket. Installation is the reverse of removal.

NOTE: *When replacing any EEC system hoses, always use hoses that are fuel-resistant or are marked "EVAP."*

TESTING

EEC System Troubleshooting

There are several things which may be checked if a malfunction of the evaporative emission control system is suspected.

1. Leaks may be traced by using a hydrocarbon tester. Run the test probe along the lines and connections. The meter will indicate the presence of a leak by a high hydrocarbon (HC) reading. This method is much more accurate than visual inspection which would only indicate the presence of a leak large enough to pass liquid.

2. Leaks may be caused by any of the following:

    a. Defective or worn hoses;

    b. Disconnected or pinched hoses;

    c. Improperly routed hoses;

    d. A defective filler cap or safety valve (sealed cap system).

NOTE: *If it becomes necessary to replace any of the hoses used in the evaporative emission control system, use only hoses which are fuel-resistant or are marked "EVAP."*

3. If the fuel tank, storage case, or thermal expansion tank collapse, it may be the fault of clogged or pinched vent lines, a defective vapor separator, or a plugged or incorrect filler cap.

4. To test the filler cap (if it is the safety valve type), clean it and place it against the mouth. Blow into the relief valve housing. If the cap passes pressure with light blowing or if it fails to release with hard blowing, it is defective and must be replaced.

NOTE: *Use the proper cap for the type of system used; either a sealed cap or safety valve cap, as required. See the chart at the end of this section for proper cap usage.*

PURGE CONTROL VALVE—1970–71

NOTE: *This valve is used only on 1970–71 engines which are also equipped with an air injection system.*

1. Disconnect the line which runs from the storage case to the valve, at the valve end.

2. Connect a tachometer to the engine in accordance with the manufacturer's instructions.

3. Start the engine and slowly increase its speed until the tachometer reads 2,500 rpm (transmission in Neutral).

4. Place a finger over the hose fitting (storage-case-to-valve) on the valve.

5. If there is no suction, check the air pump for a malfunction. (See above.) If the air pump is not defective, replace the valve.

CHECK VALVE—COROLLA 1971–72

Rough idling when the gas tank is full is probably caused by a defective check valve. To test it, proceed as follows:

1. Run the engine at idle.

2. Clamp the hose between the vacuum switching valve and the charcoal canister or case.

3. If the engine idle becomes smooth, replace the check valve.

CHECK VALVE—ALL MODELS 1973–81

The check valve is located in the line which runs from the fuel tank (or vapor separator) to the charcoal canister. On all 1973 models, as well as all Corolla models, it is located in the trunk; on all other models it is located in the engine compartment, near the charcoal canister. To test the check valve, proceed as follows:

1. Remove the check valve from the fuel tank-to-canister line. Note which end goes toward the tank and which end toward the canister.

2. Blow into the fuel tank end; a slight resistance should be felt at first.

3. Blow through the canister end; no resistance should be felt at all.

4. Replace the check valve if it is defective.

Carburetor Auxiliary Slow System

A carburetor auxiliary slow system is used on 1970–71 3K-C engines. It provides uniform combustion during deceleration. The com-

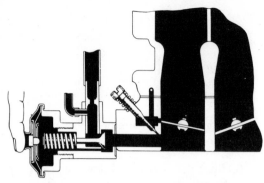

Inspecting the auxiliary slow system diaphgram

ponents of the auxiliary slow system consists of a vacuum-operated valve, a fresh air intake, and a fuel line which is connected to the carburetor float chamber.

During deceleration, manifold vacuum acts on the valve which opens it, causing additional air/fuel mixture to flow into the intake manifold. The additional mixture aids in more complete combustion.

REMOVAL AND INSTALLATION

1. Remove the hoses from the auxiliary slow system unit.

2. Unfasten the recessed screws and withdraw the system as a complete unit.

Installation is performed in the reverse order of the above.

Testing

1. Start the engine, allow it to reach normal operating temperature, and run it at normal idle speed.

2. Remove the rubber cap from the diaphragm assembly and place your finger over the opening. There should be no suction at idle speed. If there is, the diaphragm is defective and the unit must be replaced.

3. Pinch the air intake hose which runs from the air cleaner to the auxiliary slow system. There should be no change in engine idle with the hose pinched.

4. Disconnect the air intake hose at the auxiliary slow system. Race the engine. Place your finger over the air intake. Release the throttle; suction should be felt at the air intake.

5. If any of the tests indicate a defective auxiliary slow system, replace it as a unit.

Throttle Positioner

On Toyotas with an engine modification system, a throttle positioner is included to reduce exhaust emissions during declaration. The positioner prevents the throttle from closing completely. Vacuum is reduced under the throttle valve which, in turn, acts on the retard chamber of the distributor vacuum unit. This compensates for the loss of engine braking caused by the partially opened throttle.

NOTE: *For a description of the operation of the dual-diaphragm distributor, see "Dual-Diaphragm Distributor," which follows.*

Once the vehicle drops below a predetermined speed, the vacuum switching valve

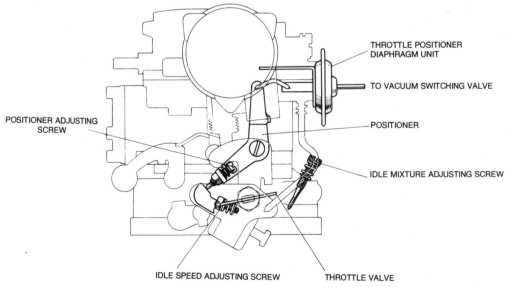

THROTTLE POSITIONER DIAPHRAGM UNIT

TO VACUUM SWITCHING VALVE

POSITIONER

IDLE MIXTURE ADJUSTING SCREW

POSITIONER ADJUSTING SCREW

IDLE SPEED ADJUSTING SCREW

THROTTLE VALVE

Components of the throttle positioner

provides vacuum to the throttle positioner diaphragm; the throttle positioner retracts allowing the throttle valve to close completely. The distributor also is returned to normal operation.

ADJUSTMENT

1. Start the engine and allow it to reach normal operating temperature.

2. Adjust the idle speed as detailed in Chapter 1.

NOTE: *Leave the tachometer connected after completing the idle adjustments, as it will be needed in Step 5.*

3. Detach the vacuum line from the positioner diaphragm unit and plug the line up.

4. Accelerate the engine slightly to set the throttle positioner in place.

5. Check the engine speed with a tachometer when the throttle positioner is set.

6. If necessary, adjust the engine speed, with the throttle positioner adjusting screw, to the specifications given in the "Throttle Positioner Settings" chart at the end of this section.

7. Connect the vacuum hose to the positioner diaphragm.

8. The throttle lever should be freed from the positioner as soon as the vacuum hose is connected. Engine idle should return to normal.

Throttle Positioner Setting
(rpm)

Year	Engine	Engine rpm (Positioner Set)
1975–77 ①	2T-C	1500 MT 1400 AT ①
	3K-C	1500 (Canada)
1978–81	2T-C	1400 MT 1200 AT
	3T-C	1600 MT 1300 AT ②
	1A-C, 3A	N.A.
1981	4K-C	2000

① 1977: 1200
② Calif.: 1400
AT Automatic transmission
MT Manual transmission

9. If the throttle positioner fails to function properly, check its linkage, and vacuum diaphragm. If there are no defects in either of these, the fault probably lies in the vacuum switching valve or the speed marker unit.

NOTE: *Due to the complexity of these two components, and also because they require special test equipment, their service is best left to an authorized facility.*

Mixture Control Valve 2T-C Engines—1971–74

The mixture control valve, used on 2T-C engines, aids in combustion of unburned fuel during periods of deceleration. The mixture control valve is operated by the vacuum switching valve during periods of deceleration to admit additional fresh air into the intake manifold. The extra air allows more complete combustion of the fuel, thus reducing hydrocarbon emissions.

NOTE: *The mixture control valve is not used on 2T-C engines on 1974 cars sold in California, nor on any 1975 or later 2T-C at all.*

REMOVAL AND INSTALLATION

1. Unfasten the vacuum switching valve line from the mixture control valve.

2. Remove the intake manifold hose from the valve.

3. Remove the valve from its engine mounting.

Installation is performed in the reverse order of removal.

TESTING

1. Start the engine and allow it to idle (warmed up).

2. Place your hand over the air intake at the bottom of the valve.

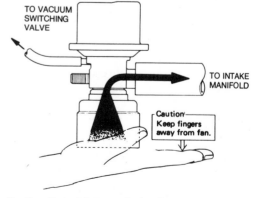

TO VACUUM SWITCHING VALVE

TO INTAKE MANIFOLD

Caution
Keep fingers away from fan.

Testing the mixture control valve

CAUTION: *Keep your fingers clear of the engine fan.*

3. Increase the engine speed and then release the throttle.

4. Suction should be felt at the air intake only while the engine is decelerating. Once the engine has returned to idle, no suction should be felt.

If the above test indicates a malfunction, proceed with the next step; if not, the mixture control valve is functioning properly and requires no further adjustment.

5. Disconnect the vacuum line from the mixture control valve. If suction can be felt underneath the valve with the engine at idle, the valve seat is defective and must be replaced.

6. Reconnect the vacuum line to the valve. Disconnect the other end of the line from the vacuum switching valve and place it in your mouth.

7. With the engine idling, suck on the end of the vacuum line to duplicate the action of the vacuum switching valve.

8. Suction at the valve air intake should only be felt for an instant. If air cannot be drawn into the valve at all, or if it is continually drawn in, replace the mixture control valve.

If the mixture control valve is functioning properly, and all of the hose and connections are in good working order, the vacuum switching valve is probably at fault.

Auxiliary Enrichment System— 1974–77

An auxiliary enrichment system, which Toyota calls an "Auxiliary Accelerator Pump (AAP) System," is used on all models, starting in 1975.

When the engine is cold, an auxiliary enrichment circuit in the carburetor is operated to squirt extra fuel into the acceleration circuit in order to prevent the mixture from becoming too lean.

A thermostatic vacuum valve (warmup-sensing valve), which is threaded into the intake manifold, controls the operation of the enrichment circuit. Below a specified temperature, the valve is opened and manifold vacuum is allowed to act on a diaphragm in the carburetor. The vacuum pulls the diaphragm down, allowing fuel to flow into a special chamber above it.

Under sudden acceleration manifold vacuum drops momentarily, allowing the dia-

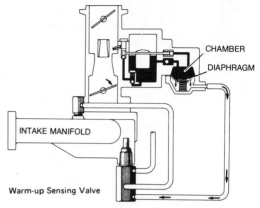

Components of the auxiliary enrichment system

phragm to be pushed up by spring tension. This in turn forces the fuel from the chamber through a passage and out the accelerator pump jet.

When the coolant temperature goes above specification, the thermostatic vacuum valve closes, preventing the vacuum from reaching the diaphragm which makes the enrichment system inoperative.

TESTS

1. Check for clogged, pinched, disconnected, or misrouted vacuum lines.

2. With the engine cold (below 75°F), remove the top of the air cleaner, and allow the engine to idle.

3. Disconnect the vacuum line from the carburetor AAP unit. Gasoline should squirt out the accelerator pump jet.

4. If gas doesn't squirt out of the jet, check for vacuum at the AAP vacuum line with the engine idling. If there is no vacuum and the hoses are in good shape, the thermostatic vacuum valve is defective and must be replaced.

5. If the gas doesn't squirt out and vacuum is present at the vacuum line in Step 4, the AAP unit is defective and must be replaced.

6. Repeat Step 3 with the engine at normal operating temperature. If gasoline squirts out of the pump jet, the thermostatic vacuum valve is defective and must be replaced.

7. Reconnect all of the vacuum lines and install the top of the air cleaner.

Auxiliary Enrichment System— 1978–81

This system is used on some engines to improve driveability. It cuts air supplied to the

CHILTON'S
FUEL ECONOMY
& TUNE-UP TIPS

Tune-Up • Spark Plug Diagnosis • Emission Controls

Fuel System • Cooling System • Tires and Wheels

General Maintenance

CHILTON'S FUEL ECONOMY & TUNE-UP TIPS

Fuel economy is important to everyone, no matter what kind of vehicle you drive. The maintenance-minded motorist can save both money and fuel using these tips and the periodic maintenance and tune-up procedures in this Repair and Tune-Up Guide.

There are more than 130,000,000 cars and trucks registered for private use in the United States. Each travels an average of 10-12,000 miles per year, and, in total they consume close to 70 billion gallons of fuel each year. This represents nearly ⅔ of the oil imported by the United States each year. The Federal government's goal is to reduce consumption 10% by 1985. A variety of methods are either already in use or under serious consideration, and they all affect your driving and the cars you will drive. In addition to "down-sizing", the auto industry is using or investigating the use of electronic fuel delivery, electronic engine controls and alternative engines for use in smaller and lighter vehicles, among other alternatives to meet the federally mandated Corporate Average Fuel Economy (CAFE) of 27.5 mpg by 1985. The government, for its part, is considering rationing, mandatory driving curtailments and tax increases on motor vehicle fuel in an effort to reduce consumption. The government's goal of a 10% reduction could be realized — and further government regulation avoided — if every private vehicle could use just 1 less gallon of fuel per week.

How Much Can You Save?

Tests have proven that almost anyone can make at least a 10% reduction in fuel consumption through regular maintenance and tune-ups. When a major manufacturer of spark plugs sur-

TUNE-UP

1. Check the cylinder compression to be sure the engine will really benefit from a tune-up and that it is capable of producing good fuel economy. A tune-up will be wasted on an engine in poor mechanical condition.

2. Replace spark plugs regularly. New spark plugs alone can increase fuel economy 3%.

3. Be sure the spark plugs are the correct type (heat range) for your vehicle. See the Tune-Up Specifications.

Heat range refers to the spark plug's ability to conduct heat away from the firing end. It must conduct the heat away in an even pattern to avoid becoming a source of pre-ignition, yet it must also operate hot enough to burn off conductive deposits that could cause misfiring.

The heat range is usually indicated by a number on the spark plug, part of the manufacturer's designation for each individual spark plug. The numbers in bold-face indicate the heat range in each manufacturer's identification system.

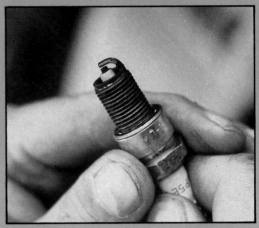

Periodically, check the spark plugs to be sure they are firing efficiently. They are excellent indicators of the internal condition of your engine.

Manufacturer	Typical Designation
AC	R **45** TS
Bosch (old)	WA **145** T30
Bosch (new)	HR **8** Y
Champion	RBL **15** Y
Fram/Autolite	**4**15
Mopar	P-**62** PR
Motorcraft	BRF-**42**
NGK	BP **5** ES-15
Nippondenso	W **16** EP
Prestolite	14GR **5** 2A

On AC, Bosch (new), Champion, Fram/Autolite, Mopar, Motorcraft and Prestolite, a higher number indicates a hotter plug. On Bosch (old), NGK and Nippondenso, a higher number indicates a colder plug.

4. Make sure the spark plugs are properly gapped. See the Tune-Up Specifications in this book.

5. Be sure the spark plugs are firing efficiently. The illustrations on the next 2 pages show you how to "read" the firing end of the spark plug.

6. Check the ignition timing and set it to specifications. Tests show that almost all cars

veyed over 6,000 cars nationwide, they found that a tune-up, on cars that needed one, increased fuel economy over 11%. Replacing worn plugs alone, accounted for a 3% increase. The same test also revealed that 8 out of every 10 vehicles will have some maintenance deficiency that will directly affect fuel economy, emissions or performance. Most of this mileage-robbing neglect could be prevented with regular maintenance.

Modern engines require that all of the functioning systems operate properly for maximum efficiency. A malfunction anywhere wastes fuel. You can keep your vehicle running as efficiently and economically as possible, by being aware of your vehicles operating and performance characterists. If your vehicle suddenly develops performance or fuel economy problems it could be due to one or more of the following:

PROBLEM	POSSIBLE CAUSE
Engine Idles Rough	Ignition timing, idle mixture, vacuum leak or something amiss in the emission control system.
Hesitates on Acceleration	Dirty carburetor or fuel filter, improper accelerator pump setting, ignition timing or fouled spark plugs.
Starts Hard or Fails to Start	Worn spark plugs, improperly set automatic choke, ice (or water) in fuel system.
Stalls Frequently	Automatic choke improperly adjusted and possible dirty air filter or fuel filter.
Performs Sluggishly	Worn spark plugs, dirty fuel or air filter, ignition timing or automatic choke out of adjustment.

Check spark plug wires on conventional point type ignition for cracks by bending them in a loop around your finger.

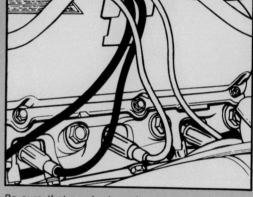

Be sure that spark plug wires leading to adjacent cylinders do not run too close together. (Photo courtesy Champion Spark Plug Co.)

have incorrect ignition timing by more than 2°.

7. If your vehicle does not have electronic ignition, check the points, rotor and cap as specified.

8. Check the spark plug wires (used with conventional point-type ignitions) for cracks and burned or broken insulation by bending them in a loop around your finger. Cracked wires decrease fuel efficiency by failing to deliver full voltage to the spark plugs. One misfiring spark plug can cost you as much as 2 mpg.

9. Check the routing of the plug wires. Misfiring can be the result of spark plug leads to adjacent cylinders running parallel to each other and too close together. One wire tends to pick up voltage from the other causing it to fire "out of time".

10. Check all electrical and ignition circuits for voltage drop and resistance.

11. Check the distributor mechanical and/or vacuum advance mechanisms for proper functioning. The vacuum advance can be checked by twisting the distributor plate in the opposite direction of rotation. It should spring back when released.

12. Check and adjust the valve clearance on engines with mechanical lifters. The clearance should be slightly loose rather than too tight.

SPARK PLUG DIAGNOSIS

Normal

APPEARANCE: This plug is typical of one operating normally. The insulator nose varies from a light tan to grayish color with slight electrode wear. The presence of slight deposits is normal on used plugs and will have no adverse effect on engine performance. The spark plug heat range is correct for the engine and the engine is running normally.

CAUSE: Properly running engine.

RECOMMENDATION: Before reinstalling this plug, the electrodes should be cleaned and filed square. Set the gap to specifications. If the plug has been in service for more than 10-12,000 miles, the entire set should probably be replaced with a fresh set of the same heat range.

Oil Deposits

APPEARANCE: The firing end of the plug is covered with a wet, oily coating.

CAUSE: The problem is poor oil control. On high mileage engines, oil is leaking past the rings or valve guides into the combustion chamber. A common cause is also a plugged PCV valve, and a ruptured fuel pump diaphragm can also cause this condition. Oil fouled plugs such as these are often found in new or recently overhauled engines, before normal oil control is achieved, and can be cleaned and reinstalled.

RECOMMENDATION: A hotter spark plug may temporarily relieve the problem, but the engine is probably in need of work.

Incorrect Heat Range

APPEARANCE: The effects of high temperature on a spark plug are indicated by clean white, often blistered insulator. This can also be accompanied by excessive wear of the electrode, and the absence of deposits.

CAUSE: Check for the correct spark plug heat range. A plug which is too hot for the engine can result in overheating. A car operated mostly at high speeds can require a colder plug. Also check ignition timing, cooling system level, fuel mixture and leaking intake manifold.

RECOMMENDATION: If all ignition and engine adjustments are known to be correct, and no other malfunction exists, install spark plugs one heat range colder.

Photos Courtesy Champion Spark Plug Co.

Carbon Deposits

APPEARANCE: Carbon fouling is easily identified by the presence of dry, soft, black, sooty deposits.

CAUSE: Changing the heat range can often lead to carbon fouling, as can prolonged slow, stop-and-start driving. If the heat range is correct, carbon fouling can be attributed to a rich fuel mixture, sticking choke, clogged air cleaner, worn breaker points, retarded timing or low compression. If only one or two plugs are carbon fouled, check for corroded or cracked wires on the affected plugs. Also look for cracks in the distributor cap between the towers of affected cylinders.

RECOMMENDATION: After the problem is corrected, these plugs can be cleaned and reinstalled if not worn severely.

MMT Fouled

APPEARANCE: Spark plugs fouled by MMT (Methycyclopentadienyl Maganese Tricarbonyl) have reddish, rusty appearance on the insulator and side electrode.

CAUSE: MMT is an anti-knock additive in gasoline used to replace lead. During the combustion process, the MMT leaves a reddish deposit on the insulator and side electrode.

RECOMMENDATION: No engine malfunction is indicated and the deposits will not affect plug performance any more than lead deposits (see Ash Deposits). MMT fouled plugs can be cleaned, regapped and reinstalled.

High Speed Glazing

APPEARANCE: Glazing appears as shiny coating on the plug, either yellow or tan in color.

CAUSE: During hard, fast acceleration, plug temperatures rise suddenly. Deposits from normal combustion have no chance to fluff-off; instead, they melt on the insulator forming an electrically conductive coating which causes misfiring.

RECOMMENDATION: Glazed plugs are not easily cleaned. They should be replaced with a fresh set of plugs of the correct heat range. If the condition recurs, using plugs with a heat range one step colder may cure the problem.

Ash (Lead) Deposits

APPEARANCE: Ash deposits are characterized by light brown or white colored deposits crusted on the side or center electrodes. In some cases it may give the plug a rusty appearance.

CAUSE: Ash deposits are normally derived from oil or fuel additives burned during normal combustion. Normally they are harmless, though excessive amounts can cause misfiring. If deposits are excessive in short mileage, the valve guides may be worn.

RECOMMENDATION: Ash-fouled plugs can be cleaned, gapped and reinstalled.

Detonation

APPEARANCE: Detonation is usually characterized by a broken plug insulator.

CAUSE: A portion of the fuel charge will begin to burn spontaneously, from the increased heat following ignition. The explosion that results applies extreme pressure to engine components, frequently damaging spark plugs and pistons.

Detonation can result by over-advanced ignition timing, inferior gasoline (low octane) lean air/fuel mixture, poor carburetion, engine lugging or an increase in compression ratio due to combustion chamber deposits or engine modification.

RECOMMENDATION: Replace the plugs after correcting the problem.

EMISSION CONTROLS

13. Be aware of the general condition of the emission control system. It contributes to reduced pollution and should be serviced regularly to maintain efficient engine operation.

14. Check all vacuum lines for dried, cracked or brittle conditions. Something as simple as a leaking vacuum hose can cause poor performance and loss of economy.

15. Avoid tampering with the emission control system. Attempting to improve fuel econ-

FUEL SYSTEM

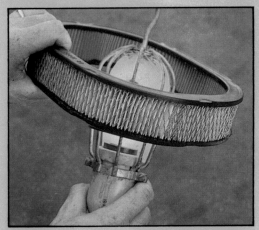

Check the air filter with a light behind it. If you can see light through the filter it can be reused.

Extremely clogged filters should be discarded and replaced with a new one.

18. Replace the air filter regularly. A dirty air filter richens the air/fuel mixture and can increase fuel consumption as much as 10%. Tests show that ⅓ of all vehicles have air filters in need of replacement.

19. Replace the fuel filter at least as often as recommended.

20. Set the idle speed and carburetor mixture to specifications.

21. Check the automatic choke. A sticking or malfunctioning choke wastes gas.

22. During the summer months, adjust the automatic choke for a leaner mixture which will produce faster engine warm-ups.

COOLING SYSTEM

29. Be sure all accessory drive belts are in good condition. Check for cracks or wear.

30. Adjust all accessory drive belts to proper tension.

31. Check all hoses for swollen areas, worn spots, or loose clamps.

32. Check coolant level in the radiator or expansion tank.

33. Be sure the thermostat is operating properly. A stuck thermostat delays engine warm-up and a cold engine uses nearly twice as much fuel as a warm engine.

34. Drain and replace the engine coolant at least as often as recommended. Rust and scale

TIRES & WHEELS

38. Check the tire pressure often with a pencil type gauge. Tests by a major tire manufacturer show that 90% of all vehicles have at least 1 tire improperly inflated. Better mileage can be achieved by over-inflating tires, but never exceed the maximum inflation pressure on the side of the tire.

39. If possible, install radial tires. Radial tires deliver as much as ½ mpg more than bias belted tires.

40. Avoid installing super-wide tires. They only create extra rolling resistance and decrease fuel mileage. Stick to the manufacturer's recommendations.

41. Have the wheels properly balanced.

omy by tampering with emission controls is more likely to worsen fuel economy than improve it. Emission control changes on modern engines are not readily reversible.

16. Clean (or replace) the EGR valve and lines as recommended.

17. Be sure that all vacuum lines and hoses are reconnected properly after working under the hood. An unconnected or misrouted vacuum line can wreak havoc with engine performance.

23. Check for fuel leaks at the carburetor, fuel pump, fuel lines and fuel tank. Be sure all lines and connections are tight.

24. Periodically check the tightness of the carburetor and intake manifold attaching nuts and bolts. These are a common place for vacuum leaks to occur.

25. Clean the carburetor periodically and lubricate the linkage.

26. The condition of the tailpipe can be an excellent indicator of proper engine combustion. After a long drive at highway speeds, the inside of the tailpipe should be a light grey in color. Black or soot on the insides indicates an overly rich mixture.

27. Check the fuel pump pressure. The fuel pump may be supplying more fuel than the engine needs.

28. Use the proper grade of gasoline for your engine. Don't try to compensate for knocking or "pinging" by advancing the ignition timing. This practice will only increase plug temperature and the chances of detonation or pre-ignition with relatively little performance gain.

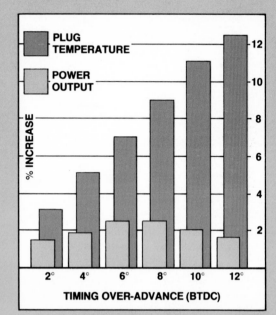

Increasing ignition timing past the specified setting results in a drastic increase in spark plug temperature with increased chance of detonation or preignition. Performance increase is considerably less. (Photo courtesy Champion Spark Plug Co.)

that form in the engine should be flushed out to allow the engine to operate at peak efficiency.

35. Clean the radiator of debris that can decrease cooling efficiency.

36. Install a flex-type or electric cooling fan, if you don't have a clutch type fan. Flex fans use curved plastic blades to push more air at low speeds when more cooling is needed; at high speeds the blades flatten out for less resistance. Electric fans only run when the engine temperature reaches a predetermined level.

37. Check the radiator cap for a worn or cracked gasket. If the cap does not seal properly, the cooling system will not function properly.

42. Be sure the front end is correctly aligned. A misaligned front end actually has wheels going in different directions. The increased drag can reduce fuel economy by .3 mpg.

43. Correctly adjust the wheel bearings. Wheel bearings that are adjusted too tight increase rolling resistance.

Check tire pressures regularly with a reliable pocket type gauge. Be sure to check the pressure on a cold tire.

GENERAL MAINTENANCE

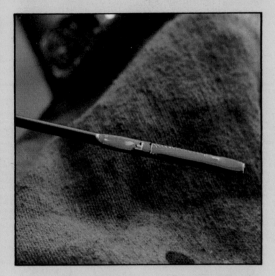

Check the fluid levels (particularly engine oil) on a regular basis. Be sure to check the oil for grit, water or other contamination.

A vacuum gauge is another excellent indicator of internal engine condition and can also be installed in the dash as a mileage indicator.

44. Periodically check the fluid levels in the engine, power steering pump, master cylinder, automatic transmission and drive axle.

45. Change the oil at the recommended interval and change the filter at every oil change. Dirty oil is thick and causes extra friction between moving parts, cutting efficiency and increasing wear. A worn engine requires more frequent tune-ups and gets progressively worse fuel economy. In general, use the lightest viscosity oil for the driving conditions you will encounter.

46. Use the recommended viscosity fluids in the transmission and axle.

47. Be sure the battery is fully charged for fast starts. A slow starting engine wastes fuel.

48. Be sure battery terminals are clean and tight.

49. Check the battery electrolyte level and add distilled water if necessary.

50. Check the exhaust system for crushed pipes, blockages and leaks.

51. Adjust the brakes. Dragging brakes or brakes that are not releasing create increased drag on the engine.

52. Install a vacuum gauge or miles-per-gallon gauge. These gauges visually indicate engine vacuum in the intake manifold. High vacuum = good mileage and low vacuum = poorer mileage. The gauge can also be an excellent indicator of internal engine conditions.

53. Be sure the clutch is properly adjusted. A slipping clutch wastes fuel.

54. Check and periodically lubricate the heat control valve in the exhaust manifold. A sticking or inoperative valve prevents engine warm-up and wastes gas.

55. Keep accurate records to check fuel economy over a period of time. A sudden drop in fuel economy may signal a need for tune-up or other maintenance.

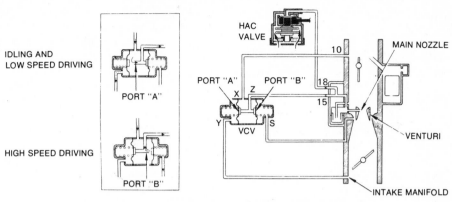

Schematic of the 1978–81 auxiliary enrichment system

main nozzle of the carburetor under certain conditions to improve performance.

If the system is suspected to be operating improperly, test the VCV valve as described below. If any of the tests are failed, replace the valve.

TESTS

1. Disconnect hoses 10 to 15 at the carburetor. Start the engine.

2. Blow air into hose No. 10 at idle speed. Check to see that air is expelled from hose 15.

3. Connect the VCV "S" pipe to the intake manifold as shown in the illustration. Again, blow air into hose 10 at idle speed. Check to see that air comes out of hose 15.

4. Stop the engine. Again blow air into hose 10. Check to see that air *does not* come out of hose.

5. Reconnect all hoses.

Spark Delay Valve

Starting 1975, non-California Corolla models have a spark delay valve (SDV) in the distributor vacuum line. The valve has a small orifice in it, which slows down the vacuum flow to the vacuum advance unit on the distributor. By delaying the vacuum to the distributor, a reduction in HC and CO emissions is possible.

When the coolant temperature is below 95°F, a coolant temperature operated vacuum control valve is opened, allowing the distributor to receive undelayed, ported vacuum through a separate vacuum line. Above 95°F, this line is blocked and all ported vacuum must go through the spark delay valve.

TESTING

1. Allow the engine to cool, so that the coolant temperature is below 95°F.

2. Disconnect the vacuum line which runs from the coolant temperature operated vacuum valve to the vacuum advance unit at the advance unit end. Connect a vacuum gauge to this line.

3. Start the engine. Increase the engine speed; the gauge should indicate a vacuum.

4. Allow the engine to warm-up to normal operating temperature. Increase the engine speed; this time the vacuum gauge should read zero.

5. Replace the coolant temperature operated vacuum valve, if it fails either of these tests. Disconnect the vacuum gauge and reconnect the vacuum lines.

6. Remove the spark delay valve from the vacuum lines, noting which side faces the distributor.

7. Connect a hand-operated vacuum pump which has a built-in vacuum gauge to the carburetor side of the spark delay valve.

8. Connect a vacuum gauge to the distributor side of the valve.

9. Operate the hand pump to create a vacuum. The vacuum gauge on the distribu-

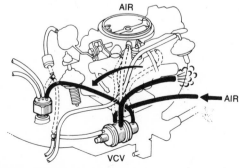

Connect hoses as shown

tor side should show a hesitation before registering.

10. The gauge reading on the pump side should drop slightly, taking several seconds for it to balance with the reading on the other gauge.

11. If Steps 9 and 10 are negative, replace the spark delay valve.

12. Remove the vacuum gauge from the distributor side of the valve. Cover the distributor side of the valve with your finger and operate the pump to create a vacuum of 15 in. Hg.

13. The reading on the pump gauge should remain steady. If the gauge reading drops, replace the valve.

14. Remove your finger; the reading of the gauge should drop slowly. If the reading goes to zero rapidly, replace the valve.

Dual-Diaphragm Distributor

Some Toyota models are equipped with a dual-diaphragm distributor unit. This distributor has a retard diaphragm, as well as a diaphragm for advance.

Retarding the timing helps to reduce exhaust emissions, as well as making up for the lack of engine braking on models equipped with a throttle positioner.

TESTING

1. Connect a timing light to the engine. Check the ignition timing.

NOTE: *Before proceeding with the tests, disconnect any spark control devices, distributor vacuum valves, etc. If these are left connected, inaccurate results may be obtained.*

2. Remove the retard hose from the distributor and plug it. Increase the engine speed. The timing should advance. If it fails to do so, then the vacuum unit is faulty and must be replced.

3. Check the timing with the engine at normal idle speed. Unplug the retard hose and connect it to the vacuum unit. The timing should instantly be retarded from 4 to 10 degrees. If this does not occur, the retard diaphragm has a leak and the vacuum unit must be replaced.

Engine Modifications System

Toyota also uses an assortment of engine modifications to regulate exhaust emissions. Most of these devices fall into the category of engine vacuum controls. There are three principal components used on the engine modifications system, as well as a number of smaller parts. The three major components are: a speed sensor; a computer (speed marker); and a vacuum switching valve.

The vacuum switching valve and computer circuit operates most of the emission control components. Depending upon year and engine usage, the vacuum switching valve and computer may operate the pure control for the evaporative emission control system; the transmission controlled spark (TCS) or speed controlled spark (SCS); the dual-diaphragm distributor, the throttle positioner systems, the EGR system, the catalyst protection system, etc.

The functions of the evaporative emissions control system, the throttle positioner, and the dual-diaphragm distributor are described in detail in the preceding sections. However,

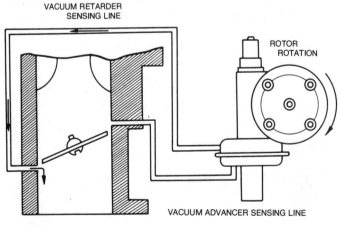

VACUUM RETARDER SENSING LINE

ROTOR ROTATION

VACUUM ADVANCER SENSING LINE

CARBURETOR

Dual-diaphgram distributor with vacuum switching valve

a word is necessary about the functions of the TCS and SCS systems before discussing the operation of the vacuum switching valve/computer circuit.

The major difference between the transmission controlled spark and speed controlled spark systems is the manner in which system operation is determined Toyota TCS systems use a mechanical switch to determine which gear is selected; SCS systems use a speed sensor built into the speedometer cable.

Below a predetermined speed, or any gear other than Fourth, the vacuum advance unit on the distributor is rendered inoperative or the timing retarded. By changing the distributor advance curve in this manner, it is possible to reduce emissions of oxides of nitrogen (NO_x).

NOTE: *Some engines are equipped with a thermo-sensor so that the TCS or SCS system only operates when the coolant temperature is 140°–212°F.*

Aside from determining the preceding conditions, the vacuum switching valve computer circuit operates other devices in the emission control system (EGR, Catalytic converter, etc.).

The computer acts as a speed marker; at certain speeds it sends a signal to the vacuum switching valve which acts as a gate, opening and closing the emission control system vacuum circuits.

The vacuum switching valve on all 1970 and some 1971 engines is a simple affair; a single solenoid operates a valve which uncovers certain vacuum ports at the same time others are covered.

The valve used on all 1972–81 and some 1971 engines contains several solenoid and valve assemblies so that different combinations of opened and closed vacuum ports are possible. This allows greater flexibility of operation for the emission control system.

SYSTEM CHECKS

Due to the complexity of the components involved, about the only engine modification system checks which can be made, are the following:

1. Examine the vacuum lines to ensure that they are not clogged, pinched, or loose.

2. Check the electrical connections for tightness and corrosion.

3. Be sure that the vacuum sources for the vacuum switching valve are not plugged.

4. On models equipped with speed controlled spark, a broken speedometer cable could also render the system inoperative.

Beyond these checks, servicing the engine modifications system is best left to an authorized service facility.

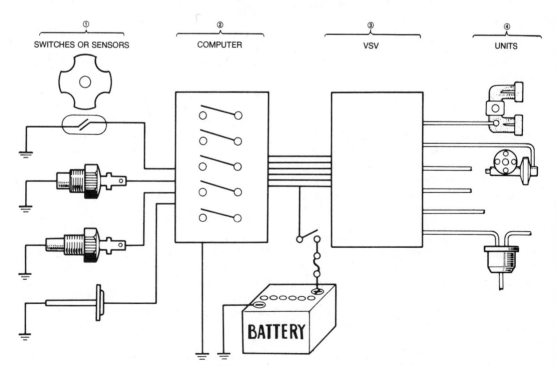

Block diagram of a typical engine modification system

NOTE: *A faulty vacuum switching valve or computer could cause more than one of the emission control systems to fail. Therefore, if several systems are out, these two units (and the speedometer cable) would be the first things to check.*

Choke Opener System

Used on all models except the 1975 Corolla and only on California Corollas in 1976, this system holds the choke open during warmup to prevent an overly rich mixture from emitting pollutants above acceptable limits. When the coolant temperature rises above 140°F, a thermostatic vacuum switching valve allows vacuum from the manifold to pull in on the choke opener diaphragm which is connected to the choke valve. Thus the choke valve is opened sooner than if just the automatic choke was operating it. When the coolant is below 95°F, the choke opener works with the automatic choke to close the choke valve and permit the choke to close until the engine is warm.

Dual Vacuum Advance Distributor

This system is available on non-California Corollas as an option starting 1976. It replaces the old dual point distributor and its function is basically the same.

SYSTEM CHECKS

1. Check all the hoses for proper connections and tightness.
2. With the engine cold, disconnect hose "D," idle the engine and see if the octane selector is drawn in. If not, check for vacuum at sub-diaphragm "B." If there is vacuum, replace the distributor diaphragm. If not, pinch hose "A" with your finger. If the octane selector is drawn in, replace TVSV 3. If it's still not drawn in, check the check valve. If the check valve is OK, replace the thermostatic valve or the choke breaker diaphragm.
3. If the octane selector is drawn in (at the beginning of Step 2), you should then disconnect hose "C" from the check valve. If octane selector isn't drawn in, replace the check valve.
4. If the octane selector is drawn in, disconnect hose "B" from the distributor and open and close the throttle valve. The octane selector should move. If not, see that TVSV 1 is open. If not, replace it. If it is open, replace the distributor diaphragm.

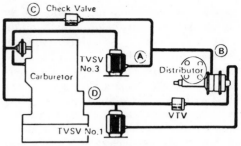

Vacuum system inspection diagram

5. If the octane selector moves in the previous step with the engine temperature around 104°F, check that the ignition timing is approximately 10°B at idle. If the timing is off, adjust it. If the ignition timing is OK, replace TVSV 3.
6. Pinch hose "A" closed and check ignition timing. The timing should change to a figure in the range of 18–22°B. If the timing doesn't change, replace the distributor. If the timing does change, rev the engine to 2,000 rpm. Check to see if the octane selector is pulled in after about four seconds. If not, replace the vacuum transmitting valve (VTV). If the octane selector is pulled in, the system is OK.

Exhaust Gas Recirculation (EGR)

All 1975–81 engines, except for 1975–80 2T-C engines, use EGR.

In all cases, the EGR valve is controlled by the same computer and vacuum switching valve which is used to operate other emission control system components.

On all engines there are two conditions, determined by the computer and vacuum switching valve, which permit exhaust gas recirculation to take place:

1. Vehicle speed.
2. Engine coolant temperature.

SYSTEM CHECKS

If, after having completed the above tests, the EGR system still doesn't work right and everything else checks out OK, the fault probably lies in the computer or the vacuum switching valve systems. If this is the case, it is best to have the car checked out by test facility which has the necessary Toyota emission system test equipment.

NOTE: *A good indication that the fault doesn't lie in the EGR system, but rather in the vacuum supply system, would be if several emission control systems were not working properly.*

Catalytic Converters

Starting 1975, all Toyota passenger cars sold in California and all Mark IIs sold in the US, are equipped with catalytic converters. The converters are used to oxidize hydrocarbons (HC) and carbon monoxide (CO). The converters are necessary because of the stricter emission level standards for the 1975 models.

The catalysts are made of noble metals (platinum and palladium) which are bonded to individual pellets. These catalysts cause the HC and CO to break down into water and carbon dioxide (CO_2) without taking part in the reaction; hence, a catalyst life of 50,000 miles may be expected under normal conditions.

An air pump is used to supply air to the exhaust system to aid in the reaction. A thermosensor, inserted into the converter, shuts off the air supply if the catalyst temperature becomes excessive.

The same sensor circuit also causes a dash warning light labeled "EXH TEMP" to come on when the catalyst temperature gets too high.

NOTE: *It is normal for the light to come on temporarily if the car is being driven downhill for long periods of time (such as descending a mountain).*

The light will come on and stay on if the air injection system is malfunctioning or if the engine is misfiring.

PRECAUTIONS

1. Use only unleaded fuel.
2. Avoid prolonged idling; the engine should run no longer than 20 minutes at curb idle, nor longer than 10 minutes at fast idle.
3. Reduce the fast idle speed, by quickly depressing and releasing the accelerator pedal, as soon as the coolant temperature reaches 120°F.
4. Do not disconnect any spark plug leads while the engine is running.
5. Make engine compression checks as quickly as possible.
6. Do not dispose of the catalyst in a place where anything coated with grease, gas, or oil is present; spontaneous combustion could result.

CATALYST TESTING

At the present time there is no known way to reliably test catalytic converter operation in the field. The only reliable test is a 12 hour and 40 minute "soak test" (CVS) which must be done in a laboratory.

An infrared HC/CO tester is not sensitive enough to measure the higher tailpipe emissions from a partially-failed converter. Thus, a bad converter may allow enough HC and CO emissions to escape, so that the car is not in compliance with Federal (or state) standards, but still will not cause the needle on the HC/CO tester to move off zero.

A *completely* failed converter should cause the tester to show a slight reading. As a result, it should be possible to spot one of these.

As long as you avoid severe overheating or use of leaded fuels and the car has less than 50,000 miles on it, it is safe to assume that the converter is working.

If you are in doubt about the converter, take your car to a diagnostic center which has an infrared tester.

WARNING LIGHT CHECKS

NOTE: *The warning light comes on while the engine is being cranked, to test its operation, just like any of the other warning lights.*

1. If the warning light comes on and stays on, check the components of the air injection system as previously outlined. If these are not defective, check the ignition system for faulty leads, plugs, points, or control box.
2. If no problems can be found in Step 1, check the wiring for the light for shorts or opened circuits.
3. If nothing else can be found wrong in Steps 1 and 2, check the operation of the emission control system vacuum switching valve or computer, either by substitution of a new unit, or by taking it to a service vacility which has Toyota's special emission control system checker.

CONVERTER REMOVAL AND INSTALLATION

CAUTION: *Do not perform this operation on a hot (or even warm) engine. Catalyst temperatures may go as high as 1,700°F, so that any contact with the catalyst could cause severe burns.*

1. Disconnect the lead from the converter thermosensor.
2. Remove the wiring shield.
3. Unfasten the pipe clamp securing bolts at either end of the converter. Remove the clamps.

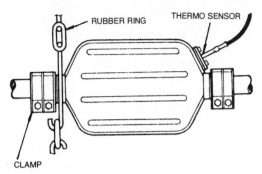

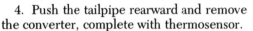
Catalytic converter installation

Removing the mechanical fuel pump

4. Push the tailpipe rearward and remove the converter, complete with thermosensor.

5. Carry the converter with the thermosensor upward to prevent the catalyst from falling out.

6. Unfasten the screws and withdraw the thermosensor and gasket.

Installation is performed in the following order:

1. Place a new gasket on the thermosensor. Push the thermosensor into the converter and secure it with its two bolts. Be careful not to drop the thermosensor.

NOTE: *Service replacement converters are provided with a plastic thermosensor guide. Slide the sensor into the guide to install it. Do not remove the guide.*

2. Install new gaskets on the converter mounting flanges.

3. Secure the converter with its mounting clamps.

4. If the converter is attached to the body with rubber O-rings, install the O-rings over the body and converter mounting hooks.

5. Install the wire protector and connect the lead to the thermosensor.

FUEL SYSTEM

Mechanical Fuel Pump

All pre-1975 Toyota vehicles use a mechanically operated fuel pump of diaphragm construction. A separate fuel filter is incorporated into the fuel line. See Chapter 1 for its required service.

REMOVAL AND INSTALLATION

1. Disconnect both of the fuel lines from the pump.

2. Unfasten the bolts which attach the fuel pump to the cylinder block.

3. Withdraw the pump assembly.

Testing mechanical fuel pump discharge pressure

Installation is performed in the reverse order of removal. Always use a new gasket when installing the fuel pump. After the pump is installed check its discharge rate against the "Tune-Up Specifications" chart at the beginning of Chapter 2.

In 1977 the 2T-C engine is equipped with a mechanical fuel pump with a fuel return cut valve installed. This valve is designed to vary the amount of fuel returned to the gas tank according to the engine load. It helps to avoid gas percolation when the engine is hot and lightly loaded.

NOTE: *Failure to use a gasket of the correct thickness could result in an improper pump discharge rate.*

Electric Fuel Pump
LOCATION

Starting 1975, all models exc. 1977 2T-C, 1981 3K-C and 1981 4K-C use an electric fuel pump.

The electric fuel pump is located inside the ges tank. It is serviced as a unit; if it breaks, replace it.

Starting 1976, all Toyotas sold in the U.S. are equipped with a rollover spill protection system for the fuel supply. The cut-off valve is located between the fuel filter and the carburetor. All models also use a check valve in-

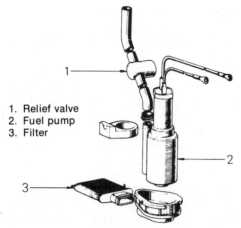

1. Relief valve
2. Fuel pump
3. Filter

Components of the electric fuel pump

side the carburetor and revised EEC system hose routing.

REMOVAL AND INSTALLATION

1. Disconnect the negative (−) cable from the battery.

2.a. On sedans and hardtops, remove the trim panel from inside the trunk;

b. On station wagons, raise the rear of the vehicle, in order to gain access to the pump. Support it securely.

3. Remove the screws which secure the pump access plate to the tank. Withdraw the plate, gasket, and pump assembly.

4. Disconnect the leads and hoses from the pump.

Installation is performed in the reverse order of removal. Use a new gasket on the pump access plate.

TESTING

CAUTION: *Do not operate the fuel pump unless it is immersed in gasoline and connected to its resistor.*

1. Disconnect the lead from the oil pressure warning light sender.

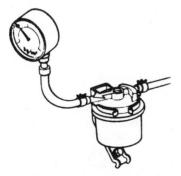

Testing electric fuel pump discharge pressure

2. Unfasten the line from the outlet side of the fuel filter.

3. Connect a pressure gauge to the filter outlet with a length of rubber hose.

4. Turn the ignition switch to the "ON" position, but do not start the engine.

5. Check the pressure gauge reading against the figure given in the "Tune-Up Specifications" chart in Chapter 2.

6. Check for a clogged filter or pinched lines if the pressure is not up to specification.

7. If there is nothing wrong with the filter or lines, replace the fuel pump.

8. Turn the ignition off and reconnect the fuel line to the filter. Connect the lead to the oil pressure sender also.

Carburetors

The carburetors used on Toyota models are conventional two-barrel, down-draft types similar to domestic carburetors. The main circuits are: *primary*, for normal operational requirements; *secondary*, to supply high-speed fuel needs; *float*, to supply fuel to the primary and secondary circuits; *accelerator*, to supply fuel for quick and safe acceleration; *choke*, for reliable starting in cold weather; and *power valve*, for fuel economy. Although slight differences in appearance may be noted, these carburetors are basically alike. Of course, different jets and settings are demanded by the different engines to which they are fitted.

REMOVAL AND INSTALLATION

1. Remove the air filter housing, disconnect all air hoses from the filter base, and disconnect the battery ground cable.

2. Disconnect the fuel line, choke pipe, and distributor vacuum line. On 20R engines, disconnect the choke coolant hose. Disconnect any electrical leads which run to the carburetor.

3. Remove the accelerator linkage. (With an automatic transmission, also remove the throttle rod to the transmission.)

4. Remove the four nuts which secure the carburetor to the manifold and lift off the carburetor and gasket.

5. Cover the open manifold with a clean rag to prevent small objects from dropping into the engine.

Installation is performed in the reverse order of removal. After the engine is warmed up, check for fuel leaks and float level settings.

GENERAL OVERHAUL NOTES

Efficient carburetion depends greatly on careful cleaning and inspection during overhaul since dirt, gum, water, or varnish in or on the carburetor parts are often responsible for poor performance.

Overhaul your carburetor in a clean, dust-free area. Carefully disassemble the carburetor, referring often to the exploded views. Keep all similar and "lookalike" parts segregated during disassembly and cleaning to avoid accidental interchange during assembly. Make a note of all jet sizes.

When the carburetor is disassembled, wash all parts (except diaphragms, electric choke units, pump plunger, and any other plastic, leather, fiber, or rubber parts) in clean carburetor solvent. Do not leave parts in the solvent any longer than is necessary to sufficiently loosen the deposits. Excessive cleaning may remove the special finish from the float bowl and choke valve bodies, leaving these parts unfit for service. Rinse all parts in clean solvent and blow them dry with compressed air or allow them o air dry. Wipe clean all cork, plastic, leather, and fiber parts with a clean, lint-free cloth.

Blow out all passages and jets with compressed air and be sure that there are no restrictions or blockages. Never use wire or similar tools to clean jets, fuel passages, or air bleeds. Clean all jets and valves separately to avoid accidental interchange.

Check all parts for wear or damage. If wear or damage is found, replace the defective parts. Especially check the following:

1. Check the float needle and seat for wear. If wear is found, replace the complete assembly.

2. Check the float hinge pin for wear and the float(s) for dents or distortion. Replace the float if fuel has leaked into it.

3. Check the throttle and choke shaft bores for wear or an out-of-round condition. Damage or wear to the throttle arm, shaft, or shaft bore will often require replacement of the throttle body. These parts require a close tolerance of fit; wear may allow air leakage, which could affect starting and idling.

NOTE: *Throttle shafts and bushings are not included in overhaul kits. They can be purchased separately.*

4. Inspect the idle mixture adjusting needles for burrs or grooves. Any such condition requires replacement of the needle, since you will not be able to obtain a satisfactory idle.

5. Test the accelerator pump check valves. They should pass air one way but not the other. Test for proper seating by blowing and sucking on the valve. Replace the valve if necessary. If the valve is satisfactory, wash the valve again to remove breath moisture.

6. Check the bowl cover for warped surfaces with a straightedge.

7. Closely inspect the valves and seats for wear and damage, replacing as necessary.

8. After the carburetor is assembled, check the choke valve for freedom of operation.

Carburetor overhaul kits are recommended for each overhaul. These kits contain all gaskets and new parts to replace those that deteriorate most rapidly. Failure to replace all parts supplied with the kit (especially gaskets) can result in poor performance later.

Some carburetor manufacturers supply overhaul kits of 3 basic types: minor repair; major repair; and gasket kits. Basically, they contain the following:

Minor Repair Kits:
• All gaskets
• Float needle valve
• Volume control screw
• All diaphragms
• Spring for the pump diaphragm
Major Repair Kits:
All jets and gaskets
• All diaphragms
• Float needle valve
• Volume control screw
• Pump ball valve
• Float
• Complete intermediate rod
• Intermediate pump lever
• Some cover hold-down screws and washers

Gasket Kits:
• All gaskets

After cleaning and checking all components, reassemble the carburetor, using new parts and referring to the exploded view. When reassembling, make sure that all screws and jets are tight in their seats, but do not overtighten, as the tips will be distorted. Tighten all screws gradually, in rotation. Do not tighten needle valves into their seats; uneven jetting will result. Always use new gaskets. Be sure to adjust the float level when reassembling.

FLOAT LEVEL ADJUSTMENT

Float level adjustments are unnecessary on models equipped with a carburetor sight glass, if the fuel level falls within the lines when the engine is running.

There are two float level adjustments which may be made on Toyota carburetors. One is with the air horn inverted, so that the float is in a fully *raised* position; the other is with the air horn in an upright position, so that the float falls to the bottom of its travel.

The float level is either measured with a special carburetor float level gauge, which comes with a rebuilding kit, or with a standard wire gauge. For the proper type of gauge, as well as the points to be measured, see the "Float Level Adjustments" chart at the end of this section.

NOTE: *Gap specifications are also given so that a float level gauge may be fabricated. Several different gauges are illustrated below.*

Adjust the float level by bending the tabs on the float levers, either upper or lower, as required.

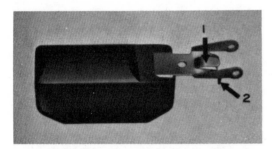

To adjust the float level bend the upper tab (1) or the lower tab (2)

Measuring The Float Level

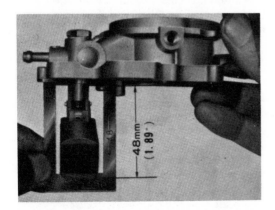

early 3K-C—lowered

early—raised

4K-C, late 3K-C, 2T-C and 3T-C—lowered

4K-C, late 3K-C, 2T-C, 3T-C—raised

FAST IDLE ADJUSTMENT

Off-Vehicle

The fast idle adjustment is performed with the choke valve fully *closed*, except on the 2T-C and 3T-C engine which should have the choke valve fully *opened*.

Adjust the gap between the throttle valve edge and bore to the specifications, where given, in the "Fast Idle Adjustment" chart. Use a wire gauge to determine the gap.

The chart also gives the proper primary throttle valve opening angle, where necessary, and the proper means of fast idle adjustment.

NOTE: *The throttle valve opening angle is measured with a gauge supplied in the car-*

Fast Idle Speed—1975–77

Engine	Speed (rpm)
2T-C (US)	3000
2T-C (Calif)	2700

US—United States
Calif—California
Not available for 3K-C engine

Fast Idle Speed—1978–81

Engine	Speed (rpm)
2T-C (US)	3,200
2T-C (Calif)	3,000
4K-C	3,500
3A-C	3,600
3A	3,000
3T-C	3,000 Canada 3,400 U.S.A

buretor rebuilding kit. It is also possible to make one out of cardboard by using a pro-tractor to obtain the correct angle.

On Vehicle—1975–81 Only

1. Perform the idle speed/mixture adjustments as outlined in Chapter 2. Leave the tachometer connected.
2. Remove the top of the air cleaner.
3. Open the throttle valve slightly and close the choke valve. Next, hold the choke

Make fast idle adjustments by bending the linkage

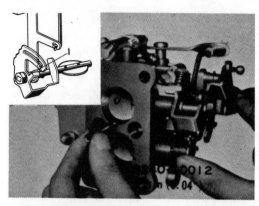
Screw-type fast idle adjustment (1)

valve with your finger and close the throttle valve. The choke valve is now fully closed.

4. Without depressing the accelerator pedal, start the engine.
5. Check the engine fast idle speed against the following chart.
6. If the reading on the tachometer is not within specifications, adjust the fast idle speed by turning the fast idle screw.
7. Disconnect the tachometer, install the air cleaner cover, and connect the EGR valve vacuum line if it was disconnected.

AUTOMATIC CHOKE ADJUSTMENT

The automatic choke should be adjusted with the carburetor installed and the engine running.

1. Check to ensure that the choke valve will close from fully opened when the coil housing is turned counterclockwise.
2. Align the mark on the coil housing with the center line on the thermostat case. In this position, the choke valve should be fully closed when the ambient temperature is 77°F.
3. If necessary, adjust the mixture by turning the coil housing. If the mixture is too *rich*, rotate the housing *clockwise;* if too *lean,* rotate the housing *counterclockwise.*
   NOTE: *Each graduation on the thermostat case is equivalent to 9°F.*

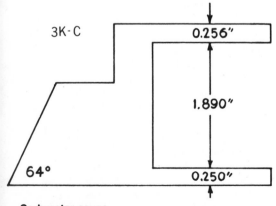

3K-C   0.256"

1.890"

64°   0.250"

Carburetor gauge

Float Level Adjustments

Engine	Float Raised			Float Lowered		
	Gauge Type	Machine Distance Between:	Gap (in.)	Gauge Type	Measure Distance Between:	Gap (in.)
3K-C	Special	Float end and air horn	0.056 ① ③	Special	Lowest point of float and upper side of gauge	1.89 ②
2T-C, 3TC	Block	Float tip and air horn	0.138 ④	Wire	Needle valve bushing pin and float lip	0.047
1A-C, 3A, 3A-C	Special	Float tip and air horn	0.158	Special	Needle valve plunger and float tab	0.047
4K-C	Special	Float tip and air horn	0.030	Special	Needle valve plunger and float tip	0.02

① 1977—0.26
② 1977—from float lip 0.035
   1978–79—float lip gap .024
   1980–81—float tip gap 0.020
③ 1978–81—0.30
④ 1978–81—0.236

Fast Idle Linkage Adjustment

Engine	Throttle Valve to Bore Clearance (in.)	Primary Throttle Angle (deg)	To Adjust Fast Idle:
3K-C through 1980	0.040 ①	9 ②	Bend the fast idle lever
4K-C and 1981 3K-C	0.040	90	Bend the fast idle lever
2T-C, 3T-C	0.032 ③	7	Turn the fast idle adjusting screw
1A-C	—	22	—
3A	—	24	—
3A-C	—	21	—

—Not available
① 0.051 in 1976; 0.056 in 1977; 0.037 in 1978–79
② 20° open
③ 1976–79: 0.043

Begin adjustment by aligning the setting marks

UNLOADER ADJUSTMENT

Make the unloader adjustment with the primary valve fully opened. Adjust by performing the procedure indicated on the "Choke Unloader Adjustment" chart. The total angle of choke valve opening, in the chart, is measured with either a special gauge, supplied in the carburetor rebuilding kit, or a gauge of the proper angle fabricated from cardboard.

Kick-Up Adjustment

Engine	Primary Throttle Valve Opening Angle (deg)
3K-C	81 from closed
2T-C	55 from closed ①

① 1977–79—64–90°

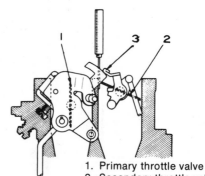

Kick-up adjustment

1. Primary throttle valve
2. Secondary throttle valve
3. Secondary throttle lever

KICK-UP ADJUSTMENT

1. Open the primary throttle valve the amount specified in the "Kick-Up Adjustment" chart.

2. Measure the secondary throttle valve-to-bore clearance with a 0.008 in. gauge.

3. Adjust the clearance by bending the secondary throttle lever.

Initial Idle Mixture Screw Adjustment

When assembling the carburetor, turn the idle mixture screw the number of turns specified below. After the carburetor is installed, perform the appropriate idle speed/mixture adjustment as outlined in Chapter 2.

• 3K-C, 4K-C 1978–81—1½ turns from seating
• 3K-C 1977—1¾ turns from seating

Choke Unloader Adjustment

Engine	Throttle Valve Fully Closed (deg)	Choke Valve Angle (deg) From Closed to Fully Open (deg)	Throttle Valve Open (total) (deg)	To Adjust Bend:
1970–75 2T-C, 3K-C	20	27	47	Fast idle cam follower or choke shaft lip
1976–81 3K-C	9	20	90	Fast idle cam follower or choke shaft tab
2T-C	7	38	90	Fast idle lever, follower or choke shaft tab
3T-C, 1A-C, 3A, 3A-C	20	—	47	Fast idle lever
4K-C	8.5	52	90	Connecting link

—Not available

• 3K-C through 1976—2 turns from seating
• 1977 3K-C 1¾ turns from seating
• 1977 and later 2T-C 3T-C—2⅝ turns out
• 1A-C—2¼ turns
• 3A, 3A-C—2¾ turns

CAUTION: *Seat the idle mixture screw lightly; overtightening will damage its tip.*

Choke Return System

1977 and later 3K-C engines and all 4K-C engines have a choke return system to protect the catalytic converter. Because of the change of overheating the exhaust system and damaging the catalytic converter by running with the choke out, a thermoswitch and return spring system automatically close the choke when the coolant temperature reaches 104°F.

A holding coil and holding plate surround the choke cable and retain it when the temperature is low enough. When the temperature reaches 104°F the thermoswitch opens, freeing the return spring to pull in the choke. There are no adjustments on the system. If a malfunction occurs, trace the loss and replace that segment of the unit.

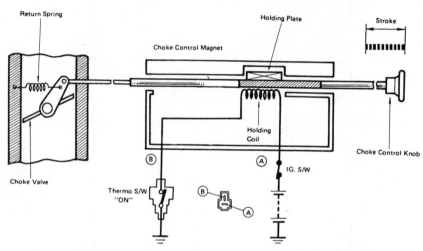

Automatic choke return system for 3K-C and 4K-C engine

Chassis Electrical

HEATER

On some models the air conditioner, if so equipped, is integral with the heater, and therefore, heater removal may differ from the procedures detailed below.

Blower

REMOVAL AND INSTALLATION

Corolla—1970-74

1. Drain the cooling system.
2. Remove the package tray from beneath the dashboard.
3. Unfasten the two water hoses from the heater.
NOTE: *Have a container ready to catch any water which remains in the system.*
4. Unfasten the clamp and remove the defroster hose.
5. Unfasten the three heater control cables from the heater box.
6. Remove the fresh air duct.
7. Unfasten the electrical connections.
8. Unfasten the four heater box attachment bolts and withdraw the heater box.
9. Loosen the fan attachment nut by tapping it lightly and then withdraw the fan from the shaft.
CAUTION: *Do not remove the balancing weight from the fan.*

10. Unfasten the blower motor securing screws and remove the motor.
Installation is the reverse of removal. Be sure that the fan does not contact the blower housing when it is assembled. Hold the fan adapter in place, on the armature shaft while tightening the fan locknut to 43 ft. lbs.

Corolla—1975 and Later, Starlet

1. Disconnect the blower wiring harness.
2. Remove the right-hand defroster hose.
3. Remove the three screws which secure the blower motor and lift out the motor.
4. Separate the fan from the motor.
Installation is the reverse of removal.

Tercel

1. Disconnect the negative battery terminal.
2. Remove the under tray (if so equipped).
3. Remove the blower duct and air duct.
NOTE: *Before removing the air duct remember to remove the two attaching clamps.*
4. Remove the glove box.
5. Remove the control cable.
6. Disconnect the electrical connector on the blower motor.
7. Remove the blower motor bolts and remove the motor.
8. Installation is the reverse of removal.

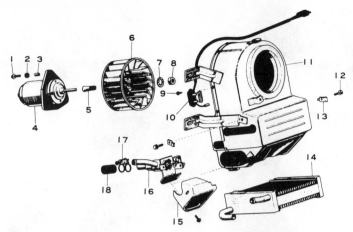

1. Screw and washer
2. Bushing
3. Bushing
4. Blower motor
5. Fan adapter
6. Fan
7. Serrated washer
8. Nut
9. Screw and washer
10. Resistor
11. Blower housing
12. Bolt and washer
13. Clamp
14. Core
15. Water valve cover
16. Water valve
17. Clamp
18. Hose

1970–74 Corolla heater assembly

Carina blower assembly

Carina

1. Working from under the instrument panel, unfasten the defroster hoses from the heater box.
2. Unplug the multiconnector.
3. Loosen the mounting screws and withdraw the blower assembly.
Installation is the reverse of removal.

Core

REMOVAL AND INSTALLATION

Corolla—1970–74

1. Perform the preceding heater blower removal procedures.
2. Separate the parts of the heater box.
3. Withdraw the core from the bottom of the case.
Assembly and installation are the reverse of removal and disassembly.

Corolla—1975 and Later, Starlet

1. Disconnect the negative battery cable and drain the cooling system.

Removing the heater assembly—1975 Corolla

2. Disconnect the heater hose from the engine compartment side.
3. Remove the knobs from the heater and fan controls.
4. Remove the two securing screws, and take the heater control panel off.
5. Remove the heater control, complete with cables.
6. Disconnect the wiring harness.
7. Unfasten the three heater assembly securing bolts and remove the assembly.
8. Separate the core from the heater assembly.
Installation is performed in the reverse order of removal.

Tercel

1. Disconnect the negative battery terminal.

2. Drain the radiator.

3. Remove the ash tray and retainer.

4. Remove the rear heater duct (optional).

5. Remove the left and right side defroster ducts.

6. Remove the under tray (optional).

7. Remove the glove box.

8. Remove the main air duct.

9. Disconnect the radio and remove it.

10. Disconnect the heater control cables and remove them.

11. Disconnect the heater hoses.

12. Remove the front and rear air ducts.

13. Remove the electrical connector.

14. Remove the heater bolts and remove the heater.

NOTE: *Slide the heater to the right side of car to remove it.*

15. Remove the heater core.

16. Installation is the reverse of removal.

Carina

1. Drain the cooling system.

2. Remove the console, if so equipped, by removing the shift knob (manual), wiring connector, and console attaching screws.

3. Remove the carpeting from the tunnel.

4. If necessary, remove the cigarette lighter and ash tray.

5. Remove the package tray, if it makes access to the heater core difficult.

6. Unfasten the securing screws and remove the center air outlet on the Mark II/6.

7. Remove the bottom cover/intake assembly screws and withdraw the assembly.

8. Remove the cover from the water valve.

9. Remove the water valve.

10. Unfasten the hose clamps and remove the hoses from the core.

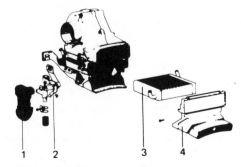

1. Water valve cover
2. Water valve
3. Core
4. Duct/cover assembly

Carina core removal

11. Withdraw the core.

Installation is performed in the reverse order of removal.

RADIO

Never operate the radio without a speaker; severe damage to the output transistors will result. If the speaker must be replaced, use a speaker of the correct impedance (ohms) or else the output transistors will be damaged and require replacement.

Removal and Installation

Corolla (1970–74)

1. Remove the knobs from the radio.

2. Remove the nuts from the radio control shafts.

3. Detach the antenna lead from the jack on the radio case.

4. Remove the cowl air intake duct.

5. Detach the power and speaker leads.

6. Remove the radio support nuts and bolts.

7. Withdraw the radio from beneath the dashboard.

8. Remove the nuts which secure the speaker through the service hole in the top of the glovebox.

9. Remove remainder of the speaker securing nuts from above the radio mounting location.

10. Withdraw the speaker.

Installation is performed in the reverse order of removal.

Corolla–1975 and Later, Starlet, and Tercel

1. Remove the two screws from the top of the dashboard center trim panel.

2. Lift the center panel out far enough to gain access to the cigarette lighter wiring and disconnect the wiring. Remove the trim panel.

3. Unfasten the screws which secure the radio to the instrument panel braces.

4. Lift out the radio and disconnect the leads from it. Remove the radio.

Installation is the reverse of removal.

Carina

1. Remove the center air outlet from under the dash.

2. Unfasten the radio control mounting bracket.

3. Remove the radio control knobs and then the retaining nuts from the control shafts.

4. Detach the speaker, and the power and antenna leads from the radio.

5. Withdraw the radio from underneath the dashboard.

6. Unfasten the speaker retaining nuts and remove the speaker.

Installation is performed in the reverse order of removal.

WINDSHIELD WIPER

Blade and Arm
REPLACEMENT

1. To remove the wiper blades, lift up on the spring release tab on the wiper blade-to-wiper arm connector.

2. Pull the blade assembly off the wiper arm.

3. There are two types of replacements for Toyotas:

    a. Pre-1973—replace the entire wiper blade as an assembly. Simply snap the replacement into place on the arm.

    b. Post-1973—press the old wiper blade insert down, away from the blade assembly, to free it from the retaining clips on the blade ends. Slide the insert out of the blade. Slide the new insert into the blade assembly and bend the insert upward slightly to engage the retaining clips.

4. To replace a wiper arm, unscrew the acorn nut which secures it to the pivot and carefully pull the arm upward and off the pivot. Install the arm by reversing this procedure.

Motor
REMOVAL AND INSTALLATION
Corolla—1970–74

1. Disconnect the car battery.

2. Unfasten the wiper motor connection.

3. Detach the wiper motor from the linkage by prying it with a screwdriver.

4. Remove the package tray.

5. Unfasten the three wiper motor securing nuts and withdraw the motor from inside the car.

Installation is performed in the reverse order of removal.

Corolla (1975–81), Carina, Starlet

1. Disconnect the wiper motor multiconnector.

2. Remove the service cover and loosen the wiper motor securing bolts.

3. Use a screwdriver to separate the wiper link-to-motor connection.

CAUTION: *Be careful not to bend the linkage.*

4. Withdraw the wiper motor assembly.

Installation is performed in the reverse order of removal.

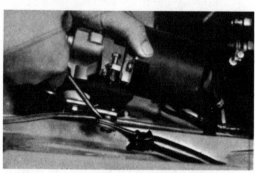

On Carina and 1975–76 Corolla, separate the wiper link from the motor with a screwdriver

Tercel

1. Disconnect the negative battery terminal.

2. Insert a screwdriver between the linkage and the motor.

3. Pry up to separate the linkage from the motor.

4. Disconnect the electrical connector from the motor.

5. Remove the mounting bolts and remove the motor.

6. Installation is the reverse of removal.

Linkage
REMOVAL AND INSTALLATION
Corolla—1970–74

1. Disconnect the battery.

2. Remove the wiper arms and the pivot caps.

3. Remove the instrument cluster.

4. Unfasten the heater's defroster hose, loosen the two screws, and then remove right-hand defroster nozzle.

5. Disconnect the wiper motor and link by prying on the link with a screwdriver.

6. Loosen the three bolts which attach the pivots. Remove both pivots.

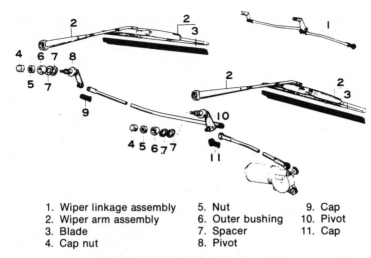

1. Wiper linkage assembly
2. Wiper arm assembly
3. Blade
4. Cap nut
5. Nut
6. Outer bushing
7. Spacer
8. Pivot
9. Cap
10. Pivot
11. Cap

Carina and 1975–76 Corolla wiper linkage assembly

7. Remove the wiper linkage assembly.

Installation is performed in the reverse order of removal. Tighten the pivot to 0.9–1.9 ft. lbs.

CAUTION: *If the pivot is overtightened, the linkage will be damaged.*

Before installing the wiper arms, operate the motor once by turning it on and off at the wiper switch so that the wipers may be easily installed in the park position

Corolla (1975–81), Carina, Starlet

1. Perform the wiper motor removal procedure.

2. Loosen the wiper arm retaining nuts and remove the arms.

3. Unfasten the wiper pivot nuts and remove the linkage assembly through the access hole.

Installation is the reverse of removal.

INSTRUMENT CLUSTER

REMOVAL AND INSTALLATION

Corolla—1970–74

1. Disconnect the battery.

2. Detach the speedometer cable from the speedometer.

3. Remove the center and right-hand trim moldings from the instrument panel.

4. Unfasten the instrument cluster and panel molding retainer screw.

5. Remove the two nuts which secure the instrument cluster from behind.

6. Pull the cluster out slightly and disconnect the wiring.

7. Remove the cluster assembly completely.

CAUTION: *Be careful not to scratch the steering column cover.*

Installation is performed in the reverse order of removal.

Corolla—1975 and Later, Starlet

1. Disconnect the negative battery cable.

2. Remove the screws which secure the instrument cluster surround (two at the top and one next to the fresh air vent).

3. Remove the center trim panel by unfastening its two retaining screws. Disconnect the cigarette lighter wiring before completely removing the panel.

4. Withdraw the speedometer cable and disconnect it.

5. Pull the instrument cluster out just far enough so that its wiring harness may be disconnected.

6. Remove the cluster.

Installation is performed in the reverse order of removal.

Carina

1. Remove the glove box door and withdraw the glove box slightly.

2. Disconnect the inspection lamp socket and glove box light wiring.

3. Remove the glove box completely.

4. Unfasten the cigarette lighter wiring and remove the ash tray.

5. Unfasten the lower crash pad screws and remove the crash pad.

NOTE: *It may be necessary to unfasten the attachment screws and lower the steering column. Be careful, the column is the collapsible type.*

6. Loosen the radio rear attaching screws and detach the heater cable at the heater.

7. Unfasten the instrument retaining screws and tilt the panel toward the rear.

8. Detach the speedometer cable and the wiring multiconnectors. Remove the cluster assembly.

Installation is performed in the reverse order of removal.

Tercel

1. Disconnect the negative battery terminal.

2. Remove the steering column cover.

NOTE: *Be careful not to damage the collapsible steer column mechanism.*

3. Remove the screws from the instrument-panel.

4. Gently pull the panel out approximately half way.

5. Disconnect the speedometer and any other electrical connections that are necessary.

6. Remove the panel at this time.

7. Installation is the reverse of removal.

HEADLIGHTS

REMOVAL AND INSTALLATION
Corolla, Tercel, Starlet

1. Unfasten the two headlight bezel (1970–74) or grille (1955–77) securing screws. Remove the bezel or grille.

2. Loosen (do not remove) the three headlight retaining ring screws and rotate the ring counterclockwise in order to remove it.

CAUTION: *Be careful not to disturb the two headlight aiming screws.*

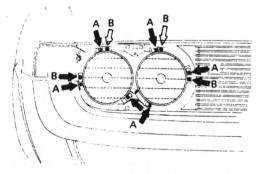

To remove the headlights, remove the retaining screws "A"; but do not loosen adjusting screws "B"

3. Detach the connector from the back of the sealed beam unit and remove the unit from the car.

Installation is performed in the reverse order of removal.

Carina

1. Remove the headlight bezel and/or radiator grille, as necessary.

2. Repeat Steps 2–3 of the "Corolla Headlight Removal" procedure for each lamp unit to be replaced.

NOTE: *On some models, the headlight retainer must be rotated clockwise in order to remove the headlight unit.*

Installation is performed in the reverse order of removal.

CAUTION: *Do not interchange inner and outer headlight units.*

TURN SIGNAL AND HAZARD FLASHER LOCATIONS

All Models—Except 1975–81 Corolla and Tercel

These models' turn signals and hazard warning flashers are combined in a single unit. It is located on the left-hand side, underneath the dashboard, next to the fuse block.

NOTE: *On some models it may be necessary to remove the fuse block bracket in order to gain access to the flasher.*

Corolla—1975 and Later and Tercel

The combination turn signal/hazard flasher is located behind the kick panel on the driver's side. In order to remove the flasher, first remove the panel retaining screws and lift out the kick panel.

WIRING DIAGRAMS

Wiring diagrams have been left out of this book. As cars have become more complex, and available with longer and longer option lists, wiring diagrams have grown in size and complexity also. It has become virtually impossible to provide a readable reproduction in a reasonable number of pages. Information on ordering wiring diagrams from the vehicle manufacturer can be found in the owners manual.

Clutch and Transmission

MANUAL TRANSMISSION

LINKAGE ADJUSTMENT

All Toyota passenger cars sold in the US have floor-mounted shifters, and internally-mounted shift linkages. On some older models, the linkage is contained in the side cover which is bolted on the transmission case. All of the other models have the linkage mounted inside the top of the transmission case, itself.

No external adjustments are needed or possible.

REMOVAL AND INSTALLATION

Corolla and Carina

Working from inside of the car, perform the following:

1. Place the gear selector in Neutral. Remove the center console, if so equipped.

2. Remove the trim boot at the base of the shift lever and the boot underneath it on the shift tower.

3. On Corolla 1200 and Starlet models only:

    a. Unfasten the snap-ring from the base of the shift lever;

    b. Withdraw the council spring and the shift lever itself.

4. On Corolla 1600 and Carina models only:

    a. Unfasten the four shift lever plate returning screws;

    b. Withdraw the shift lever assembly;

    c. Remove the gasket.

NOTE: *Cover the hole with a clean cloth to prevent anything from falling into the transmission case.*

Working in the engine compartment perform the following:

5. Drain the cooling system and disconnect the cable from the positive side of the battery.

6. Remove the radiator hoses.

7. On Corolla 1200 models, only:

    a. Unfasten the back-up lamp switch connector;

    b. Remove the engine fan.

8. On Corolla 1600 and Carina models, only:

    a. Remove the air cleaner, complete with hoses;

    b. Unfasten the accelerator torque rod at the carburetor;

    c. Remove the clutch hydraulic line support bracket;

    d. Remove the starter assembly from the left-side of the engine;

    e. Remove the upper left-hand clutch housing bolt, from the flat at the top of the clutch housing.

9. On Starlet:

    a. Remove the water outlet hose.

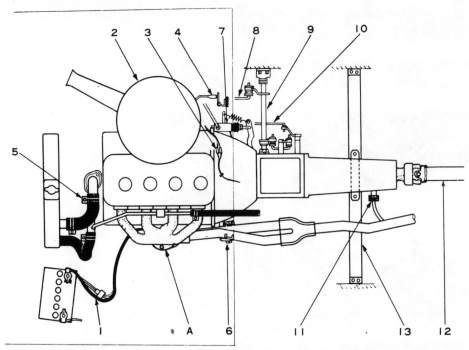

A. Exhaust pipe flange
1. Positive battery cable (+)
2. Air cleaner
3. Back-up lamp connector
4. Torque rod
5. Radiator hose

6. Exhaust pipe clamp
7. Master cylinder w/line support bracket
8. Accelerator linkage
9. Pivot—not applicable in USA

10. Bellcrank—not applicable in the USA
11. Speedometer cable
12. Driveshaft
13. Rear supporting crossmember

Removing the transmission from the Corolla and Carina

b. Remove the air cleaner.

c. Disconnect the accelerator pump lever.

d. Disconnect the wiring harness connector.

e. Wrap the steering rack boot with a rag.

f. Remove the starter.

Working from beneath the car:

CAUTION: *Be sure that the car is securely supported with jackstands. Remember, you will be working underneath it.*

10. Drain the transmission oil.

11. Detach the exhaust pipe from the manifold and remove the exhaust pipe support bracket.

12. Remove the driveshaft.

NOTE: *It will be necessary to plug the opening in the end of the transmission with an old yoke or, if none is available, cover it with a plastic bag secured by a rubber band.*

13. Unfasten the speedometer cable from the right-side of the transmission.

14. On Corolla 1600 and Carina models, only:

a. Remove the clutch release cylinder

assembly from the transmission and tie it aside, so that it is out of the way;

b. Unplug the back-up lamp switch connector.

15. Support the front of the transmission with a jack.

16. Unfasten the engine rear mounts. (See Chapter 3). Remove the rear crossmember.

17. Remove the jack from under the transmission.

18. On Corolla 1600 and Carina models, unbolt the clutch housing from the engine and withdraw the transmission assembly.

NOTE: *Remove the brace, if so equipped.*

19. Perform the following on Corolla 1200 and Starlet models, before removing the transmission:

a. Remove the cotter pin from the clutch release linkage;

b. Remove the clutch release cable;

c. Separate the clutch housing from the engine by removing the bolts which secure it.

Installation is performed in the reverse order of removal, but remember to perform the following during installation.

Apply a light coating of multipurpose

grease to the input shaft end, input shaft spline, clutch release bearing, and driveshaft end. On Corolla 1200 and Starlet models, apply multipurpose grease to the ball on the end of the gearshaft lever assembly and clutch release cable end.

On Corolla 1200 and Starlet models, install the clutch housing-to-engine bolts in two or three stages. After installation:

1. Fill the transmission and cooling system. (See the "Capacities" chart in Chapter 1).

2. Adjust the clutch as detailed following.

3. Check to ensure that the back-up lamps come on when Reverse is selected.

Tercel

1. Disconnect the negative battery cable.

2. Drain the coolant from the radiator tank and remove the top radiator hose.

3. Remove the air cleaner intake duct.

4. Remove the intermediate steering shaft.

5. Drain the gear oil from the transmission.

NOTE: *Remove all three drain plugs.*

6. Remove the exhaust pipe.

7. Remove the No. 1 gear shift rod and shift lever housing rod.

8. Remove the speedometer cable and back up light switch connector.

9. Remove the rear engine support crossmember.

NOTE: *Support the transaxle with a jack and a block of wood.*

10. Remove the nine transmission bolts.

11. Install 4 bolts on the transaxle side to an equal depth.

12. Separate the transmission by tightening the bolts a little at a time on the transmission side.

13. Remove the transmission.

14. Installation is the reverse of removal. Tighten the transmission bolts 8–11 ft. lbs. Fill the transmission with 6.5 pints of gear oil.

CLUTCH

The clutch is a single-plate, dry disc type. Some early models use a coil-spring pressure plate. Later models use a diaphragm-spring pressure plate. Clutch release bearings are sealed ball bearing units which need no lubrication and should never be washed in any kind of solvent. All clutches, except those on the Corolla 1200 series, are hydraulically operated.

Pedal Height Specifications

Model/Year	Height (in.)	Measure Between
Corolla 1200 1975–77	2.2 ①	Pedal pad and floor mat
Corolla 1200 1978–81	6.7	Pedal pad and floor mat
Tercel 1980–81	6.65	Pedal pad and floor mat
Corolla 1600 1975–81	6.5	Pedal pad and floor mat
Starlet	6.93	Pedal pad and floor mat

① Pedal depressed

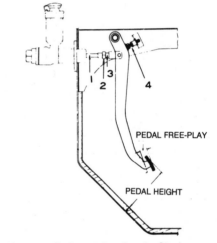

1. Master cylinder pushrod
2. Pushrod locknut
3. Clevis
4. Pedal stop (bolt)

Clutch pedal adjustment

PEDAL HEIGHT ADJUSTMENT

Adjust the pedal height to the specification given in the following chart, by rotating the pedal stop (nut).

FREE-PLAY ADJUSTMENT
Starlet

1. Depress the pedal several times.

2. Depress the pedal by hand until resistance is felt. Free play should be 0.08–1.18 in.

3. Check the clutch release sector pawl. Six notches should remain between the pawl and the end of the sector. If less than 6, re-

Clutch Pedal Free-Play Adjustments

Model	Master Cylinder Piston to Pushrod Clearance (in.)	Release Cylinder to Release Fork Free-Play (in.)	Pedal Free-Play (in.)
Starlet	—	—	0.08–1.18
Corolla 1200	0.02	1.00–1.40	1.00–1.80 ①
1600	0.02	0.08–0.14 ②	0.79–1.58
1800	Not adj.	Not adj.	0.51–0.91
Carina	0.04–0.12	0.08–0.14	1.00–1.75

① 1978–79: 0.8–1.4
② 1978–81: Not adjustable

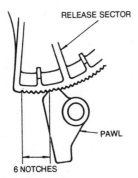

Minimum Pawl and sector position for a used clutch: Starlet

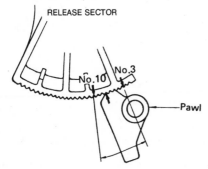

Pawl and sector position for a new clutch: Starlet

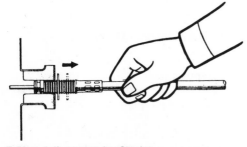

E-Ring Adjustment for Starlet

place the clutch disc. If the clutch disc has been replaced, the pawl should be between the 3rd and 10th notch.

4. To obtain either the used or new position, change the position of the E-ring.

Corolla 1200

1. Pull on the clutch release cable at the clutch support flange until a resistance is felt

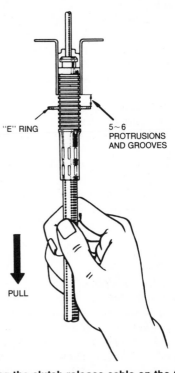

Adjusting the clutch release cable on the Corolla 1200

Clutch Torque Specifications (ft. lbs.)

Model	Release Fork	Retracting Spring Bolts	Clutch Cover-to-Flywheel Bolts
Corolla 1200	13.7–22.4	—	10.9–15.9
Corolla 1600, 1800 and Carina	—	10.9–15.9	10.9–15.9 ①
Starlet	—	—	11–15

① 1975 Corolla—15–16 ft. lbs.; 1976–79—10.9–15.9 ft. lbs.

when the release bearing contacts the clutch diaphragm spring.

2. Holding the cable in this position, measure the distance between the E-ring and the end of the wire support flange. The distance should be 5–6 threads.

3. If adjustment is required, change the position of the E-ring.

4. After completing the adjustment, check the clutch pedal free-play which should be 0.8–1.4 in. after the pedal is depressed several times.

All—Except Corolla 1200 and Starlet

NOTE: *The Tercel clutch is self-adjusting.*

1. Adjust the clearance between the master cylinder piston and the pushrod to the specifications given in the "Clutch Pedal Free-Play Adjustments" chart. Loosen the pushrod locknut and rotate the pushrod while depressing the clutch pedal lightly with your finger.

2. Tighten the locknut when finished with the adjustment.

3. Adjust the release cylinder free-play by loosening the release cylinder pushrod locknut and rotating the pushrod until the specification in the chart is obtained.

4. Measure the clutch pedal free-play after performing the above adjustments. If it fails to fall within specifications, repeat Steps 1–3 until it does.

REMOVAL AND INSTALLATION

CAUTION: *Do not allow grease or oil to get on any of the disc, pressure plate, or flywheel surfaces.*

All Exc. Tercel

1. Remove the transmission from the car as previously detailed.

2. Remove the clutch cover and disc from the bellhousing.

3. Unfasten the release fork bearing clips. Withdraw the release bearing hub, complete with the release bearing.

4. Remove the tension spring from the clutch linkage.

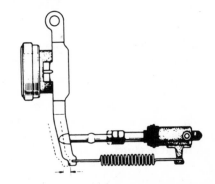

Release cylinder free-play is the distance between the arrows

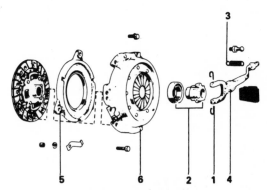

1. Release bearing hub clips
2. Release bearing hub w/bearing
3. Tension spring
4. Release fork
5. Clutch pressure plate
6. Clutch cover w/spring

Clutch components (all models similar)

5. Remove the release fork and support.

6. Punch matchmarks on the clutch cover and the pressure plate so that the pressure plate can be returned to its original position during installation.

7. Slowly unfasten the screws which attach the retracting springs.

NOTE: *If the screws are released too fast, the clutch assembly will fly apart, causing possible injury or loss of parts.*

8. Separate the pressure plate from the clutch cover/spring assembly.

Inspect the parts for wear or deterioration. Replace parts as required.

Installation is performed in the reverse order of removal. Several points should be noted, however:

1. Be sure to align the matchmarks on the clutch cover and pressure plate which were made during disassembly.

2. Apply a thin coating of multipurpose grease to the release bearing hub and release fork contact points. Also, pack the groove inside the clutch hub with multipurpose grease.

3. Center the clutch disc by using a clutch pilot tool or an old input shaft. Insert the pilot into the end of the input shaft front bearing and bolt the clutch to the flywheel.

NOTE: *Bolt the clutch assembly to the flywheel in two or three stages, evenly and to the torque specified in the chart below.*

4. Adjust the clutch as outlined below.

Tercel

In order to replace the clutch, the engine must be removed. See the engine removal section.

Lightly apply multipurpose grease to points "1" and "2"

1. After the engine has been removed tie the bell housing to the cowl.

2. Place matchmarks on the clutch cover and flywheel.

3. Remove the clutch cover.

NOTE: *Loosen each bolt gradually to prevent distortion of the cover.*

4. Remove the disc.

5. Installation is the reverse of removal.

NOTE: *Do not allow grease to get on the disc lining, flywheel, or cover. When reinstalling the clutch be sure to use a spline alignment tool or an old input shaft to properly align the clutch. Tighten the cover bolts 11–15 ft. lbs.*

Master Cylinder

REMOVAL AND INSTALLATION

1. Remove the clevis pin.

2. Detach the hydraulic line from the tube.

CAUTION: *Do not spill brake fluid on the painted surfaces of the vehicle.*

3. Unfasten the bolts which secure the master cylinder to the firewall. Withdraw the assembly.

Installation is performed in the reverse order of removal. Blend the system as detailed

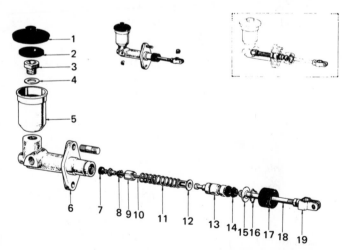

1. Filler cap
2. Float
3. Reservoir setbolt
4. Washer
5. Reservoir
6. Master cylinder body
7. Inlet valve
8. Spring
9. Inlet valve housing
10. Connecting rod
11. Spring
12. Spring retainer
13. Piston
14. Cylinder cup
15. Plate
16. Snap-ring
17. Boot
18. Pushrod
19. Clevis

Clutch master cylinder components

following. Adjust the clutch pedal height and free-play as previously detailed.

OVERHAUL

1. Clamp the master cylinder body in a vise with soft jaws.
2. Separate the reservoir assembly from the master cylinder.
3. Remove the snap-ring and remove the pushrod/piston assembly.
4. Inspect all of the parts and replace any which are worn or defective.

Assembly is performed in the following order:
1. Coat all parts with clean brake fluid, prior to assembly.
2. Install the piston assembly in the cylinder bore.
3. Fit the pushrod over the washer and secure them with the snap-ring.
4. Install the reservoir.

Clutch Slave Cylinder

REMOVAL AND INSTALLATION

CAUTION: *Do not spill brake fluid on the painted surface of the vehicle.*
1. Raise the front of the car and support it with jackstands. Be sure that it is supported *securely.*
2. If necessary, remove the rear gravel shield to gain access to the release cylinder.
3. Remove the clutch fork return spring.
4. Unfasten the hydraulic line from the release cylinder by removing its retaining nut.
5. Screw the threaded end of the pushrod in.
6. Remove the release cylinder retaining nuts and remove the cylinder.

Installation is performed in the reverse order of removal. Adjust the pushrod freeplay and bleed the hydraulic system.

OVERHAUL

1. Remove the pushrod assembly and the rubber boot.
2. Withdraw the piston, complete with its cup; don't remove the cup unless it is being replaced.
3. Wash all the parts in brake fluid.
4. Replace any worn or damaged parts.
5. Replace the cylinder assembly if the piston-to-bore clearance is greater than 0.006 in.

Assembly is the reverse of disassembly. Coat all parts in clean brake fluid, prior to assembly.

Clutch Hydraulic System
BLEEDING

1. Fill the master cylinder reservoir with brake fluid.
CAUTION: *Do not spill brake fluid on the painted surfaces of the vehicle.*
2. Remove the cap and loosen the bleeder plug. Block the outlet hole with your finger.
3. Pump the clutch pedal several times, then take your finger from the hole while depressing the clutch pedal. Allow the air to flow out. Place your finger back over the hole and release the pedal.
4. After fluid pressure can be felt (with your finger), tighten the bleeder plug.
5. Fit a bleeder tube over the plug and place the other end into a clean jar half-filled with brake fluid.
6. Depress the clutch pedal, loosen the bleeder plug with a wrench, and allow the fluid to flow into the jar.
7. Tighten the plug and then release the clutch pedal.

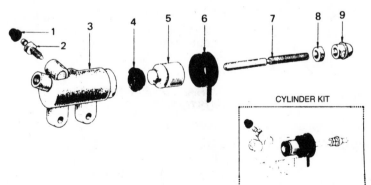

CYLINDER KIT

1. Cap
2. Bleeder plug
3. Release cylinder body
4. Cylinder cup
5. Piston
6. Boot
7. Pushrod
8. Nut
9. Nut

Clutch release cylinder—exploded view

8. Repeat Steps 6–7 until no air bubbles are visible in the bleeder tube.

9. When there are no more air bubbles, tighten the plug while keeping the clutch-pedal fully depressed. Replace the cap.

10. Fill the master cylinder to the specified level. (See Chapter 1.)

11. Check the system for leaks.

AUTOMATIC TRANSMISSION

PAN REMOVAL

1. Unfasten the oil plug and drain the fluid from the transmission.

2. Unfasten the pan securing bolts.

3. Withdraw the pan.

Installation is performed in the reverse order of removal. Torque the pan securing bolts to 4–6 ft. lb. (17–20 ft. lbs.—A-40). Refill the transmission with fluid as outlined in Chapter 1.

LOW SERVO AND BAND ADJUSTMENT

2-Speed—Corolla

The low and band adjusting bolt is located on the outside of the transmission case, so that it is unnecessary to remove the oil pan in order to perform the adjustment

1. Loosen the locknut on the adjusting bolt.

2. Tighten the bolt until it is bottomed.

3. Back off 3½ turns and hold the adjusting bolts securely while tightening the locknut.

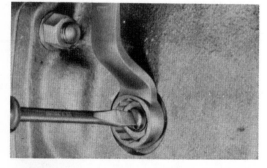

Adjusting the low servo and band on the two-speed Toyoglide

FRONT BAND ADJUSTMENT

3-Speed Toyoglide

1. Remove the oil pan as previously outlined.

2. Pry the band engagement lever toward band with a screwdriver.

3. The gap between end of the piston rod and the engagement bolt should be 0.138 in.

4. If the gap does not meet the specification, adjust it by turning the engagement bolt.

5. Install the oil pan and refill the transmission as previously outlined.

REAR BAND ADJUSTMENT

3-Speed Toyoglide

The rear band adjusting bolt is located on the outside of the case, so it is not necessary to remove the oil pan in order to adjust the band.

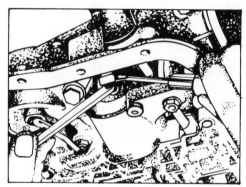

Adjusting the three-speed Toyoglide front band

1. Loosen the adjusting bolt locknut and fully screw in the adjusting bolt.

2. Loosen the adjusting bolt one turn.

3. Tighten the locknut while holding the bolt so that it cannot turn.

BAND ADJUSTMENTS

3-Speed A-40

The A-40 transmission has no bands, and therefore no band adjustments are possible. The only external adjustments are throttle and shift linkages.

NEUTRAL SAFETY SWITCH ADJUSTMENT

2-Speed—Corolla

The neutral safety switch used on Corolla models is not adjustable. If it malfunctions, it must be replaced. To do so, proceed in the following manner:

1. Remove the center console.

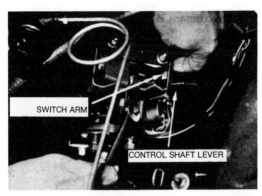

Adjusting the neutral safety switch on cars with column shift

Adjusting the neutral safety switch on cars with three-speed automatic and floorshift

2. Unfasten and remove the three screws securing the transmission selector assembly.

3. Disconnect the neutral safety switch multiconnector.

4. Slightly lift transmission selector assembly and unfasten the two neutral safety switch attaching screws.

5. Withdraw the switch.

Installation is performed in the reverse order of removal. Position the selector lever in Neutral (N) and install the switch so that installation marks align with each other.

3-Speed—Column Selector

The neutral safety switch/reverse lamp switch on the Toyoglide transmission with a column-mounted selector is located under the hood on the shift linkage. If the switch is not functioning properly, adjust as follows:

1. Loosen the switch securing bolt.

2. Move the switch so that its arm just contacts the control shaft lever when the gear selector is in Drive (D) position.

3. Tighten the switch securing bolt.

4. Check the operation of the switch; the car should start only in Park (P) or Neutral (N) and the back-up lamps should come on only when Reverse (R) is selected.

5. If the switch cannot be adjusted so that it functions properly, replace it with a new one. Perform the adjustment as previously outlined.

3-Speed—Console Shift

Models with a console-mounted selector have the neutral safety switch on the linkage located beneath the console.

To adjust it, proceed in the following manner:

1. Remove the screws securing the center console.

2. Unfasten the console multiconnector, if so equipped, and completely remove the console.

3. Adjust the switch in the manner outlined in the preceding column selector section.

4. Install the console in the reverse order of removal after completion of the switch adjustment.

SHIFT LINKAGE ADJUSTMENT

2 and 3-Speed Toyoglide

The transmission should be engaged, in the gear selected as indicated on the shift quadrant. If it is not, then adjust the linkage as follows:

1. Check all of the shift linkage bushings for wear. Replace any worn bushings.

2. Loosen the connecting rod swivel locknut.

3. Move the selector lever and check movement of the pointer in the shift quadrant.

4. When the control shaft is set in the

Loosening the column shift swivel locknut

Adjusting the column shift indicator drive cord

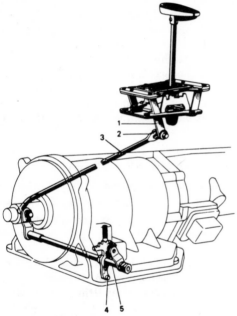

1. Gear selector lever
2. Intermediate rod
3. Control rod
4. Manual valve lever
5. Shaft

Toyoglide floorshift components

neutral position the quadrant pointer should indicate "N" as well.

Steps 5–7 apply only to cars equipped with column-mounted gear selectors.

5. If the pointer does not indicate Neutral (N), then check the drive cord adjustment.

6. Remove the steering column shroud.

7. Turn the drive cord adjuster with a phillips screwdriver until the pointer indicates Neutral (N).

Steps 8–10 apply to both column-mounted and floor-mounted selectors:

8. Position the manual valve lever on the

transmission so that it is in the Neutral position.

9. Lock the connecting rod swivel with the locknut so that the pointer, selector, and manual valve lever are all positioned in Neutral.

10. Check the operation of the gear selector by moving it through all ranges.

3-Speed A-40

1. Loosen the adjusting nut on the linkage and check the linkage for freedom of movement.

2. Push the manual valve lever toward the front of the car, as far as it will go.

3. Bring the lever back to its third notch (Neutral).

4. Have an assistant hold the shift lever in Neutral, while you tighten the linkage adjusting nut so that it can't slip.

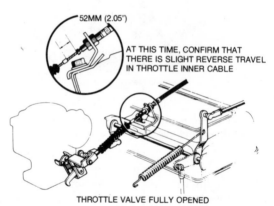

A-40 throttle linkage adjustment

THROTTLE LINKAGE ADJUSTMENT

2-Speed—Corolla

1. Loosen the locknuts on the throttle linkage connecting rod turnbuckle.

2. Have an assistant depress the accelerator pedal fully.

3. Hold the throttle butterfly in the fully opened position.

4. Adjust the length of the rod so that the pointer lines up with the mark on the transmission case.

5. Tighten the locknut.

3-Speed Toyoglide

1. Loosen the locknut at each end of the linkage adjusting turnbuckle.

2. Detach the throttle linkage connecting rod from the carburetor.

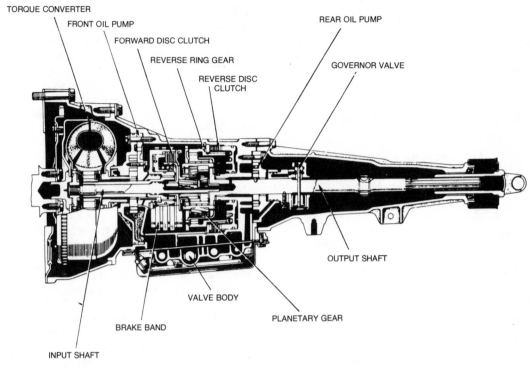

Cutaway view of the two-speed Toyoglide transmission

3. Align the pointer on the throttle valve lever with the mark stamped on the transmission case.

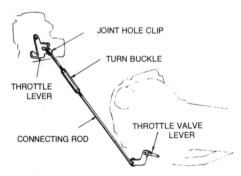

Toyoglide throttle linkage components

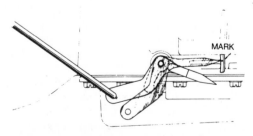

Toyoglide throttle linkage aligning marks

4. Rotate the turnbuckle so that the end of the throttle linkage rod and the carburetor throttle lever are aligned.

NOTE: *The carburetor throttle valve must be fully opened during this adjustment.*

5. Tighten the turnbuckle locknuts and reconnect the throttle rod to the carburetor.

6. Open the throttle valve and check the pointer alignment with the mark on the transmission case.

7. Road-test the car. If the transmission "hunts," i.e., keeps shifting rapidly back and forth between gears at certain speeds or if it fails to downshift properly when going up hills, repeat the throttle linkage adjustment.

3-Speed A-40 and A-40D

1. Remove the air cleaner.

2. Conform that the accelerator linkage opens the throttle fully. Adjust the link as necessary.

3. Peel the rubber dust boot back from the throttle cable.

4. Loosen the adjustment nuts on the throttle cable bracket (rocker cover) just enough to allow cable housing movement.

5. Have an assistant depress the accelerator pedal fully.

6. Adjust the cable housing so that the dis-

tance between its end and the cable stop collar is 2.05 in.

7. Tighten the adjustment nuts. Make sure that the adjustment hasn't changed. Install the dust boot and the air cleaner.

REMOVAL AND INSTALLATION

Tercel

1. Disconnect the negative battery cable.
2. Drain the coolant from the radiator tank and remove the top hose.
3. Remove the air cleaner inlet duct.
4. Remove the intermediate steering shaft.
5. Drain the fluid from the transmission.
6. Remove the exhaust pipe.
7. Remove the shift lever rod.
8. Remove the speedometer cable, backup light connector and any throttle linkage.
9. Remove the cooling lines from the transmission.
10. Support the transaxle with a jack.
11. Remove the rear crossmember.
12. Separate the transmission from the transaxle.
13. Remove the transmission.
14. Installation is the reverse of removal.

3-Speed Toyoglide

1. Disconnect the battery.
2. Remove the air cleaner and disconnect the accelerator torque link or the cable.
3. Disconnect the throttle link rod at the carburetor side, then disconnect the backup light wiring at the firewall (on early models).
4. Jack up the car and support it on stands, then drain the transmission. (Use a clean receptacle so that the fluid can be checked for color, smell and foreign matter.)
5. Disconnect all shift linkage.
6. On early models, remove the cross shaft from the frame.
7. Disconnect the throttle link rod at the transmission side and remove the speedometer cable, cooler lines and parking brake equalizer bracket.
8. Loosen the exhaust flange nuts and remove the exhaust pipe clamp and bracket.
9. Remove the drive shaft and the rear mounting bracket, then lower the rear end of the transmission carefully.
10. Unbolt the torque converter from the drive plate. Support the engine with a suit-

able jack stand and remove the seven bolts that hold the transmission to the engine.

Reverse the order of the removal procedures with the following precautions.

1. Install the drive plate and ring gear, tighten the attaching bolts to 37–43 ft. lbs.
2. After assembling the torque converter to the transmission, check the clearance, it should be about 0.59 in.
3. Before installing the transmission, install the oil pump locator pin on the torque converter to facilitate installation.
4. While rotating the crankshaft, tighten the converter attaching bolts, a little at a time.
5. After installing the throttle connecting second rod, make sure the throttle valve lever indicator aligns with the mark on the transmission with the carburetor throttle valve fully opened. If required, adjust the rod.
6. To install the transmission control rod correctly, move the transmission lever to N (Neutral), and the selector lever to Neutral. Fill the transmission with automatic transmission fluid (Type F only), then start the engine. Run the engine at idle speed and apply the brakes while moving the selector lever through all positions, then return it to Neutral.
7. After warming the engine, move the selector lever through all positions, then back to Neutral, and check the fluid level. Fill as necessary.
8. Adjust the engine idle to 550–650 rpm with the selector lever at Drive. Road test the vehicle.
9. With the selector lever at 2 or Drive, check the point at which the transmission shifts. Check for shock, noise and slipping with the selector lever in all positions. Check for leaks from the transmission.

3-Speed A-40

To remove and install the transmission, proceed in the following manner:

1. Perform Steps 1 through 3 of the three-speed Toyoglide removal procedure.
2. Remove the upper starter mounting nuts using a socket wrench with a long extension.
3. Raise the car and support it securely with jack stands. Drain the transmission.
4. Remove the lower starter mounting bolt and lay the starter along side of the engine. Don't let it hang by the wires.

5. Unbolt the parking brake equalizer support.

6. Matchmark the driveshaft and the companion flange, to ensure correct installation. Remove the bolts securing the driveshaft to the companion flange.

7. Slide the driveshaft straight back and out of the transmission. Use a spare U-joint yoke or tie a plastic bag over the end of the transmission to keep any fluid from dripping out.

8. Remove the bolts from the cross-shaft body bracket, the cotter pin from the manual lever, and the cross-shaft socket from the transmission.

9. Remove the exhaust pipe bracket from the torque converter bell housing.

10. Disconnect the oil cooler lines from the transmission and remove the line bracket from the bell housing.

11. Disconnect the speedometer cable from the transmission.

12. Unbolt both support braces from the bell housing.

13. Use a transmission jack to raise the transmission slightly.

14. Unbolt the rear crossmember and lower the transmission about 3 in.

15. Pry the two rubber torque converter access plugs out of their holes at the back of the engine.

16. Remove the six torque converter mounting bolts through the access hole. Rotate the engine with the crankshaft pulley.

17. Cut the head off a bolt to make a guide pin for the torque converter. Install the pin on the converter.

18. Remove the converter bell housing-to-engine bolts.

19. Push on the end of the guide pin in order to remove the converter with the transmission. Remove the transmission rearward and then bring it out from under the car.

CAUTION: *Don't catch the throttle cable during removal.*

Installation is the reverse of removal. Be sure to note the following, however.

1. Install the two long bolts on the upper converter housing and tighten them to 36–58 ft. lbs.

2. Tighten the converter-to-flex-plate bolts finger-tight, and then tighten them with a torque wrench to 11–16 ft. lbs.

3. When installing the speedometer cable, make sure that the felt dust protector and washer are on the cable end.

4. Tighten the cooling line and exhaust pipe bracket mounting bolts to 37–58 ft. lbs. Tighten the cooling lines to 14–22 ft. lbs.

5. Align the matchmarks made on the driveshaft and the companion flange during removal. Tighten the driveshaft mounting bolts to 11–16 ft. lbs.

6. Be sure to install the oil pan drain plug. Tighten it to 11–14 ft. lbs.

7. Adjust the throttle cable.

8. Fill the transmission to the proper capacity. Use only type "F" (ATF) fluid. Start the engine, run the selector through all gear ranges and place it in Park (P). Check the level on the dipstick and add type F fluid, as necessary.

9. Road test the car and check for leaks.

Drive Train

7

DRIVELINE

Driveshaft and U-Joints

REMOVAL AND INSTALLATION

Except Tercel

1. Raise the rear of the car with jacks and support the rear axle housing with jack-stands.

CAUTION: *Be sure that the car is securely supported. Remember, you will be working underneath it.*

2. Unfasten the bolts which attach the driveshaft universal joint yoke flange to the mounting flange on the differential drive pinion.

3. On models equipped with three universal joints, perform the following:

a. Withdraw the driveshaft subassembly from the U-joint sleeve yoke;

b. Unfasten the center support bearing from its bracket.

4. Remove the driveshaft end from transmission.

5. Install an old U-joint yoke in the transmission or, if none is available, use a plastic bag secured with a rubber band over the hole to keep the transmission oil from running out.

6. Withdraw the driveshaft from beneath the vehicle.

Installation is performed in the following order:

1. Apply multipurpose grease on the section of the U-joint sleeve which is to be inserted into the transmission.

2. Insert the driveshaft sleeve into the transmission.

CAUTION: *Be careful not to damage any of the seals.*

3. For models equipped with three U-joints and center bearings, perform the following:

a. Adjust the center bearing clearance with no load placed on the driveline components; the top of the rubber center cushion should be 0.04 in. *behind* the center of the elongated bolt hole;

b. Install the center bearing assembly.

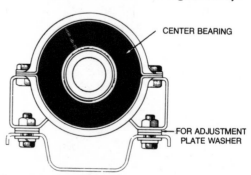

Center bearing adjustment

NOTE: *Use the same number of washers on the center bearing bracket as were removed.*

4. Secure the U-joint flange to the differential pinion flange with the mounting bolts.

CAUTION: *Be sure that the bolts are of the same type as those removed and that they are tightened securely.*

5. Remove the jackstands and lower the vehicle.

U-JOINT OVERHAUL

1. Matchmark the yoke and the driveshaft.

2. Remove the lockrings from the bearings.

3. Position the yoke on vise jaws. Using a bearing remover and a hammer, gently tap the remover until the bearing is driven out of the yoke about ½ in.

4. Place the tool in the vise and drive the yoke away from the tool until the bearing is removed.

5. Repeat Steps 3 and 4 for the other bearings.

6. Check for worn or damaged parts. Inspect the bearing journal surfaces for wear.

U-joint assembly is performed in the following order:

1. Install the bearing cups, seals, and O-rings in the spider.

2. Grease the spider and the bearings.

3. Position the spider in the yoke.

4. Start the bearings in the yoke and then press them into place, using a vise.

Press the bearing into place with a vise

5. Repeat Step 4 for the other bearings.

6. If the axial-play of the spider is greater than 0.002 in., select lockrings which will provide the correct play. Be sure that the lockrings are the same size on both sides or driveshaft noise and vibration will result.

7. Check the U-joint assembly for smooth operation.

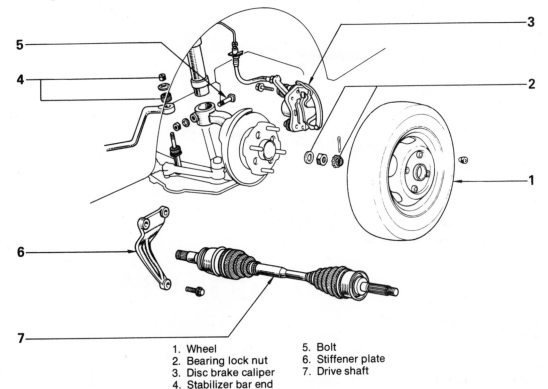

1. Wheel	5. Bolt
2. Bearing lock nut	6. Stiffener plate
3. Disc brake caliper	7. Drive shaft
4. Stabilizer bar end	

Tercel front drive axle

TERCEL

1. Jack up your vehicle and support it with jackstands.

2. Remove the front wheel.

3. Remove the brake caliper and tie it out of the way.

4. Remove the cotter pin, locknut and adjusting nut, from the hub.

5. Remove the bottom nut from the shock absorber.

6. Pull down on the hub to separate it from the shock.

7. Using a suitable puller pull the axle hub from the driveshaft.

8. Remove the transaxle support bracket.

9. Remove the driveshaft from the transaxle using special tool #09648-16010 available from your Toyota dealer.

NOTE: *Be careful not to damage the rubber boots on the driveshaft.*

10. Installation is the reverse of removal.

Tripod Removal

INNER ONLY

1. Remove the snap-ring and boot clamp.

2. Matchmark the driveshaft and the inboard joint shaft.

3. Remove the inner boot.

4. Place matchmarks on the tripod and the shaft.

NOTE: *When making these matchmarks be sure to use paint, or chalk. Do not punch mark any of these parts.*

6. Drive the tripod off with a drift pin.

NOTE: *Do not tap on the roller portion of the tripod.*

7. Check for worn or damaged parts.

8. When reinstalling the tripod fill the boot with a lithium base grease.

9. Installation is the reverse of removal.

The manufacturer recommends that the outboard shaft be serviced as a complete unit only.

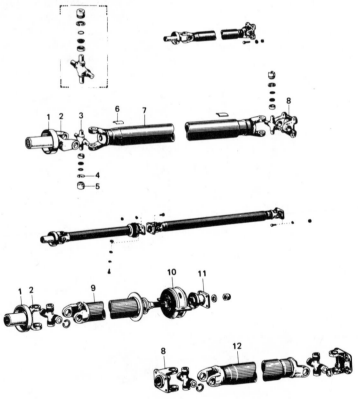

1. Transmission end of driveshaft	7. Driveshaft
2. U-joint yoke and sleeve	8. U-joint yoke flange
3. U-joint spider	9. Intermediate driveshaft assembly
4. Snap-ring	10. Center bearing support
5. U-joint spider bearing	11. U-joint flange assembly
6. Balancing weight	12. Driveshaft

Two-piece driveshaft only

Driveshaft components—upper illustration shows a single-piece driveshaft; lower, a two-piece driveshaft

TERCEL

1. Jack up your vehicle and support it with jackstands.

2. Remove the front wheel.

3. Remove the brake caliper and tie it out of the way.

4. Remove the stabilizer bar end.

5. Remove the strut bar end.

6. Remove the tie rod end, with a suitable puller.

7. Support the lower control arm with a jack.

8. Remove the lower control arm bolt.

9. Remove the bolt at the ball joint.

10. Lower the jack and remove the control arm.

11. Remove the bottom shock bolt.

12. Pull the hub from the driveshaft with a suitable puller.

13. Remove the steering knuckle from the shock absorber.

14. Installation is the reverse of removal.

The following torque specifications are needed: bottom shock bolt 40–52 ft. lbs., ball joint bolt 40–52 ft. lbs., stabilizer bar 11–15 ft. lbs., tie rod end 37–50 ft. lbs., lower control arm 51–65 ft. lbs., strut bar 29–39 ft. lbs., brake caliper 33–39 ft. lbs.

REAR AXLE

Determining Axle Ratio

The drive axle of a car is said to have a certain axle ratio. This number (usually a whole number and a decimal fraction) is actually a comparison of the number of gear teeth on the ring gear and the pinion gear. For example, a 4.11 rear means that theoretically, there are 4.11 teeth on the ring gear and one tooth on the pinion gear or, put another way, the driveshaft must turn 4.11 times to turn the wheels once. Actually, on a 4.11 rear, there might be 37 teeth on the ring gear and 9 teeth on the pinion gear. By dividing the number of teeth on the pinion gear into the number of teeth on the ring gear, the numerical axle ratio (4.11) is obtained. This also provides a good method of ascertaining exactly which axle ratio one is dealing with.

Another method of determining gear ratio is to jack up and support the car so that both rear wheels are off the ground. Make a chalk mark on the rear wheel and the drive shaft. Put the transmission in neutral. Turn the rear wheel one complete turn and count the number of turns that the driveshaft makes. The number of turns that the driveshaft makes in one complete revolution of the rear wheel is an approximation of the rear axle ratio.

Axle Shaft
REMOVAL AND INSTALLATION
Except Tercel

1. Raise the rear of the car and support it securely by using jackstands.

CAUTION: *Be sure that the vehicle is securely supported. Remember, you will be working underneath it.*

2. Drain the oil from the axle housing.

3. Remove the wheel disc, unfasten the lug nuts, and remove the wheel.

4. Punch matchmarks on the brake drum and the axle shaft to maintain rotational balance.

Using a slide hammer to remove the axle shaft

5. Remove the brake drum and related components, as detailed in Chapter 9.

6. Remove the rear bearing retaining nut.

7. Remove the backing plate attachment nuts through the access holes in the rear axle shaft flange.

8. Use a slide hammer with a suitable adapter to withdraw the axle shaft from its housing.

CAUTION: *Use care not to damage the oil seal when removing the axle shaft.*

9. Repeat the procedure for the axle shaft on the opposite side. Be careful not to mix the components of the two sides.

Installation is performed in the reverse order of removal. Coat the lips of the rear housing oil seal with multipurpose grease prior to installation of the rear axle shaft. Torque the bearing retaining nut to the specifications given in the chart below.

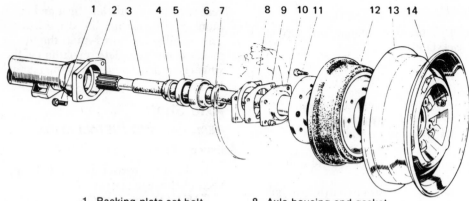

1. Backing plate set bolt
2. Rear axle housing
3. Rear axle shaft
4. Axle bearing inner retainer
5. Oil seal
6. Bearing
7. Spacer
8. Axle housing end gasket
9. Bearing retainer gasket
10. Axle bearing inner retainer
11. Hub bolt
12. Brake drum assembly
13. Wheel
14. Hub nut

Rear axle shaft and related components

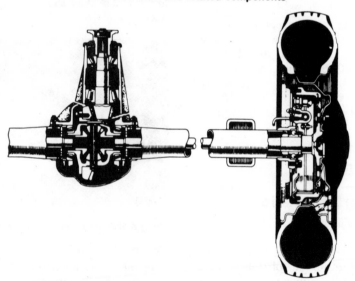

Cutaway view of a typical rear axle

Axle Bearing Retaining Nut Specifications

Model	Torque Range (ft. lbs.)
Corolla ('70–'74)	15–22
Corolla 1600	26–38
Tercel	22
Corolla 1800	19–23
Starlet	44–53

NOTE: *Always use new nuts, as they are of the self-locking type.*

DIFFERENTIAL

Removal and Installation

NOTE: *Rear axle servicing is a complex operation. Repair should not be attempted unless the special tools and knowledge required are readily available.*

REAR CARRIER—ALL MODELS, EXCEPT TERCEL

1. Remove the axle shafts.
2. Disconnect the driveshaft from the pinion shaft flange.
3. Unfasten the carrier securing nuts and remove the carrier assembly.

Installation is performed in the reverse order of removal. Be sure to apply liquid sealer to both the carrier gasket and the lower carrier securing nuts.

TERCEL

1. Disconnect the negative battery terminal.
2. Drain the water from the radiator tank.
3. Remove the top radiator hose from the engine.
4. Remove the clutch cable if so equipped.
5. Remove the starter.

NOTE: *On cars equipped with automatic transmissions you must remove the torque converter bolts via the starter inset. Also remember to disconnect the oil cooling lines.*

6. Remove the intermediate steering shaft.
7. Remove the bottom bolt on the engine shock absorber.
8. Remove the front driveshafts. See the section relating to this procedure.
9. Remove the exhaust pipe.
10. Remove the shifting linkage.
11. Remove the back-up light connector and the speedometer.

NOTE: *On cars with automatic transmissions remove any necessary throttle linkage if so equipped.*

12. Drain the oil from the transaxle and the transmission.

NOTE: *Remove all three drain plugs on manual transmission cars.*

13. Support the rear of the engine with a jack.
14. Remove the rear crossmember.
15. Place a jack under the transaxle.
16. Separate the transmission from the transaxle and remove the transmission.
17. Remove the bellhousing bolts and remove the transaxle.
18. Installation is the reverse of removal.

Because of the many specialized tools required to work on the differential, it is recommended that this work be performed by your dealer or a professional mechanic qualified to handle this type of work.

Overhaul

1. Thoroughly wash and rinse the carrier and blow dry with compressed air.
2. Securely clamp the carrier in a vise or suitable stand.
3. Apply a light coating of mechanic's blue to the teeth of the ring gear.
4. Applying a slight drag on the ring gear to avoid backlash, rotate the pinion in a smooth and continuous manner to obtain a good tooth pattern on the ring gear.
5. Next, attach a dial indicator gauge to the carrier base and check the ring gear backlash.

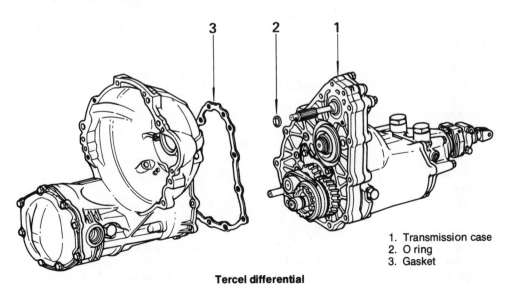

1. Transmission case
2. O ring
3. Gasket

Tercel differential

6. Also check ring gear runout at this time. If the tooth pattern obtained is correct, and the backlash and runout are within limits, any gear noise must come from the side gears.

7. With the dial indicator gauge set up on the carrier, check the backlash between the pinion gears and side gears. Excessive backlash usually is due to either worn thrust washers or a worn pinion shaft.

8. Check side gear thrust clearance with a feeler gauge.

9. If everything is within specifications, test the preload on the differential drive pinion nut. Punch mark both pinion and nut in their original positions, then loosen the pinion nut about ½ turn and torque to specifications. If the punch marks line up again (within 60°) the pinion preload was correct.

10. Punch mark both the carrier and the side bearing caps for identification, remove the locknuts and take off the caps.

11. Remove the differential case assembly from the carrier. Do not mix the bearing cups; paint mark them for identification.

12. Remove the differential pinion nut (do not let the pinion drop out), then remove the pinion spacer, yoke and oil seal.

13. With a brass punch, drive out the pinion bearing cups.

NOTE: *This should be done only when the bearings are to be replaced.*

14. Press or pull off the drive pinion rear bearing. Avoid damaging the flat spacer behind the bearing.

15. Measure the spacer thickness and note the measurement for future use. Remove both side bearings from the differential case and mark them "L" and "R" for identification.

NOTE: *Remove side bearings only if they must be replaced.*

16. Punch mark the differential case and cover, then remove the cover bolts and the cover (where fitted).

17. Remove the shaft and pinions, the side gears and all thrust washers.

NOTE: *Some differential types have four spider pinion gears; punch mark the gears before removal so they can be correctly reinstalled.*

Check all bearing cones and cups for wear. Inspect the tooth surfaces of all gears carefully and inspect all thrust washers for wear and signs of slipping in their seats. Check all gear shafts for scoring, wear or distortion. Finally, inspect the case and carrier housing for cracks or other damage. Also check the case for signs of wear at the side gear bores, bearing cap and mounting hubs.

Assembly is performed in the following order:

1. Wash and clean all parts before installation.

2. Lightly oil all bearings and gear shafts, except the ring gear and drive pinion teeth.

3. Place the side gears and the pinion gears, with their thrust washers, into the differential case.

4. Insert the shaft and align the lock pin holes in the case and shaft.

5. Install the case cover in place and install the lock pin (bolt) and tighten the cover bolts to specification; check the play.

6. If the side bearings were removed, install them now. If the ring gear was removed, install it now. Tighten the bolts in symmetrical sequence to avoid distortion and runout.

7. Install the drive pinion bearing cups into the carrier housing, using a suitable installing tool. Make sure the cups are seated solidly.

8. Assemble the drive pinion rear bearing to the drive pinion and insert it into the carrier housing. Install the spacer and front bearing to the drive pinion; install the yoke and tighten the nut to specifications.

CAUTION: *The drive pinion oil seal is NOT installed at this point.*

9. The drive pinion preload is measured in in. lbs. (not ft. lbs.). Adjust the preload by changing the length of the bearing spacer (between the front and rear bearings) until the required preload is obtained.

10. Place the previously assembled differential case into position in the bearing hubs and put the caps into position as marked(L and R).

11. Set the case so that there will be the least amount of backlash between the ring gear and pinion (in order to save time adjusting).

12. Install the adjusting nuts (also marked L and R) and take care not to cross-thread them.

13. Finger-tighten the bearing caps until the threads are lined up correctly, then tighten slowly.

14. Back off the right-hand adjusting nut (ring gear teeth side) and screw in the other nut until almost no backlash is felt.

15. Attach a dial indicator gauge so that it reads at right angles to the back of the ring gear, then screw in the right-hand adjusting

nut until the gauge indicates that all side play has been eliminated.

16. Tighten the adjusting nut another 1 or 1½ notches (depending on the fit of the lock tabs).

17. Recheck the preload on the drive pinion as before; this time the specifications are different.

18. If too loose, readjust the side bearing preload; if too tight, adjust the ring gear backlash.

19. Install the dial indicator gauge so that it contacts the ring gear teeth at right angles. Adjust the backlash to specifications.

20. If too great, adjust by loosening the bearing cap bolts slightly and screwing the right-hand adjusting nut (ring gear teeth side) out about two notches.

21. Tighten the left-hand adjusting nut the same amount.

NOTE: *One notch of the adjusting nut equals about 0.002 in. of backlash.*

22. Recheck the backlash, then tighten the bearing cap nuts.

23. Using a dial indicator recheck all run-out dimensions (ring gear back, ring gear outer circumference and differential case).

24. Apply a thin coat of mechanic's blue, red lead or even lipstick to the ring gear teeth. Rotate the gear several times, applying a light drag to the ring gear. Rotate the gear in both directions.

25. Inspect the tooth pattern. There are four basic tooth patterns: heel, toe, flank and face. Most often the tooth pattern obtained will be a combination of two of these patterns and the adjustments must be made accordingly.

Heel contact Move the drive pinion in by increasing the thickness of the spacer (between the pinion head and rear bearing). Readjust backlash by moving the ring gear away from the pinion.

Face contact Adjust same as above.

Toe contact Adjust by moving the drive pinion out by reducing the thickness of the spacer. Readjust backlash.

Flank contact Adjust same as toe contact.

Continue assembling as follows:

26. Remove the drive pinion nut and install the seal into the differential carrier housing, then install the oil slinger, dust shield and yoke and retorque the pinion nut as specified.

27. Install the differential carrier assembly into the axle housing.

Differential Specifications

Model/Year	Backlash (in.)		Run-Out (in.)	Torque (ft. lbs.)		Pinion Bearing Preload (in. lbs.)	
	Ring Gear and Pinion	Side Gears	Ring Gear	Side Bearing Cap	Differential Pinion Nut	New	Old
Corolla 1200	0.0040–0.0060	0.0010–0.0060	0.0028	40–47	65–145	7–12	4–6
1600 1975–78	0.0040–0.0060	0.0010–0.0060	0.0028	40–47	65–145	7–12	4–6
1600 1979	0.0051–0.0071	0.0020–0.0080	0.0030	37–50	80–173	8.7–13.9	4.3–6.9
1800	0.0051–0.0071	0.0010–0.0079	0.0028	37–50	80–173	8.7–13.9	4.3–6.9
Tercel	0.0039–0.0059	0.0016–0.0094	0.0028	33–39	109–267	4.3–8.7	2.6–4.3
Starlet	0.0051–0.0071	0.0008–0.0059	0.0028	40–47	80–173	5.6–10.9	5.2–9.5

Suspension and Steering

FRONT SUSPENSION

Springs

REMOVAL AND INSTALLATION

Corolla, Carina, Starlet

1. Remove the hubcap and loosen the lug nuts.

2. Raise the front of the car and support it, on the chassis jacking plates provided, with jackstands.

CAUTION: *Do not support the weight of the car on the suspension arm; the arm will deform under its weight.*

3. Unfasten the lug nuts and remove the wheel.

4. Detach the front brake line from its clamp.

5. Remove the brake caliper as detailed in Chapter 9 and wire it out of the way.

6. Unfasten the three nuts which secure the upper shock absorber mounting plate to the top of the wheel arch.

7. Remove the two bolts which attach the shock absorber lower end to the steering knuckle lower arm.

NOTE: *Press down on the suspension lower arm, in order to remove the shock absorber assembly. This must be done to clear the collars on the steering knuckle*

arm bolt holes when removing the *shock/spring assembly.*

8. Fabricate the shock absorber/spring assembly mounting stand, as illustrated. Bolt the assembly on the stand and mount the stand on a vise.

9. Use a coil spring compressor to compress the spring until it can be moved freely.

10. Remove the bearing dust cap from the top of the shock absorber assembly.

11. Use an adjustable wrench or a large open-end wrench to keep the upper spring seat from turning and unfasten the 10 mm nut at the top of the shock absorber assembly.

CAUTION: *Do not use an impact wrench when loosening the nut.*

12. Remove the components from the top

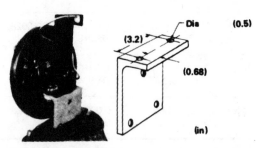

Fabricate the shock absorber stand and mount it in a vise as shown

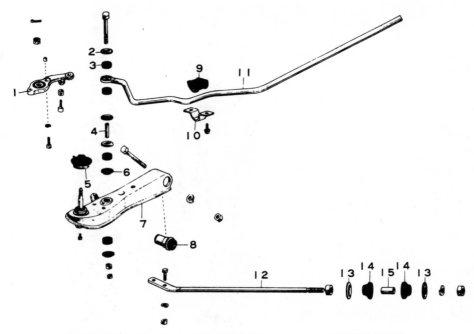

1. Steering knuckle arm
2. Retainer
3. Cushion
4. Collar
5. Dust cover
6. Retainer
7. Lower control arm
8. Bushing
9. Bushing
10. Bracket
11. Stabilizer bar
12. Strut
13. Retainer
14. Cushion
15. Collar

Components of the Corolla and Carina MacPherson strut front suspension

of the shock and withdraw the spring in its compressed state.

Check the spring for cracks and weakness. Check the dust seals and spring seats for wear or deterioration. Replace parts, as necessary.

Installation is performed in the reverse order of removal. Be sure to note the following, however:

1. Align the hole in the upper suspension support with the shock absorber piston rod end so that they fit properly.

2. Always use a *new* nut and nylon washer on the shock absorber piston rod end when securing it to the upper suspension support. Torque the nut to 29–40 ft. lbs.

CAUTION: *Do not use an impact wrench to tighten the nut.*

3. Coat the suspension support bearing with multipurpose grease prior to installation. Pack the space in the upper support with multipurpose grease, also, after installation.

4. Tighten the suspension support-to-wheel arch bolts to the following specification:

Corolla—11–16 ft. lbs.
Carina—14–23 ft. lbs.

Starlet—15–21 ft. lbs.

5. Tighten the shock absorber-to-steering knuckle arm bolts to the following specifications:

Starlet—42–56 ft. lbs.
Corolla—50–65 ft. lbs.
Carina—58–87 ft. lbs.

6. Adjust the front wheel bearing preload as outlined in Chapter 9.

7. Bleed the brake system as outlined in Chapter 9.

Tercel

1. Jack up your vehicle and support it with jack stands.

2. Remove the front wheel.

3. Remove the brake caliper and tie it out of the way.

4. Remove the stabilizer bar end.

5. Remove the bottom shock bolt.

6. Push down on the steering knuckle to free the bottom of the shock absorber.

7. Remove the top shock bolts.

8. Remove the shock and spring combination.

9. Place the shock portion in a vise, being careful not to crush the shock.

NOTE: *You will need special tool #09741-*

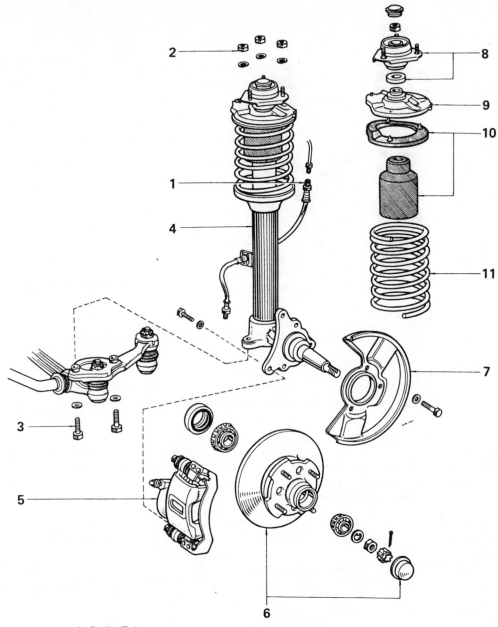

1. Brake Tube
2. Upper Support
3. Shell Lower Bolt Nut
4. Shock Absorber
5. Brake Caliper
6. Brake Disc & Hub
7. Backing Plate
8. Upper Support & Dust Seal
9. Spring Upper Seat
10. Spring Insulator & Spring Bumper
11. Spring

Components of the Starlet front suspension

16010 available from your Toyota dealer for the above procedure.

10. Use a spring compressor to compress the spring.

CAUTION: *Make sure that the spring compressor is properly secured to the*

spring when removing it, otherwise serious body harm could result.

11. Remove the upper nut, dust cover, upper seat and insulator.

12. Remove the spring.

NOTE: *Do not release the tension on the*

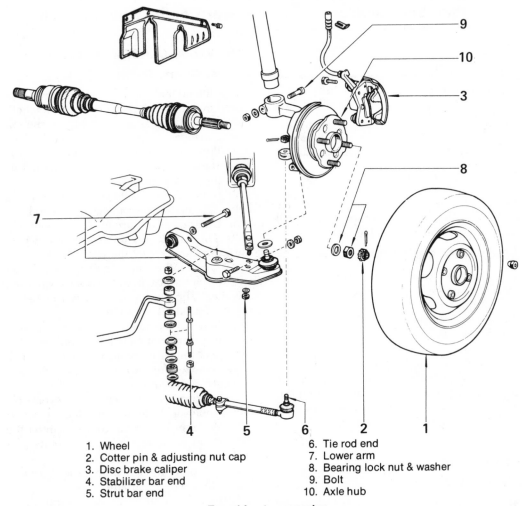

1. Wheel
2. Cotter pin & adjusting nut cap
3. Disc brake caliper
4. Stabilizer bar end
5. Strut bar end
6. Tie rod end
7. Lower arm
8. Bearing lock nut & washer
9. Bolt
10. Axle hub

Tercel front suspension

spring compressor unless you need to re-place the spring.

13. Installation is the reverse of removal.

The torque specifications needed are Shock seat bolt 29–39 ft. lbs., Top shock bolts 15–21 ft. lbs., Bottom shock bolt 40–52 ft. lbs.

Use a spring compressor to remove the load from the coil spring

Front Shock Absorber

REMOVAL AND INSTALLATION

Corolla, Carina

1. Perform the "Front Coil Spring Removal" procedure as previously outlined for the Corolla, Carina, and Starlet.

2. Remove the wheel hub and brake disc as outlined in Chapter 9.

Inspect the shock absorber and test it as outlined following. Inspect the other parts of the front suspension system which were removed.

Installation is performed in the reverse order of removal. See the notes at the end of coil spring installation for specific details and torque specifications.

Tercel

Follow the procedure outlined for front spring removal. After you have removed the

Torque Specifications

Part(s)	Torque (ft. lbs.)
Control arm-to-strut	29–40
Stabilizer bar (upper nut)	10–16
Stabilizer bar (lower nut)	7–12
Ball joint-to-knuckle arm	36–51
Knuckle arm-to-shock	51–65

spring from the shock you can then replace the shock. The reinstallation procedure will be the same as previously detailed.

SHOCK ABSORBER INSPECTION

With the shock absorber removed from the vehicle, examine it for the following:
1. Fluid leaks;
2. Damaged housing;
3. Weakness;
4. Wear;
5. Bent or cracked studs.

Test shock absorber operation by placing it in an upright position; push and pull on the shock. If the shock presents little resistance or binds, replace it with a new one.

Lower Ball Joints

INSPECTION

All Except Tercel

Check the front wheel play. Replace the lower ball joint if the play at the wheel rim exceeds 0.04 in. vertical motion or 0.08 in. horizontal motion. Be sure that the dust covers are not torn and that they are securely glued to the ball joints.

CAUTION: *Do not jack up the control arm on Corolla or Carina models; damage to the arm will result.*

Tercel

1. Jack up the vehicle and place wooden blocks under the front wheels. The block height should be 7.09–7.87 inches.
2. Use jack stands for additional safety.
3. Make sure the front wheels are in a straight forward position.
4. Check the wheels.
5. Lower the jack until there is approximately half a load on the front springs.
6. Move the lower control arm up and down to check that there is no ball joint play.

Lower Control Arm and Ball Joint

REMOVAL AND INSTALLATION

Corolla, Carina, Starlet

The ball joint and control arm cannot be separated from each other. If one fails, then both must be replaced as an assembly, in the following manner:

1. Perform Steps 1–7 of the "Corolla, Carina, Starlet. Front Coil Spring Removal" procedure. Skip Step 6.
2. Remove the stabilizer bar securing bolts. On Starlet, disconnect the tie rod.
3. Unfasten the torque strut mounting bolts. On Starlet, jack up the opposite wheel until the frame clears the jackstand.
4. Remove the control arm mounting bolt and detach the arm from the front suspension member. The Starlet uses a caster adjusting spacer, be careful not to lose it.
5. Remove the steering knuckle arm from the control arm with a ball joint puller.

Inspect the suspension components which were removed for wear or damage. Replace any parts, as required.

Installation is performed in the reverse order of removal. Note the following, however:

1. When installing the control arm on the suspension member, tighten the bolts partially at first.
2. Complete the assembly procedure and lower the car to the ground.

Bounce the front of the car several times. Allow the suspension to settle, then tighten the lower control arm bolts to 51–65 ft. lbs. Tighten knuckle arm bolts to 42–56 ft. lb.; the tie rod end-to-knuckle bolt to 37–50 ft. lb. and the stabilizer bar nut to 66–90 ft. lb.

CAUTION: *Use only the bolt which was designed to fit the lower control arm. If a replacement is necessary, see an authorized dealer for the proper part.*

4. Remember to lubricate the ball joint as outlined in Chapter 1. Check front-end alignment.

Tercel

1. Jack up your vehicle and support it with jack stands.

CAUTION: *Do not jack up your car on the lower control arms.*

2. Remove the front wheels.
3. Remove the tie rod end.
4. Remove the stabilizer bar end.
5. Remove the strut bar end.

Wheel Alignment Specifications

Model	Caster Range (deg)	Caster Pref Setting (deg)	Camber Range (deg)	Camber Pref Setting (deg)	Toe-In (in.)	Steering Axis Inclination	Wheel Pivot Ratio (deg) Inner Wheel	Wheel Pivot Ratio (deg) Outer Wheel
Corolla 1200	1½P–2⅓	—	½P–1½P	½P	0.04–0.20 ④	7½P–8½P	38½–41½ ⑤	30–36 ⑥
1600 (1970–75)	1½P–2P ①	1¾P	½P–1½P	½P	0.04–0.20	7½P–8½P	38½–41½ ②	27½–33½
(1976–79)	1¼P–1½P	2P	½P–1½P	1P	0.08–0.16 ③	7¼P–8¼P	37–39 ⑤	29¼–33¼ ⑥
1800 exc. sta. wgn.	1°16'P–2°16'P	1°46'P	33'P–1°33'P	1°3'P	0–.08 ⑦	7°55'P–8°55'P	38–40	29–33
1800 sta. wgn.	1°1/16'P–2°1/16'P	1°34'P	35'P–1°35'P	1°5'P	0–.08 ⑦	7°50'P–8°50'P	38–40	29–33
Tercel	1°40'P–2°40'P	2°10'P	0–1°P	30'P	0.04–0.12	10°50'P–11°50'P	34–36	33
Carina	½P–1½P	1P	0–1½P	1P	0.20–0.28	7½P	37–39	30–34
Starlet Sedan	1°40'P–2°20'P	2P	20'P–1°P	40'P	—	9¾P	36°50'	34
Wagon	1°25'P–2°5'P	1°45'P	15'P–55'P	35'P	—	9°50'P	36°50'	33°55'

① 1975 Wagon: ¾P–1½P
② 1975 inner: 37–39 deg
③ 1976–77 (radial): 0–0.08 in.
④ 1978–79 w/bias ply: 0.079"
   w/radial ply: 0.039"
⑤ 1978–79: 37–39
⑥ 1978–79: 29–33
⑦ w/bias tires: 0.12±0.04
P Positive
N Negative

6. Place a jack under the lower control arm for support.

7. Remove the bolt from the bottom of the steering knuckle.

8. Remove the bolt from the lower control arm.

9. Remove the control arm.

NOTE: *The lower ball joint can not be separated from the lower control arm. It must be replaced as a complete unit.*

The following torques are required: bottom steering knuckle nut 40–52 ft. lbs., stabilizer bar 11–15 ft. lbs. tie rod end 37–50 ft. lbs., strut bar 29–39 ft. lbs., lower control arm 51–65 ft. lbs.

Front-end Alignment

Front-end alignment measurements require the use of special equipment. Before measuring alignment or attempting to adjust it, always check the following points:

1. Be sure that the tires are properly inflated.

2. Ensure that the wheels are properly balanced.

3. Check the ball joints to determine if they are worn or loose.

4. Check front wheel bearing adjustment. (See Chapter 9.)

5. Be sure that the car is on a level surface.

6. Check all suspension parts for tightness.

CASTER AND CAMBER ADJUSTMENTS

NOTE: *Caster and camber adjustments do not apply to Tercel, Corolla and Carina front suspension. On Starlet, Caster is adjustable by means of shims on the lower arm. If measurements are incorrect, there is distortion or severe wear in the system and part(s) must be replaced. Toe-in is adjusted as described below.*

TOE-IN ADJUSTMENT

Measure the toe-in. Adjust it, if necessary, by loosening the tie-rod end clamping bolts and rotating the tie-rod adjusting tubes. Tighten the clamping bolts when finished.

NOTE: *Both tie-rod ends should be the same length. If they are not, perform the adjustment until the toe-in is within specifications and the tie-rod ends are equal in length.*

Toe-in (tie-rod) adjustment

REAR SUSPENSION

Springs
REMOVAL AND INSTALLATION
Leaf Springs

1. Loosen the rear wheel lug nuts.

2. Raise the rear of the vehicle. Support the frame and rear axle housing with stands.

CAUTION: *Be sure that the vehicle is securely supported.*

3. Remove the lug nuts and the wheel.

4. Remove the cotter pin, nut, and washer from the lower end of the shock absorber.

5. Detach the shock absorber from the spring seat pivot pin.

6. Remove the parking brake cable clamp.

NOTE: *Remove the parking brake equalizer, if necessary.*

7. Unfasten the U-bolt nuts and remove the spring seat assemblies.

8. Adjust the height of the rear axle housing so that the weight of the rear axle is removed from the rear springs.

9. Unfasten the spring shackle retaining nuts. Withdraw the spring shackle inner plate. Carefully pry out the spring shackle with a bar.

10. Remove the spring bracket pin from the front end of the spring hanger and remove the rubber bushings.

11. Remove the spring.

CAUTION: *Use care not to damage the hydraulic brake line or the parking brake cable.*

Installation is performed in the following order:

1. Install the rubber bushings in the eye of the spring.

2. Align the eye of the spring with the

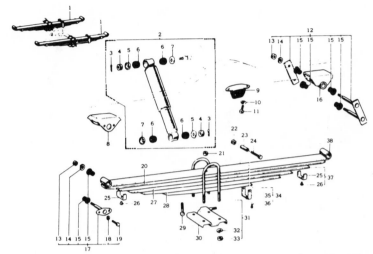

1. Rear spring	14. Spring washer	27. Rear spring leaf
2. Rear shock absorber	15. Bushing	28. Rear spring leaf
3. Cotter pin	16. Spring bracket	29. Rear spring center bolt
4. Castle nut	17. Rear spring hanger pin	30. U-bolt seat
5. Shock absorber cushion washer	18. Spring washer	31. U-bolt
6. Bushing	19. Bolt	32. Spring washer
7. Shock absorber cushion washer	20. Rear spring leaf	33. Nut
8. Spring bracket	21. Nut	34. Rear spring leaf
9. Rear spring bumper	22. Nut	35. Rear spring clip
10. Spring washer	23. Rear spring clip bolt	36. Round rivet
11. Bolt	24. Clip bolt	37. Rear spring leaf
12. Rear spring shackle	25. Rear spring clip	38. Rear spring leaf
13. Nut	26. Round rivet	

Leaf spring rear suspension—all models similar

spring hanger bracket and drive the pin through the bracket holes and rubber bushings.

NOTE: *Use soapy water as lubricant, if necessary, to aid in pin installation. Never use oil or grease.*

3. Finger-tighten the spring hanger nuts and/or bolts.

4. Install the rubber bushings in the spring eye at the opposite end of the spring.

5. Raise the free end of the spring. Install the spring shackle through the bushings and the bracket.

6. Fit the shackle inner plate and finger-tighten the retaining nuts.

7. Center the bolt head in the hole which is provided in the spring seat on the axle housing.

8. Fit the U-bolts over the axle housing. Install the lower spring seat.

9. Tighten the U-bolt nuts to 22–32 ft. lb.; the shackle bolts to 37–50 ft. lb.; the front bracket pins to 29–39 ft. lb. and the rear bracket pins to 8–11 ft. lb.

NOTE: *Some models have two sets of nuts, while others have a nut and lockwasher.*

10. Install the parking brake cable clamp. Install the equalizer, if it was removed.

11. Install the shock absorber end at the spring seat. Tighten the nuts to the specified torque.

12. Install the wheel and lug nuts. Lower the car to the ground.

13. Bounce the car several times.

14. Tighten the spring bracket pins and shackles.

15. Repeat Step 13 and check all of the torque specifications again.

Coil Springs

1. Remove the hubcap and loosen the lug nuts.

2. Jack up the rear axle housing and support the frame with jackstands. Leave the jack in place under the rear axle housing.

CAUTION: *Support the car securely. Remember; you will be working underneath it.*

3. Remove the lug nuts and wheel.

4. Unfasten the lower shock absorber end.

5. Slowly lower the jack under the rear

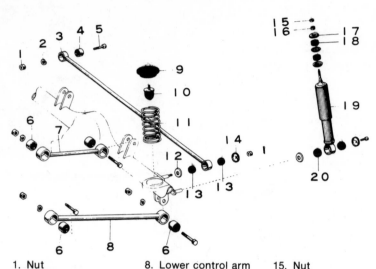

1. Nut
2. Washer
3. Lateral control rod
4. Bushing
5. Bolt
6. Bushing
7. Upper control arm
8. Lower control arm
9. Spring insulator
10. Spring bumper
11. Coil spring
12. Washer
13. Bushing
14. Washer
15. Nut
16. Nut
17. Washer
18. Bushing
19. Shock absorber
20. Bushing

Typical coil spring rear suspension

axle housing until the axle is at the bottom of its travel.

6. Withdraw the coil spring, complete with its insulator.

Inspect the coil spring and insulator for wear, cracks, or weakness; replace either or both, as necessary.

Installation is performed in the reverse order of removal. Tighten the lower shock absorber mounting to the specifications listed in the "Shock Absorber Tightening Torque" chart at the end of the "Rear Shock Absorber Removal and Installation" section.

Rear Shock Absorbers

REMOVAL AND INSTALLATION

1. Jack up the rear end of the vehicle. CAUTION: *Be sure that the vehicle is securely supported. Remember: you will be working underneath it.*

2. Support the rear axle housing with jackstands. On the Corolla and Starlet sedan, remove the rear seat to get at the upper shock retaining bolt.

3. Unfasten the upper shock absorber retaining nuts and/or bolts from the upper frame member.

4. Depending upon the type of rear springs used, either disconnect the lower end of the shock absorber from the spring seat or the rear axle housing by removing its cotter pins, nuts, and/or bolts.

5. Remove the shock absorber.

Inspect the shock for wear, leaks, or other signs of damage. Test it as outlined in the "Front Suspension Shock Absorber" section.

Installation is performed in the reverse order of removal. Tighten the shock absorber securing nuts and bolts to the specifications given in the following chart.

Shock Absorber Tightening Torque (ft. lbs.)

Model	Upper Mounting	Lower Mounting
Starlet	14–22	22–32
Corolla ('70–'74)	—	25–40
Corolla ('75–'81) Tercel	—	14–22
Carina	14–22	26–33 ①

① 1977—28.9–39.8 ft. lbs.

STEERING

Steering Wheel
REMOVAL AND INSTALLATION
Three-Spoke

CAUTION: *Do not attempt to remove or install the steering wheel by hammering on it. Damage to the energy-absorbing steering column could result.*

1. Unfasten the horn and turn signal multiconnector(s) at the base of the steering column shroud.
2. Loosen the trim pad retaining screws from the back side of the steering wheel.
3. Lift the trim pad and horn button assembly(ies) from the wheel.
4. Remove the steering wheel hub retaining nut.
5. Scratch matchmarks on the hub and shaft to aid in correct installation.
6. Use a steering wheel puller to remove the steering wheel.

Installation is performed in the reverse order of removal. Tighten the wheel retaining nut to 15–22 ft. lbs., except for the Starlet and 1975–77 Corolla which should be tightened to 22–29 ft. lbs.

Two-Spoke

The two-spoke steering wheel is removed in the same manner as the three-spoke, except that the trim pad should be pried off with a screwdriver. Remove the pad by lifting it toward the top of the wheel.

Remove the pad on the two-spoke steering wheel the direction of arrow

Four-Spoke

CAUTION: *Do not attempt to remove or install the steering wheel by hammering on it. Damage to the energy absorbing steering column could result.*

1. Unfasten the horn and turn signal multiconnectors at the base of the steering col-

Removing the four-spoke wheel with a puller

umn shroud (underneath the instrument panel).
2. Gently pry the center emblem off the front of the steering wheel.
3. Insert a wrench through the hole and remove the steering wheel retaining nut.
4. Scratch matchmarks on the hub and shaft to aid installation.
5. Use a steering wheel puller to remove the steering wheel.

Installation is the reverse of removal. Tighten the steering wheel retaining nut to 22–29 ft. lbs.

Turn Signal Switch
REMOVAL AND INSTALLATION
All Models

1. Disconnect the negative (−) battery cable.
2. Remove the steering wheel, as outlined in the appropriate preceding section.
3. Unfasten the screws which secure the upper and lower steering column shroud halves.
4. Unfasten the screws which retain the turn signal switch and remove the switch from the column. On some models, the hazard warning and windshield wiper switches are part of the assembly, and will be removed as well.

Installation is performed in the reverse order of removal.

Ignition Lock/Switch
REMOVAL AND INSTALLATION
All Models

1. Disconnect the negative (−) battery cable.
2. Unfasten the ignition switch multiconnector underneath the instrument panel.
3. Remove the screws which secure the

Depress the stop in order to remove the lock cylinder

upper and lower halves of the steering column cover.

4. Turn the lock cylinder to the "ACC" position with the ignition key.

5. Push the lock cylinder stop in with a small, round object (cotter pin, punch, etc.)

NOTE: *On some models it may be necessary to remove the steering wheel and turn signal switch first.*

6. Withdraw the lock cylinder from the lock housing while depressing the stop tab.

7. To remove the ignition switch, unfasten its securing screws and withdraw the switch from the lock housing.

Installation is performed in the following order:

1. Align the locking cam with the hole in the ignition switch and insert the switch in the lock housing.

2. Secure the switch with its screw(s).

3. Make sure that both the lock cylinder and the column lock are in the "ACC" position. Slide the cylinder into the lock housing until the stop tab engages the hole in the lock.

4. The rest of installation is performed in the reverse order of removal.

Power Steering Pump
REMOVAL AND INSTALLATION

1. Remove the fan shroud.

2. Unfasten the nut from the center of the pump pulley.

NOTE: *Use the drive belt as a brake to keep the pulley from rotating.*

3. Withdraw the drive belt.

4. Remove the pulley and the woodruff key from the pump shaft.

5. Detach the intake and outlet hoses from the pump reservoir.

NOTE: *Tie the hose ends up high, so that*

the fluid cannot flow out of them. Drain or plug the pump to prevent fluid leakage.

6. Remove the bolt from the rear mounting brace.

7. Remove the front bracket bolts and withdraw the pump.

Installation is performed in the reverse order of removal. Note the following, however:

1. Tighten the pump pulley mounting bolt to 25–39 ft. lbs.

2. Adjust the pump drive belt tension.

The belt should deflect 0.31–0.39 in. when 22 lbs. pressure is applied midway between the air pump and the power steering pump.

3. Fill the reservoir with Dexron® automatic transmission fluid. Bleed the air from the system, as detailed following.

Power steering pump removal showing (1) front mounting bolts and (2) pump

BLEEDING

1. Raise the front of the car and support it securely with jackstands.

2. Fill the pump reservoir with "DEXRON®" automatic transmission fluid.

3. Rotate the steering wheel from lock-to-lock several times. Add fluid as necessary.

4. With the steering wheel turned fully to one lock, crank the starter while watching the fluid level in the reservoir.

NOTE: *Disconnect the high-tension lead from the coil; do not start the engine. Operate the starter with a remote starter switch or have an assistant do it from inside of the car. Do not run the starter for prolonged periods.*

5. Repeat Step 4 with the steering wheel turned to the opposite lock.

6. Start the engine. With the engine idling, turn the steering wheel from lock-to-lock two or three times.

7. Lower the front of the car and repeat Step 6.

8. Center the wheel at the midpoint of its travel. Stop the engine.

9. The fluid level should not have risen more than 0.2 in. If it does, repeat Step 7 again.

10. Check for fluid leakage.

Steering Linkage

REMOVAL AND INSTALLATION

Corolla, Carina

1. Raise the front of the vehicle and support it with jackstands.

CAUTION: *Be sure that the vehicle is securely supported. Do not support it by the lower control arms.*

2. Remove the gravel shields if they prevent access to the steering linkage.

3. Unfasten the nut and, using a puller, disconnect the pitman arm from the sector shaft.

4. Unfasten the idler arm support securing bolts and remove the support from the frame.

5. Detach the tie rod ends with a puller after removing the cotter pins and castellated nuts.

6. Remove the steering linkage as an assembly.

Installation is performed in the reverse order of removal. Note the following however:

1. Tighten the tie rod ends-to-knuckle arms to 36–51 ft. lb.; the idler arm support-to-frame bolts to 22–36 ft. lb.; the pitman arm-to-sector shaft nut to 72–101 ft. lb. on Carina and 1975–81 Corolla, and to 36–58 ft. lb. on 1970–74 Corolla.

2. Align the marks on pitman arm and sector shaft before installing the pitman arm.

3. The self-locking nut used on some models, on the idler arm, may be reused if it cannot be turned by hand when fitted to the bolt.

4. Adjust the toe-in to specifications after completing the steering linkage installation procedure.

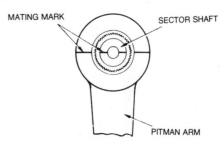

Align the marks on the pitman arm and the sector shaft

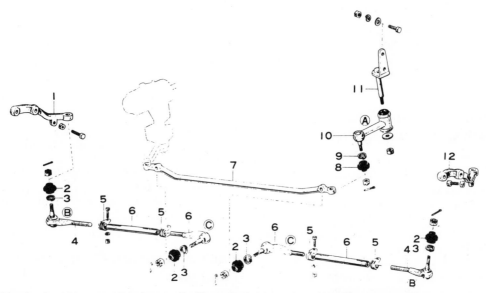

1. Steering knuckle arm—right-hand	6. Tie-rod adjusting tube
2. Dust seal	7. Steering relay rod
3. Clip	8. Dust seal
4. Tie-rod end	9. Lock ring
5. Tie-rod end clamp	10. Steering idler arm

11. Idler arm support
12. Steering knuckle arm—left-hand
A. Idler arm assembly
B. Tie-rod end assembly
C. Tie-rod adjusting tube

Corolla and Carina Steering linkage components

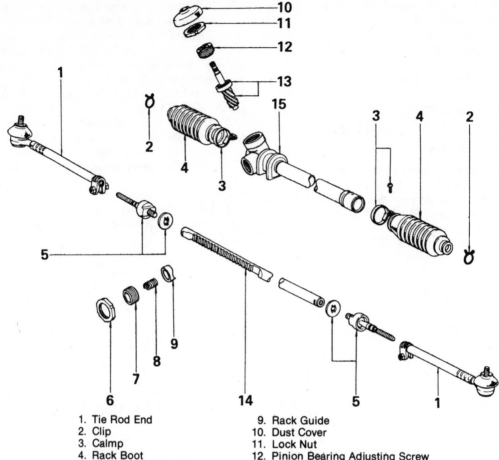

1. Tie Rod End
2. Clip
3. Calmp
4. Rack Boot
5. Rack End & Claw Washer
6. Lock Nut
7. Rack Guide Spring Cap
8. Spring
9. Rack Guide
10. Dust Cover
11. Lock Nut
12. Pinion Bearing Adjusting Screw
13. Pinion & Bearing
14. Rack
15. Rack Housing

Starlet steering gear and linkage

Manual Steering Gear

REMOVAL AND INSTALLATION

Corolla

1. Remove the bolt attaching the coupling yoke to the steering worm.

2. Disconnect the relay rod from the pitman arm.

3. Remove the steering gear housing down and to the left.

4. Install in reverse of removal. Torque the housing-to-frame bolts to 25–36 ft. lbs.; the coupling yoke bolt to 15–20 ft. lbs.; the relay rod to 36–50 ft. lbs.

Carina

1. Remove the Pitman arm from the sector shaft with a puller.

2. Loosen the flexible coupling-to-worm-shaft bolt.

3. Unbolt and remove the steering gear housing.

4. Install in reverse of removal. Torque the housing bolts to 25–36 ft. lb.; the Pitman arm to 72–101 ft. lbs.; the coupling yoke bolts to 15–20 ft. lbs.

Rack and Pinion Gear and Linkage

REMOVAL AND INSTALLATION

Tercel and Starlet

1. Jack up the vehicle and support it with jack stands.

2. Remove both front wheels.

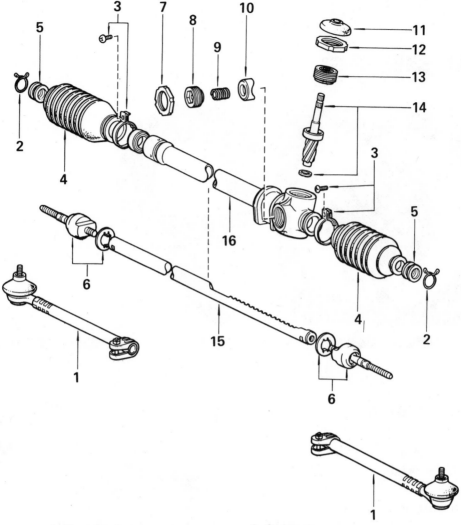

1. Tie rod end
2. Clip
3. Clamp
4. Rack boot
5. Rack end dust seal
6. Rack end & claw washer
7. Lock nut
8. Rack guide spring cap
9. Spring
10. Rack guide
11. Dust cover
12. Lock nut
13. Pinion bearing adjusting screw
14. Pinion & spacer
15. Rack
16. Rack housing

Tercel steering gear

3. Remove the intermediate shaft from the worm gear shaft.

4. Remove both tie rod ends.

5. Remove the lower suspension crossmember on Tercel.

6. Remove the rack housing bracket mounting bolts and brackets.

NOTE: *Be careful not to damage the rubber boots.*

7. Remove the steering linkage.

8. Installation is the reverse of removal. Torque the rack housing bracket bolts to 22–32 ft. lb.; the tie rod end nuts to 37–50 ft. lb.; the intermediate shaft to 22–28 ft. lb.

ADJUSTMENTS

Adjustments to the manual steering gear are not necessary during normal service. Adjustments are performed only as part of overhaul.

Brakes

BRAKE SYSTEM

ADJUSTMENTS

Rear Drum Brakes

COROLLA 1200

Corolla 1200 models are equipped with rear drum brakes which require manual adjustment. Perform the adjustment in the following order:

1. Chock the front wheels and fully release the parking brake.

2. Raise the rear of the car and support it with jackstands.

   CAUTION: *Be sure that the car is securely supported. Remember; you will be working underneath it.*

3. Remove the adjusting hole plug from the backing plate.

4. Expand the brake shoes by turning the adjusting wheel with a starwheel adjuster or a thin-bladed screwdriver.

5. Pump the brake pedal several times, while expanding the shoes, so that the shoe contacts the drum evenly.

   NOTE: *If the wheel still turns when your foot is removed from the brake pedal, continue expanding the shoes until the wheel locks.*

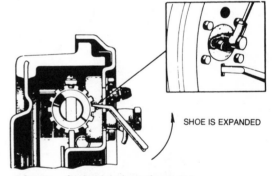

SHOE IS EXPANDED

Adjusting the brake shoe clearance

6. Back off on the adjuster, just enough so that the wheel rotates without dragging.

7. After this point is reached, continue backing off for *five* additional notches.

8. If the wheel still does not turn freely, back off one or two more notches. If after this, it still drags, check for worn or defective parts.

9. Pump the brake pedal again, and check wheel rotation.

10. Reverse Steps 1–3.

ALL MODELS—EXCEPT COROLLA 1200

These models are equipped with self-adjusting rear drum brakes. No adjustment is possible or necessary.

Front Disc Brakes

Front disc brakes require no adjustment, as hydraulic pressure maintains the proper brake pad-to-disc contact at all times.

NOTE: *Because of this, the brake fluid level should be checked regularly. (See Chapter 1).*

Master Cylinder

REMOVAL AND INSTALLATION

CAUTION: *Be careful not to spill brake fluid on the painted surfaces of the vehicle; it will damage the paint.*

1. Unfasten the hydraulic lines from the master cylinder.

2. Detach the hydraulic fluid pressure differential switch writring connectors. On models with ESP, disconnect the fluid level sensor wiring connectors, as well.

3. Loosen the master cylinder reservoir mounting bolt.

4. Then do one of the following:

a. On models with manual brakes remove the master cylinder securing bolts and the clevis pin from the brake pedal. Remove the master cylinder;

b. On the other models with power brakes, unfasten the nuts and remove the master cylinder assembly from the power brake unit.

Installation is performed in the reverse order of removal. Note the following, however:

1. Before tightening the master cylinder mounting nuts or bolts, screw the hydraulic line into the cylinder body, a few turns.

2. After installation is completed, bleed the master cylinder and the brake system, as outlined following. Check the power booster piston rod-to-piston clearance, which should be 0.0039–0.020 in. at idle.

OVERHAUL

1. Remove the reservoir caps and floats. Unscrew the bolts which secure the reservoirs to the main body.

2. Remove the pressure differential warning switch assembly. Then, working from the rear of the cylinder, remove the boot, snapring, stop washer, piston No. 1, spacer, cylinder cup, spring retainer, and spring, in that order.

3. Remove the end-plug and gasket from the front of the cylinder, then remove the front piston stop-bolt from underneath. Pull out the spring, retainer, piston no. 2, spacer, and the cylinder cup.

4. Remove the two outlet fittings, washers, check valves and springs.

5. Remove the piston cups from their seats only if they are to be replaced.

After washing all parts in clean brake fluid, dry them with compressed air (if available). Inspect the cylinder bore for wear, scuff marks, or nicks. Cylinders may be honed slightly, but the limit is 0.006 in. In view of the importance of the master cylinder, it is recommended that it is replaced rather than overhauled if worn or damaged.

Assembly is performed in the reverse order of disassembly. Absolute cleanliness is important. Coat all parts with clean brake fluid prior to assembly.

Bleed the hydraulic system after the master cylinder is installed, as detailed following.

Proportioning Valve

A proportioning valve is used on all models to reduce the hydraulic pressure to the rear brakes because of weight transfer during high-speed stops. This helps to keep the rear brakes from locking up by improving front-to-rear brake balance.

The proportioning valve is located in the engine compartment, near the master cylinder.

REMOVAL AND INSTALLATION

1. Disconnect the brake lines from the valve unions.

2. Unfasten the valve mounting bolt, if used.

3. Remove the proportioning valve assembly.

NOTE: *If the proportioning valve is defective, it must be replaced as an assembly; it cannot be rebuilt.*

Installation is the reverse of removal. Bleed the brake system after it is completed.

Bleeding

CAUTION: *Do not reuse brake fluid which has been bled from the brake system.*

1. Insert a clear vinyl tube into the bleeder plug on the master cylinder or the wheel cylinders.

NOTE: *If the master cylinder has been overhauled or if air is present in it, start the bleeding procedure with the master cylinder. Otherwise (and after bleeding the master cylinder), start with the wheel cyl-*

Bleeding the disc brake caliper

inder which is farthest from the master cylinder.

2. Insert the other end of the tube into a jar which is half filled with brake fluid.

3. Slowly depress the brake pedal (have an assistant do it) and turn the bleeder plug ¹/₃–¹/₂ of a turn at the same time.

NOTE: *If the brake pedal is depressed too fast, small air bubbles will form in the*

brake fluid which will be very difficult to remove.

4. Bleed the cylinder before hydraulic pressure decreases in the cylinder.

5. Repeat this procedure until the air bubbles are removed and then go on to the next wheel cylinder.

CAUTION: *Replenish the brake fluid in the master cylinder reservoir, so that it does not run out during bleeding.*

FRONT DISC BRAKES

Disc Brake Pads
REMOVAL AND INSTALLATION
Corolla, Carina

1. Remove the hub cap and loosen the lug nuts.

2. Raise the front of the vehicle with a jack and support it with stands on the chassis pads provided.

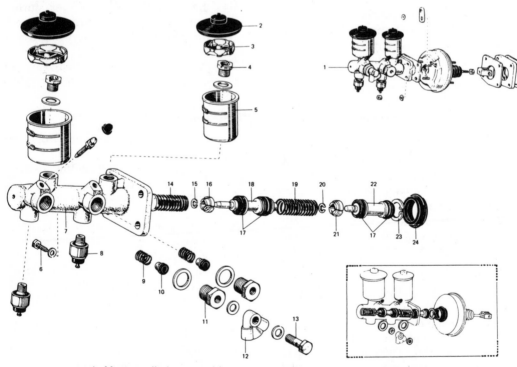

1. Master cylinder assembly	9. Spring	17. Cylinder cup
2. Reservoir cap	10. Check valve	18. No. 2 piston
3. Strainer	11. Plug	19. Spring
4. Reservoir set bolt	12. Union	20. Snap-ring
5. Reservoir	13. Union bolt	21. Retainer
6. Bolt	14. Spring	22. No. 1 piston
7. Master cylinder body	15. Snap-ring	23. Snap-ring
8. Pressure differential switch	16. Retainer	24. Rubber boot

Early type-Tandem master cylinder assembly

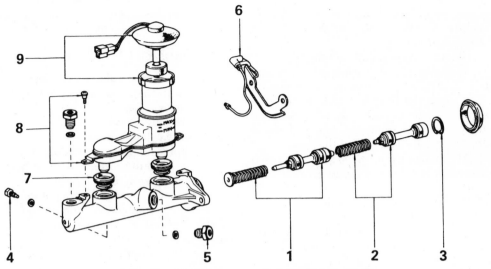

1. Piston No. 2 & Spring
2. Piston No. 1 & Spring
3. Snap Ring
4. Piston Stopper Bolt
5. Outlet Check Valve

6. Brake Tube with Way
7. Grommet
8. Reservoir
9. Cap & Strainer

Later type master cylinder

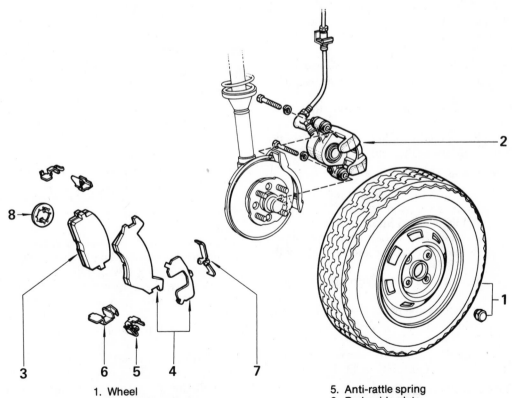

1. Wheel
2. Disc brake cylinder
3. Inner pad
4. Outer pad & anti-squeal shim

5. Anti-rattle spring
6. Pad guide plate
7. Pad support plate
8. Anti-squeal shim

Tercel front brake; Starlet is similar

CAUTION: *Be sure that the car is securely supported. Do not support the car by the lower control arm.*

3. Remove the lug nuts and the wheel.

4. Unfasten the four clips which secure the caliper guides and remove the guides.

5. Detach the flexible line from the caliper, if the caliper assembly is to be completely removed from the can. Otherwise safety-wire the caliper out of the way.

NOTE: *Be sure that the master cylinder is closed to prevent brake fluid from leaking out.*

6. Remove the caliper assembly.

7. Remove the pads.

Inspect the pads for wear. If the grooves are worn out of the pads, they must be replaced. Check pad thickness against the specifications given in the "Disc and Pad Specifications" chart at the end of the "Disc Inspection" section. Check the caliper guides for wear or deformation.

Installation is performed in the following order:

1. Clean the exposed portions of the piston.

2. Carefully insert the piston in caliper. If the piston is difficult to install, loosen the bleeder plug.

3. Insert the brake pads.

CAUTION: *Replace the pads on one side at a time, to prevent the opposite piston from falling out.*

4. Install the caliper assembly, the guides and the clips.

5. Bleed the brake line, as previously detailed, and lower the vehicle.

Tercel and Starlet

1. Jack up your vehicle and support it with jack stands.

2. Remove both front wheels.

3. Remove the two bolts from the caliper.

4. Remove the caliper and tie it out of the ay.

5. Remove the brake pads and anti-squeal snim.

6. Remove some brake fluid from the mastery cylinder. Press the piston in as far as it will go.

7. Install all parts in reverse of removal. Torque the caliper bolts to 11–15 ft. lb.

Disc Brake Calipers

REMOVAL AND INSTALLATION

Caliper removal and installation for these models is given as part of the "Brake Pad Removal and Installation" procedure. Consult the appropriate preceding section for details.

OVERHAUL

1. Remove the caliper cylinder from the car. (See the appropriate preceding "Brake Pad Removal" procedure).

2. Carefully remove the dust boot from around the cylinder bore.

3. Apply compressed air to the brake line union to force the piston out of its bore. Be careful, the piston may come out forcefully.

4. Remove the seal from the piston. Check the piston and cylinder bore for wear and/or corrosion. Replace components as necessary.

Assembly is performed in the following order:

1. Coat all components with clean brake fluid.

2. Install the seal and piston in the cylinder bore, after coating them with the rubber lubricant supplied in the rebuilding kit. Seat the piston in the bore with your fingers.

3. Fit the boot into the groove in the cylinder bore.

4. Install the caliper cylinder assembly.

Brake Disc

REMOVAL AND INSTALLATION

All Models except Tercel

1. Remove the brake pads and the caliper, as detailed in the appropriate preceding section.

2. On Corolla and Carina models only:

  a. Loosen the bolts which secure the caliper mounting bracket;

  b. Withdraw the bracket, complete with the caliper support plates and springs attached.

3. Check the disc run-out, as detailed following, at this point. Make a note of the results for use during installation.

4. Remove the grease cap from the hub. Remove the cotter pin and the castellated nut.

5. Remove the wheel hub with the brake disc attached.

Perform the disc inspection procedure, as outlined in the following section.

Installation is performed in the following order:

1. Coat the hub oil seal lip with multipurpose grease and install the disc/hub assembly.

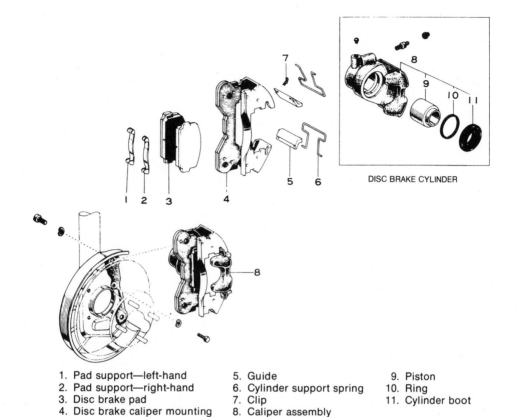

DISC BRAKE CYLINDER

1. Pad support—left-hand
2. Pad support—right-hand
3. Disc brake pad
4. Disc brake caliper mounting
5. Guide
6. Cylinder support spring
7. Clip
8. Caliper assembly
9. Piston
10. Ring
11. Cylinder boot

Corolla and Carina disc brake assembly

2. Adjust the wheel bearing preload, as detailed following.

3. Measure the disc run-out. Check it against the specifications in the "Disc and Pad Specifications" chart and against the figures noted during removal.

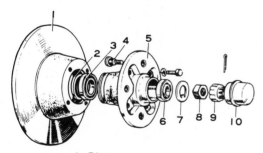

1. Disc
2. Oil seal
3. Tapered roller bearing
4. Hub bolt
5. Hub
6. Tapered roller bearing
7. Washer
8. Nut
9. Adjusting lock cap
10. Grease cap

Brake disc and hub assembly

NOTE: *If the wheel bearing nut is improperly tightened, disc run-out will be affected.*

4. On Corolla and Carina, models only:

a. Install the caliper support, complete with springs. Tighten the securing nuts to 20–40 ft. lbs.;

CAUTION: *Be careful not to distort the support springs during installation.*

b. Install the support plates and the brake pads in the same positions from which they were removed.

NOTE: *Install the pad support plate with the arrow pointing in the same direction as when it was removed.*

5. Install the remainder of the components as outlined in the appropriate preceding section.

6. Bleed the brake system.

7. Road-test the car. Check the wheel bearing preload.

Tercel

1. Jack up your vehicle and support it with jack stands.

2. Remove the front wheels.

Brake Specifications

All measurements given are in. unless noted

Model	Lug Nut Torque (ft. lbs.)	Master Cylinder Bore	Brake Disc		Brake Drum			Minimum Lining Thickness	
			Minimum Thickness	Maximum Run-Out	Diameter	Max. Machine O/S	Max. Wear Limit	Front	Rear
Corolla									
1200	65–86	0.626	0.350	0.0060	8.00	8.050	8.14	0.25	0.04
1600	65–86	0.813	0.350	0.0060	9.08	9.070	9.16	0.25	0.04
1800	66–86	—	0.453	0.0059	9.00	9.079	—	0.04	0.04
Carina	65–86	0.813	0.350	0.006	9.08	9.15	9.23	0.25	0.04
Tercel	65–86	—	0.354	0.0059	7.087	7.126	—	0.04	0.04
Starlet	65–86	0.813	0.350	0.0059	7.870	7.950	—	0.039	0.039

NOTE: Minimum lining thickness is as recommended by the manufacturer. Due to variations in state inspection regulations, the minimum allowable thickness may be different than recommended by the manufacturer.

3. Remove the brake caliper (see the brake removal section).

4. Check the disc run-out.

NOTE: *It is necessary to use a dial indicator to measure run-out.*

5. Check the disc thickness, limit 0.354 in., standard 0.394 in.

6. Remove the front axle hub if necessary (see front hub removal section).

7. Installation is the reverse of removal.

INSPECTION

Examine the disc. If it is worn, warped or scored, it must be replaced.

Check the thickness of the disc against the specifications given in the "Brake Specifications" chart. If it is below specifications, replace it. Use a micrometer to measure the thickness.

Checking disc run-out

The disc run-out should be measured *before* the disc is removed and again, *after* the disc is installed. Use a dial indicator mounted on a stand to determine run-out. If run-out exceeds 0.006 in. (all models), replace the disc.

NOTE: *Be sure that the wheel bearing nut is properly tightened. If it is not, an inaccurate run-out reading may be obtained. If different run-out readings are obtained with the same disc, between removal and installation, this is probably the cause.*

Wheel Bearings
REMOVAL AND INSTALLATION

1. Remove the caliper and the disc/hub assembly, as previously detailed.

2. If either the disc or the entire hub assembly is to be replaced, unbolt the hub from the disc.

NOTE: *If only the bearings are to be replaced, do not separate the disc and hub.*

3. Using a brass rod as a drift, tap the inner bearing cone out. Remove the oil seal and the inner bearing.

NOTE: *Throw the old oil seal away.*

4. Drift out the inner bearing cup.

5. Drift out the outer bearing cup.

Inspect the bearings and the hub for signs of wear or damage. Replace components, as necessary.

Installation is performed in the following order:

1. Install the inner bearing cup and then the outer bearing cup, by drifting them into place.

CAUTION: *Use care not to cock the bearing cups in the hub.*

2. Pack the bearings, hub inner well and grease cap with multipurpose grease.

3. Install the inner bearing into the hub.

4. Carefully install a new oil seal with a soft drift.

5. Install the hub on the spindle. Be sure to install all of the washers and nuts which were removed.

6. Adjust the bearing preload, as detailed following.

7. Install the caliper assembly, as previously detailed.

Preload Adjustment

1. With the front hub/disc assembly installed, tighten the castellated nut to the torque figure specified in the "Preload Specifications" chart.

2. Rotate the disc back and forth, two or three times, to allow the bearing to seat properly.

Preload Specifications

Model/Year	Initial Torque Setting (ft. lbs.)	Preload (oz.)
Starlet	22	1–1.5
Tercel 1980–81	22	13–30
Corolla 1975	19–23	6–13
1976–77	19–23	10–24
1978–80	19–23	11–25
Carina	19–24	10–22

Measuring wheel bearing preload with a spring scale

3. Loosen the castellated nut until it is only finger-tight.

4. Tighten the nut firmly, using a box wrench.

5. Measure the bearing preload with a spring scale attached to a wheel mounting stud. Check it against the specifications given in the "Preload Specifications" chart.

6. Install the cotter pin.

NOTE: *If the hole does not align with the nut (or cap) holes, tighten the nut slightly until it does.*

7. Finish installing the brake components and the wheel.

REAR DRUM BRAKES

Brake Drums

REMOVAL AND INSTALLATION

All Models

1. Remove the hub cap (if used) and loosen the lug nuts. Release the parking brake.

2. Block the front wheels, raise the rear of the car, and support it with jackstands.

CAUTION: *Support the car securely.*

3. Remove the lug nuts and the wheel.

4. Unfasten the brake drum retaining screws.

5. Tap the drum lightly with a mallet in order to free it. If the drum is difficult to remove use a puller; but first be sure that the parking brake is released.

CAUTION: *Don't depress the brake pedal once the drum has been removed.*

6. Inspect the brake drum as detailed following.

Brake drum installation is performed in the reverse order of removal.

INSPECTION

1. Clean the drum.

2. Inspect the drum for scoring, cracks,

grooves and out-of-roundness. Replace or turn the drum, as required.

3. Light scoring may be removed by dressing the drum with *fine* emery cloth.

4. Heavy scoring will require the use of a brake drum lathe to turn the drum.

Brake Shoes

REMOVAL AND INSTALLATION

Corolla, Carina, Starlet

1. Perform the "Brake Drum Removal" procedure as previously detailed.

2. Unhook the shoe tension springs from the shoes with the aid of a brake spring removing tool.

3. Remove the brake shoe securing springs.

4. Disconnect the parking brake cable at the parking brake shoe lever.

5. Withdraw the shoes, complete with the parking brake shoe lever.

6. Unfasten the C-clip and remove the adjuster assembly from the shoes.

Inspect the shoes for wear and scoring. Have the linings replaced if their thickness is less than 0.04 in.

Check the tension springs to see if they are weak, distorted or rusted.

Inspect the teeth on the automatic adjuster wheel for chipping or other damage.

Installation is performed in the following order:

NOTE: *Grease the point of the shoe which slides against the backing plate. Do not get grease on the linings.*

1. Attach the parking brake shoe lever and the automatic adjuster lever to the rear side of the shoe.

2. Fasten the parking brake cable to the lever on the brake shoe.

3. Install the automatic adjuster and fit the tension spring on the adjuster lever.

4. Install the securing spring on the *rear* shoe and then install the securing spring on the *front* shoe.

NOTE: *The tension spring should be installed on the anchor, before performing Step 4.*

5. Hook one end of the tension spring over the rear shoe with the tool used during removal; hook the other end over the front shoe.

CAUTION: *Be sure that the wheel cylinder boots are not being pinched in the ends of the shoes.*

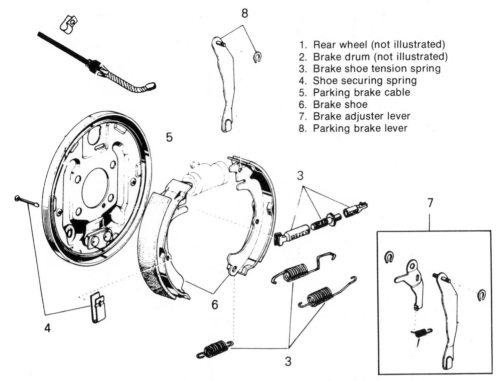

1. Rear wheel (not illustrated)
2. Brake drum (not illustrated)
3. Brake shoe tension spring
4. Shoe securing spring
5. Parking brake cable
6. Brake shoe
7. Brake adjuster lever
8. Parking brake lever

Corolla and Carina brake shoe removal sequence

6. Test the automatic adjuster by operating the parking brake shoe lever.

7. Install the drum and adjust the brakes as previously detailed.

Tercel

1. Jack up your vehicle and support it with jack stands.

2. Remove the rear wheel.

3. Remove the bearing cap, cotter pin, locknut and adjusting nut.

4. Remove the brake drum.

NOTE: *When you remove the brake drum, the outer bearing, inner bearing and grease seal will come out at this time.*

5. Remove the brake shoe return spring and the hold down springs.

6. Remove the lower return spring.

7. Remove the front brake shoe.

8. Remove the parking brake strut.

9. Remove the rear shoe.

10. Disconnect the parking brake cable from the rear shoe.

11. Remove the parking brake lever from the rear shoe.

NOTE: *When reinstalling the parking brake lever be sure to use a new C-washer.*

12. Installation is the reverse of removal. On Starlet, the parking brake lever must have a 0.0138 in clearance at the shoe. Adjust this clearance with shims.

Wheel Cylinders

REMOVAL AND INSTALLATION

1. Plug the master cylinder inlet to prevent hydraulic fluid from leaking.

2. Remove the brake drums and shoes as detailed in the appropriate preceding section.

3. Working from behind the backing plate, disconnect the hydraulic line from the wheel cylinder.

4. Unfasten the screws retaining the wheel cylinder and withdraw the cylinder.

Installation is performed in the reverse order of removal. However, once the hydraulic line has been disconnected from the wheel cylinder, the union seat must be replaced. To replace the seat, proceed in the following manner:

NOTE: *This procedure is not required on Crown models.*

1. Use a screw extractor with a diameter

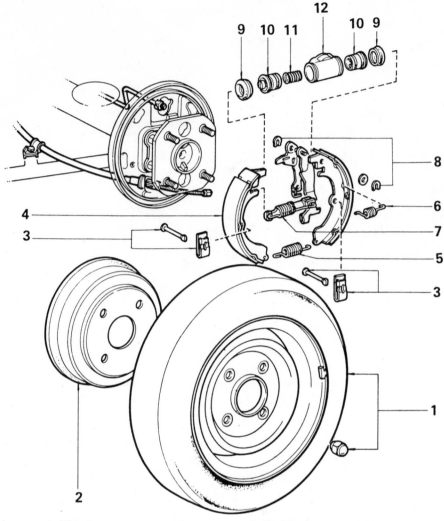

1. Wheel
2. Brake Drum
3. Shoe Hold Down Spring & Pin
4. Brake Shoe
5. Spring
6. Spring
7. Parking Brake Shoe Strut Set
8. Brake Shoe with Lever
9. Boot
10. Piston
11. Spring
12. Wheel Cylinder

Starlet Drum Brake Components

of 0.1 in. and having reverse threads, to remove the union seat from the wheel cylinder.

2. Drive in the new union seat with a $^5/_{16}$ in. bar, used as a drift.

Remember to bleed the brake system after completing wheel cylinder, brake shoe and drum installation.

OVERHAUL

It is not necessary to remove the wheel cylinder from the backing plate if it is only to be inspected or rebuilt.

1. Remove the brake drum and shoes. Re-

move the wheel cylinder only if it is going to be replaced.

2. Remove the rubber boots from either end of the wheel cylinder.

3. Withdraw the piston and cup assemblies.

4. Take the compression spring out of the wheel cylinder body.

5. Remove the bleeder plug (and ball), if necessary.

Check all components for wear or damage. Inspect the bore for signs of wear, scoring, and/or scuffing. If in doubt, replace or hone

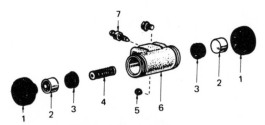

1. Wheel cylinder boot
2. Wheel cylinder piston
3. Cylinder cup
4. Compression spring
5. Union seat
6. Wheel cylinder body
7. Bleeder plug

Wheel-cylinder assembly

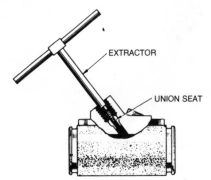

Replacing the wheel cylinder union seat

the wheel cylinder (with a special hone). The limit for honing a cylinder is 0.005 in. oversize. Wash all the residue from the cylinder bore with clean brake fluid and blow dry.

Assembly is performed in the following order:

1. Soak all components in clean brake fluid, or coat them with the rubber grease supplied in the wheel cylinder rebuilding kit.

2. Install the spring, cups (recesses toward the center), and pistons in the cylinder body, in that order.

3. Insert the boots over the ends of the cylinder.

4. Install the bleeder plug (and ball), if removed.

5. Assemble the brake shoes and install the drum.

PARKING BRAKE

ADJUSTMENTS

NOTE: *On Corolla 1200 models, the rear brake shoes must be adjusted before performing this procedure. See the section on brake adjustments at the beginning of this chapter for details.*

1. Slowly pull the parking brake lever up-

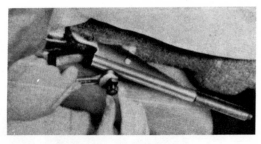

Parking brake lever adjustment

ward, without depressing the button on the end of it, and while counting the number of notches required until the parking brake is applied.

NOTE: *Two "clicks" are equal to one notch.*

2. Check the number of notches against the specifications given in the "Parking Brake Adjustment" chart.

3. If the brake requires adjustment, loosen the cable adjusting nut cap which is located at the rear of the parking brake lever. Hold the cap with an open-end wrench.

4. Take up the slack in the parking brake cable by rotating the adjusting nut with another open-end wrench.

Parking Brake Adjustment

Model	Range of Adjustment (Notches)
Corolla 1200	7–8 ①
Corolla 1600 ('75–'77) Tercel	2–4
Corolla 1600, 1800 ('78–'81)	4–12
Carina ('72–'73)	3–7
Starlet	3–6

NOTE: *Every notch equals two clicks.*
① 1978–79—4–12

　　a. If the number of notches is *less* than specified, turn the nut *counterclockwise;*

　　b. If the number of notches is *more* than specified, turn the nut *clockwise.*

5. Tighten the adjusting cap, using care not to disturb the setting of the adjusting nut.

6. Check the rotation of the rear wheels to be sure that the brakes are not dragging.

Body

10

You can repair most minor auto body damage yourself. Minor damage usually falls into one of several categories: (1) small scratches and dings in the paint that can be repaired without the use of body filler, (2) deep scratches and dents that require body filler, but do not require pulling, or hammering metal back into shape and (3) rust-out repairs. The repair sequences illustrated in this chapter are typical of these types of repairs. If you want to get involved in more complicated repairs including pulling or hammering sheet metal back into shape, you will probably need more detailed instructions. Chilton's *Minor Auto Body Repair, 2nd Edition* is a comprehensive guide to repairing auto body damage yourself.

TOOLS AND SUPPLIES

The list of tools and equipment you may need to fix minor body damage ranges from very basic hand tools to a wide assortment of specialized body tools. Most minor scratches, dings and rust holes can be fixed using an electric drill, wire wheel or grinder attachment, half-round plastic file, sanding block, various grades of sandpaper (#36, which is coarse through #600, which is fine) in both wet and dry types, auto body plastic,

primer, touch-up paint, spreaders, newspaper and masking tape.

Most manufacturers of auto body repair products began supplying materials to professionals. Their knowledge of the best, most-used products has been translated into body repair kits for the do-it-yourselfer. Kits are available from a number of manufacturers and contain the necessary materials in the required amounts for the repair identified on the package.

Kits are available for a wide variety of uses, including:

- Rusted out metal
- All purpose kit for dents and holes
- Dents and deep scratches
- Fiberglass repair kit
- Epoxy kit for restyling.

Kits offer the advantage of buying what you need for the job. There is little waste and little chance of materials going bad from not being used. The same manufacturers also merchandise all of the individual products used—spreaders, dent pullers, fiberglass cloth, polyester resin, cream hardener, body filler, body files, sandpaper, sanding discs and holders, primer, spray paint, etc.

CAUTION: *Most of the products you will be using contain harmful chemicals, so be extremely careful. Always read the complete label before opening the containers. When* *you put them away for future use, be sure they are out of children's reach!*

Most auto body repair kits contain all the materials you need to do the job right in the kit. So, if you have a small rust spot or dent you want to fix, check the contents of the kit before you run out and buy any additional tools.

ALIGNING BODY PANELS

Doors

There are several methods of adjusting doors. Your vehicle will probably use one of those illustrated.

Whenever a door is removed and is to be reinstalled, you should matchmark the position of the hinges on the door pillars. The holes of the hinges and/or the hinge attaching points are usually oversize to permit alignment of doors. The striker plate is also moveable, through oversize holes, permitting up-and-down, in-and-out and fore-and-aft movement. Fore-and-aft movement is made by adding or subtracting shims from behind the striker and pillar post. The striker should be adjusted so that the door closes fully and remains closed, yet enters the lock freely.

DOOR HINGES

Don't try to cover up poor door adjustment with a striker plate adjustment. The gap on each side of the door should be equal and uniform and there should be no metal-to-metal contact as the door is opened or closed.

1. Determine which hinge bolts must be loosened to move the door in the desired direction.

2. Loosen the hinge bolt(s) just enough to allow the door to be moved with a padded pry bar.

3. Move the door a small amount and check the fit, after tightening the bolts. Be sure that there is no bind or interference with adjacent panels.

4. Repeat this until the door is properly positioned, and tighten all the bolts securely.

Hood, Trunk or Tailgate

As with doors, the outline of hinges should be scribed before removal. The hood and trunk can be aligned by loosening the hinge bolts in their slotted mounting holes and moving the hood or trunk lid as necessary.

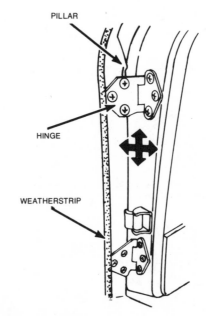

Door hinge adjustment

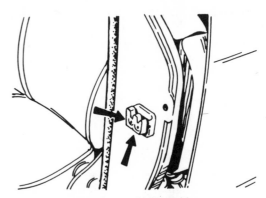

Move the door striker as indicated by arrows

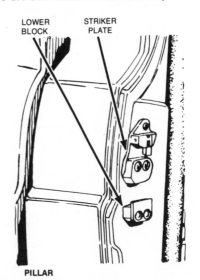

Striker plate and lower block

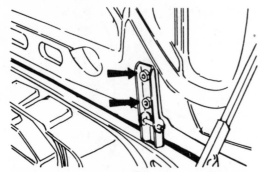

Loosen the hinge boots to permit fore-and-aft and horizontal adjustment

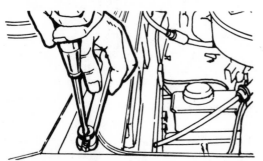

The hood is adjusted vertically by stop-screws at the front and/or rear

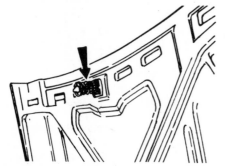

The hood pin can be adjusted for proper lock engagement

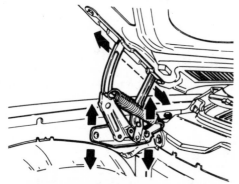

The height of the hood at the rear is adjusted by loosening the bolts that attach the hinge to the body and moving the hood up or down

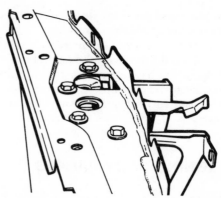

The base of the hood lock can also be repositioned slightly to give more positive lock engagement

The hood and trunk have adjustable catch locations to regulate lock engagement. Bumpers at the front and/or rear of the hood provide a vertical adjustment and the hood lockpin can be adjusted for proper engagement.

The tailgate on the station wagon can be adjusted by loosening the hinge bolts in their slotted mounting holes and moving the tailgate on its hinges. The latchplate and latch striker at the bottom of the tailgate opening can be adjusted to stop rattle. An adjustable bumper is located on each side.

RUST, UNDERCOATING, AND RUSTPROOFING

Rust

Rust is an electrochemical process. It works on ferrous metals (iron and steel) from the inside out due to exposure of unprotected surfaces to air and moisture. The possibility of rust exists practically nationwide—anywhere humidity, industrial pollution or chemical salts are present, rust can form. In coastal areas, the problem is high humidity and salt air; in snowy areas, the problem is chemical salt (de-icer) used to keep the roads clear, and in industrial areas, sulphur dioxide is present in the air from industrial pollution and is changed to sulphuric acid when it rains. The rusting process is accelerated by high temperatures, especially in snowy areas, when vehicles are driven over slushy roads and then left overnight in a heated garage.

Automotive styling also can be a contributor to rust formation. Spot welding of panels creates small pockets that trap moisture and form an environment for rust formation. Fortunately, auto manufacturers have been working hard to increase the corrosion protection of their products. Galvanized sheet metal enjoys much wider use, along with the increased use of plastic and various rust retardant coatings. Manufacturers are also designing out areas in the body where rust-forming moisture can collect.

To prevent rust, you must stop it before it gets started. On new vehicles, there are two ways to accomplish this.

First, the car or truck should be treated with a commercial rustproofing compound. There are many different brands of franchised rustproofers, but most processes involve spraying a waxy "self-healing" compound under the chassis, inside rocker panels, inside doors and fender liners and similar places where rust is likely to form. Prices for a quality rustproofing job range from $100–$250, depending on the area, the brand name and the size of the vehicle.

Ideally, the vehicle should be rustproofed as soon as possible following the purchase. The surfaces of the car or truck have begun to oxidize and deteriorate during shipping. In addition, the car may have sat on a dealer's lot or on a lot at the factory, and once the rust has progressed past the stage of light, powdery surface oxidation rustproofing is not likely to be worthwhile. Professional rustproofers feel that once rust has formed, rustproofing will simply seal in moisture already present. Most franchised rustproofing operations offer a 3–5 year warranty against rust-through, but will not support that warranty if the rustproofing is not applied within three months of the date of manufacture.

Undercoating should not be mistaken for rustproofing. Undercoating is a black, tar-like substance that is applied to the underside of a vehicle. Its basic function is to deaden noises that are transmitted from under the car. It simply cannot get into the crevices and seams where moisture tends to collect. In fact, it may clog up drainage holes and ventilation passages. Some undercoatings also tend to crack or peel with age and only create more moisture and corrosion attracting pockets.

The second thing you should do immediately after purchasing the car is apply a paint sealant. A sealant is a petroleum based product marketed under a wide variety of brand names. It has the same protective properties as a good wax, but bonds to the paint with a chemically inert layer that seals it from the air. If air can't get at the surface, oxidation cannot start.

The paint sealant kit consists of a base coat and a conditioning coat that should be applied every 6–8 months, depending on the manufacturer. The base coat must be applied before waxing, or the wax must first be removed.

Third, keep a garden hose handy for your car in winter. Use it a few times on nice days during the winter for underneath areas, and it will pay big dividends when spring arrives. Spraying under the fenders and other areas which even car washes don't reach will help remove road salt, dirt and other build-ups which help breed rust. Adjust the nozzle to a high-force spray. An old brush will help break up residue, permitting it to be washed away more easily.

It's a somewhat messy job, but worth it in the long run because rust often starts in those hidden areas.

At the same time, wash grime off the door sills and, more importantly, the under portions of the doors, plus the tailgate if you have a station wagon or truck. Applying a coat of wax to those areas at least once before and once during winter will help fend off rust.

When applying the wax to the under parts of the doors, you will note small drain holes. These holes often are plugged with undercoating or dirt. Make sure they are cleaned out to prevent water build-up inside the doors. A small punch or penknife will do the job.

Water from the high-pressure sprays in car washes sometimes can get into the housings for parking and taillights, so take a close look. If they contain water merely loosen the retaining screws and the water should run out.

Repairing Scratches and Small Dents

Step 1. This dent (arrow) is typical of a deep scratch or minor dent. If deep enough, the dent or scratch can be pulled out or hammered out from behind. In this case no straightening is necessary

Step 2. Using an 80-grit grinding disc on an electric drill grind the paint from the surrounding area down to bare metal. This will provide a rough surface for the body filler to grab

Step 3. The area should look like this when you're finished grinding

Step 4. Mix the body filler and cream hardener according to the directions

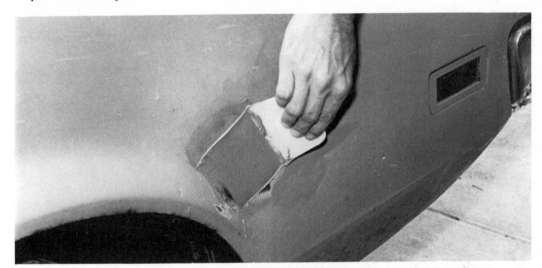

Step 5. Spread the body filler evenly over the entire area. Be sure to cover the area completely

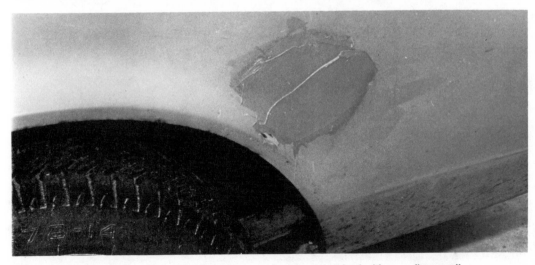

Step 6. Let the body filler dry until the surface can just be scratched with your fingernail

Step 7. Knock the high spots from the body filler with a body file

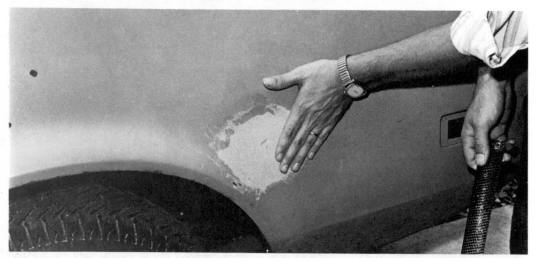

Step 8. Check frequently with the palm of your hand for high and low spots. If you wind up with low spots, you may have to apply another layer of filler

Step 9. Block sand the entire area with 320 grit paper

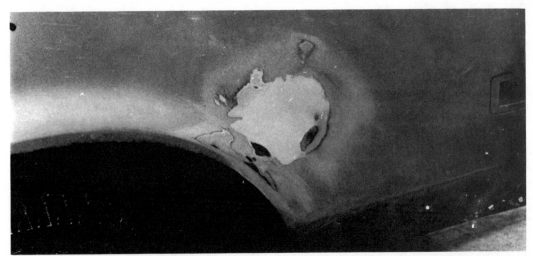

Step 10. When you're finished, the repair should look like this. Note the sand marks extending 2—3 inches out from the repaired area

Step 11. Prime the entire area with automotive primer

Step 12. The finished repair ready for the final paint coat. Note that the primer has covered the sanding marks (see Step 10). A repair of this size should be able to be spotpainted with good results

REPAIRING RUST HOLES

One thing you have to remember about rust: even if you grind away all the rusted metal in a panel, and repair the area with any of the kits available, *eventually* the rust will return. There are two reasons for this. One, rust is a chemical reaction that causes pressure under the repair from the inside out. That's how the blisters form. Two, the back side of the panel (and the repair) is wide open to moisture, and unpainted body filler acts like a sponge. That's why the best solution to rust problems is to remove the rusted panel and install a new one or have the rusted area cut out and a new piece of sheet metal welded in its place. The trouble with welding is the expense; sometimes it will cost more than the car or truck is worth.

One of the better solutions to do-it-your-self rust repair is the process using a fi-berglass cloth repair kit (shown here). This will give a strong repair that resists cracking and moisture and is relatively easy to use. It can be used on large or small holes and also can be applied over contoured surfaces.

Step 1. Rust areas such as this are common and are easily fixed

Step 2. Grind away all traces of rust with a 24-grit grinding disc. Be sure to grind back 3—4 inches from the edge of the hole down to bare metal and be sure all traces of rust are removed

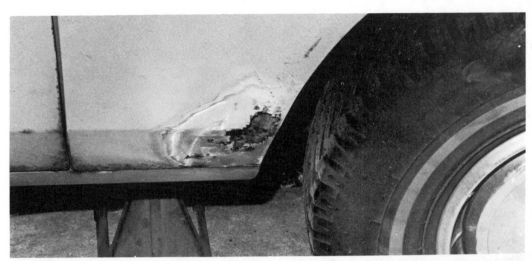

Step 3. Be sure all rust is removed from the edges of the metal. The edges must be ground back to un-rusted metal

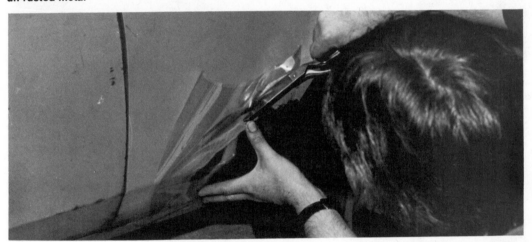

Step 4. If you are going to use release film, cut a piece about 2″ larger than the area you have sanded. Place the film over the repair and mark the sanded area on the film. Avoid any unnecessary wrinkling of the film

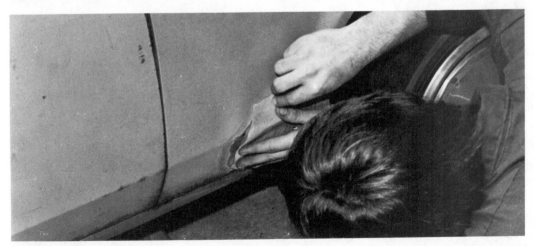

Step 5. Cut 2 pieces of fiberglass matte. One piece should be about 1″ smaller than the sanded area and the second piece should be 1″ smaller than the first. Use sharp scissors to avoid loose ends

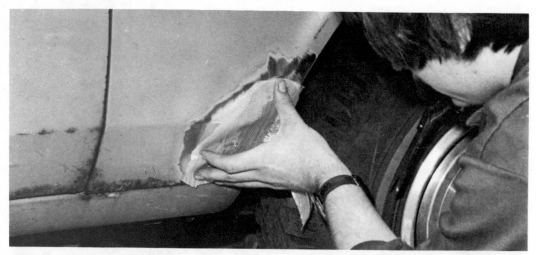

Step 6. Check the dimensions of the release film and cloth by holding them up to the repair area

Step 7. Mix enough repair jelly and cream hardener in the mixing tray to saturate the fiberglass material or fill the repair area. Follow the directions on the container

Step 8. Lay the release sheet on a flat surface and spread an even layer of filler, large enough to cover the repair. Lay the smaller piece of fiberglass cloth in the center of the sheet and spread another layer of repair jelly over the fiberglass cloth. Repeat the operation for the larger piece of cloth. If the fiberglass cloth is not used, spread the repair jelly on the release film, concentrated in the middle of the repair

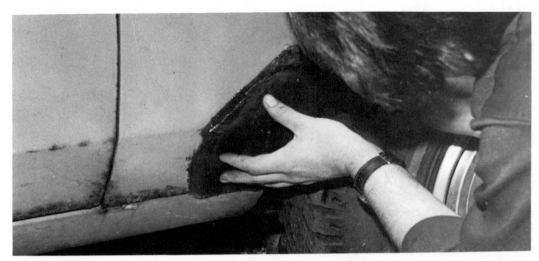

Step 9. Place the repair material over the repair area, with the release film facing outward

Step 10. Use a spreader and work from the center outward to smooth the material, following the body contours. Be sure to remove all air bubbles

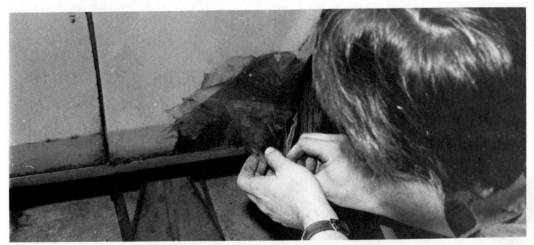

Step 11. Wait until the repair has dried tack-free and peel off the release sheet. The ideal working temperature is 65—90° F. Cooler or warmer temperatures or high humidity may require additional curing time

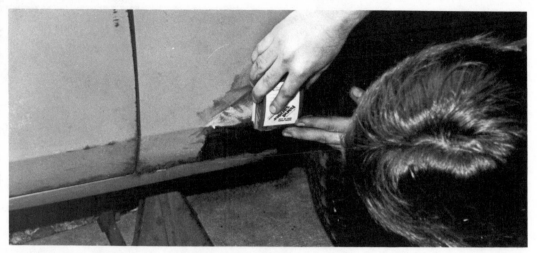

Step 12. Sand and feather-edge the entire area. The initial sanding can be done with a sanding disc on an electric drill if care is used. Finish the sanding with a block sander

Step 13. When the area is sanded smooth, mix some topcoat and hardener and apply it directly with a spreader. This will give a smooth finish and prevent the glass matte from showing through the paint

Step 14. Block sand the topcoat with finishing sandpaper

Step 15. To finish this repair, grind out the surface rust along the top edge of the rocker panel

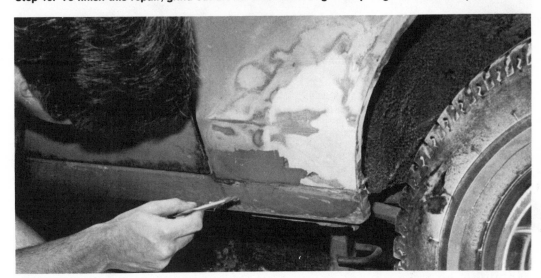

Step 16. Mix some more repair jelly and cream hardener and apply it directly over the surface

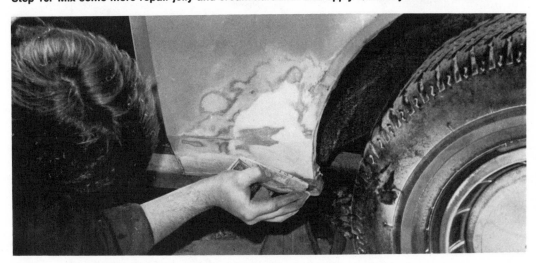

Step 17. When it dries tack-free, block sand the surface smooth

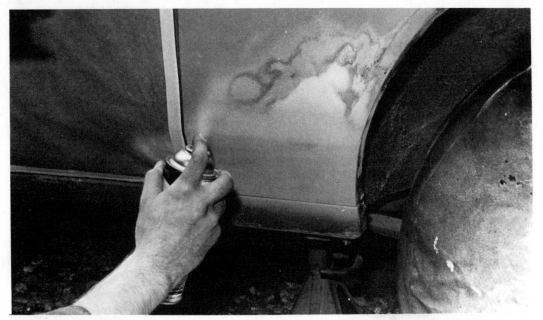

Step 18. If necessary, mask off adjacent panels and spray the entire repair with primer. You are now ready for a color coat

AUTO BODY CARE

There are hundreds—maybe thousands—of products on the market, all designed to protect or aid your car's finish in some manner. There are as many different products as there are ways to use them, but they all have one thing in common—the surface must be clean.

Washing

The primary ingredient for washing your car is water, preferably "soft" water. In many areas of the country, the local water supply is "hard" containing many minerals. The little rings or film that is left on your car's surface after it has dried is the result of "hard" water.

Since you usually can't change the local water supply, the next best thing is to dry the surface before it has a chance to dry itself.

Into the water you usually add soap. Don't use detergents or common, coarse soaps. Your car's paint never truly dries out, but is always evaporating residual oils into the air. Harsh detergents will remove these oils, causing the paint to dry faster than normal. Instead use warm water and a non-detergent soap made especially for waxed surfaces or a liquid soap made for waxed surfaces or a liquid soap made for washing dishes by hand.

Other products that can be used on painted surfaces include baking soda or plain soda water for stubborn dirt.

Wash the car completely, starting at the top, and rinse it completely clean. Abrasive grit should be loaded off under water pressure; scrubbing grit off will scratch the finish. The best washing tool is a sponge, cleaning mitt or soft towel. Whichever you choose, replace it often as each tends to absorb grease and dirt.

Other ways to get a better wash include:
• Don't wash your car in the sun or when the finish is hot.
• Use water pressure to remove caked-on dirt.
• Remove tree-sap and bird effluence immediately. Such substances will eat through wax, polish and paint.

One of the best implements to dry your car is a turkish towel or an old, soft bath towel. Anything with a deep nap will hold any dirt in suspension and not grind it into the paint.

Harder cloths will only grind the grit into the paint making more scratches. Always start drying at the top, followed by the hood and trunk and sides. You'll find there's always more dirt near the rocker panels and wheelwells which will wind up on the rest of the car if you dry these areas first.

Cleaners, Waxes and Polishes

Before going any farther you should know the function of various products.

Cleaners—remove the top layer of dead pigment or paint.

Rubbing or polishing compounds—used to remove stubborn dirt, get rid of minor scratches, smooth away imperfections and partially restore badly weathered paint.

Polishes—contain no abrasives or waxes; they shine the paint by adding oils to the paint.

Waxes—are a protective coating for the polish.

CLEANERS AND COMPOUNDS

Before you apply any wax, you'll have to remove oxidation, road film and other types of pollutants that washing alone will not remove.

The paint on your car never dries completely. There are always residual oils evaporating from the paint into the air. When enough oils are present in the paint, it has a healthy shine (gloss). When too many oils evaporate the paint takes on a whitish cast known as oxidation. The idea of polishing and waxing is to keep enough oil present in the painted surface to prevent oxidation; but when it occurs, the only recourse is to remove the top layer of "dead" paint, exposing the healthy paint underneath.

Products to remove oxidation and road film are sold under a variety of generic names—polishes, cleaner, rubbing compound, cleaner/polish, polish/cleaner, self-polishing wax, pre-wax cleaner, finish restorer and many more. Regardless of name there are two types of cleaners—abrasive cleaners (sometimes called polishing or rubbing compounds) that remove oxidation by grinding away the top layer of "dead" paint, or chemical cleaners that dissolve the "dead" pigment, allowing it to be wiped away.

Abrasive cleaners, by their nature, leave thousands of minute scratches in the finish, which must be polished out later. These should only be used in extreme cases, but are usually the only thing to use on badly oxidized paint finishes. Chemical cleaners are much milder but are not strong enough for severe cases of oxidation or weathered paint.

The most popular cleaners are liquid or paste abrasive polishing and rubbing compounds. Polishing compounds have a finer abrasive grit for medium duty work. Rubbing compounds are a coarser abrasive and for heavy duty work. Unless you are familiar with how to use compounds, be very careful. Excessive rubbing with any type of compound or cleaner can grind right through the paint to primer or bare metal. Follow the directions on the container—depending on type, the cleaner may or may not be OK for your paint. For example, some cleaners are not formulated for acrylic lacquer finishes.

When a small area needs compounding or heavy polishing, it's best to do the job by hand. Some people prefer a powered buffer for large areas. Avoid cutting through the paint along styling edges on the body. Small, hand operations where the compound is applied and rubbed using cloth folded into a thick ball allow you to work in straight lines along such edges.

To avoid cutting through on the edges when using a power buffer, try masking tape. Just cover the edge with tape while using power. Then finish the job by hand with the tape removed. Even then work carefully. The paint tends to be a lot thinner along the sharp ridges stamped into the panels.

Whether compounding by machine or by hand, only work on a small area and apply the compound sparingly. If the materials are spread too thin, or allowed to sit too long, they dry out. Once dry they lose the ability to deliver a smooth, clean finish. Also, dried out polish tends to cause the buffer to stick in one spot. This in turn can burn or cut through the finish.

WAXES AND POLISHES

Your car's finish can be protected in a number of ways. A cleaner/wax or polish/cleaner followed by wax or variations of each all provide good results. The two-step approach (polish followed by wax) is probably slightly better but consumes more time and effort. Properly fed with oils, your paint should never need cleaning, but despite the best polishing job, it won't last unless it's protected with wax. Without wax, polish must be renewed at least once a month to prevent oxidation. Years ago (some still swear by it today), the best wax was made from the Brazilian palm, the Carnuba, favored for its vegetable base and high melting point. However, modern synthetic waxes are harder, which means they protect against moisture better, and chemically inert silicone is used for a long lasting protection. The only problem with silicone wax is that it penetrates all layers of paint. To repaint or touch up a panel or car protected by silicone wax, you have to completely strip the finish to avoid "fish-eyes."

Under normal conditions, silicone waxes will last 4–6 months, but you have to be careful of wax build-up from too much waxing. Too thick a coat of wax is just as bad as no wax at all; it stops the paint from breathing.

Combination cleaners/waxes have become popular lately because they remove the old layer of wax plus light oxidation, while putting on a fresh coat of wax at the same time. Some cleaners/waxes contain abrasive cleaners which require caution, although many cleaner/waxes use a chemical cleaner.

Applying Wax or Polish

You may view polishing and waxing your car as a pleasant way to spend an afternoon, or as a boring chore, but it has to be done to keep the paint on your car. Caring for the paint doesn't require special tools, but you should follow a few rules.

1. Use a good quality wax.

2. Before applying any wax or polish, be sure the surface is completely clean. Just because the car looks clean, doesn't mean it's ready for polish or wax.

3. If the finish on your car is weathered, dull, or oxidized, it will probably have to be compounded to remove the old or oxidized paint. If the paint is simply dulled from lack of care, one of the non-abrasive cleaners known as polishing compounds will do the trick. If the paint is severely scratched or really dull, you'll probably have to use a rubbing compound to prepare the finish for waxing. If you're not sure which one to use, use the polishing compound, since you can easily ruin the finish by using too strong a compound.

4. Don't apply wax, polish or compound in direct sunlight, even if the directions on the can say you can. Most waxes will not cure properly in bright sunlight and you'll probably end up with a blotchy looking finish.

5. Don't rub the wax off too soon. The result will be a wet, dull looking finish. Let the wax dry thoroughly before buffing it off.

6. A constant debate among car enthusiasts is how wax should be applied. Some maintain pastes or liquids should be applied in a circular motion, but body shop experts have long thought that this approach results in barely detectable circular abrasions, especially on cars that are waxed frequently. They advise rubbing in straight lines, especially if any kind of cleaner is involved.

7. If an applicator is not supplied with the wax, use a piece of soft cheesecloth or very soft lint-free material. The same applies to buffing the surface.

SPECIAL SURFACES

One-step combination cleaner and wax formulas shouldn't be used on many of the special surfaces which abound on cars. The one-step materials contain abrasives to achieve a clean surface under the wax top coat. The abrasives are so mild that you could clean a car every week for a couple of years without fear of rubbing through the paint. But this same level of abrasiveness might, through repeated use, damage decals used for special trim effects. This includes wide stripes, wood-grain trim and other appliques.

Painted plastics must be cleaned with care. If a cleaner is too aggressive it will cut through the paint and expose the primer. If bright trim such as polished aluminum or chrome is painted, cleaning must be performed with even greater care. If rubbing compound is being used, it will cut faster than polish.

Abrasive cleaners will dull an acrylic finish. The best way to clean these newer finishes is with a non-abrasive liquid polish. Only dirt and oxidation, not paint, will be removed.

Taking a few minutes to read the instructions on the can of polish or wax will help prevent making serious mistakes. Not all preparations will work on all surfaces. And some are intended for power application while others will only work when applied by hand.

Don't get the idea that just pouring on some polish and then hitting it with a buffer will suffice. Power equipment speeds the operation. But it also adds a measure of risk. It's very easy to damage the finish if you use the wrong methods or materials.

Caring for Chrome

Read the label on the container. Many products are formulated specifically for chrome, but others contain abrasives that will scratch the chrome finish. If it isn't recommended for chrome, don't use it.

Never use steel wool or kitchen soap pads to clean chrome. Be careful not to get chrome cleaner on paint or interior vinyl surfaces. If you do, get it off immediately.

Troubleshooting

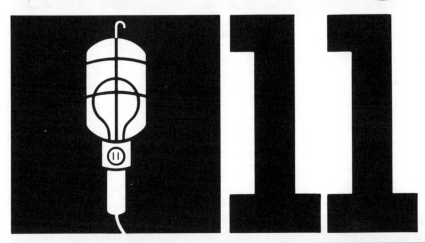

This section is designed to aid in the quick, accurate diagnosis of automotive problems. While automotive repairs can be made by many people, accurate troubleshooting is a rare skill for the amateur and professional alike.

In its simplest state, troubleshooting is an exercise in logic. It is essential to realize that an automobile is really composed of a series of systems. Some of these systems are interrelated; others are not. Automobiles operate within a framework of logical rules and physical laws, and the key to troubleshooting is a good understanding of all the automotive systems.

This section breaks the car or truck down into its component systems, allowing the problem to be isolated. The charts and diagnostic road maps list the most common problems and the most probable causes of trouble. Obviously it would be impossible to list every possible problem that could happen along with every possible cause, but it will locate MOST problems and eliminate a lot of unnecessary guesswork. The systematic format will locate problems within a given system, but, because many automotive systems are interrelated, the solution to your particular problem may be found in a number of systems on the car or truck.

USING THE TROUBLESHOOTING CHARTS

This book contains all of the specific information that the average do-it-yourself mechanic needs to repair and maintain his or her car or truck. The troubleshooting charts are designed to be used in conjunction with the specific procedures and information in the text. For instance, troubleshooting a point-type ignition system is fairly standard for all models, but you may be directed to the text to find procedures for troubleshooting an individual type of electronic ignition. You will also have to refer to the specification charts throughout the book for specifications applicable to your car or truck.

TOOLS AND EQUIPMENT

The tools illustrated in Chapter 1 (plus two more diagnostic pieces) will be adequate to troubleshoot most problems. The two other tools needed are a voltmeter and an ohmmeter. These can be purchased separately or in combination, known as a VOM meter.

In the event that other tools are required, they will be noted in the procedures.

Troubleshooting Engine Problems

See Chapters 2, 3, 4 for more information and service procedures.

Index to Systems

System	To Test	Group
Battery	Engine need not be running	1
Starting system	Engine need not be running	2
Primary electrical system	Engine need not be running	3
Secondary electrical system	Engine need not be running	4
Fuel system	Engine need not be running	5
Engine compression	Engine need not be running	6
Engine vacuum	Engine must be running	7
Secondary electrical system	Engine must be running	8
Valve train	Engine must be running	9
Exhaust system	Engine must be running	10
Cooling system	Engine must be running	11
Engine lubrication	Engine must be running	12

Index to Problems

Problem: Symptom	Begin at Specific Diagnosis, Number ___
Engine Won't Start:	
Starter doesn't turn	1.1, 2.1
Starter turns, engine doesn't	2.1
Starter turns engine very slowly	1.1, 2.4
Starter turns engine normally	3.1, 4.1
Starter turns engine very quickly	6.1
Engine fires intermittently	4.1
Engine fires consistently	5.1, 6.1
Engine Runs Poorly:	
Hard starting	3.1, 4.1, 5.1, 8.1
Rough idle	4.1, 5.1, 8.1
Stalling	3.1, 4.1, 5.1, 8.1
Engine dies at high speeds	4.1, 5.1
Hesitation (on acceleration from standing stop)	5.1, 8.1
Poor pickup	4.1, 5.1, 8.1
Lack of power	3.1, 4.1, 5.1, 8.1
Backfire through the carburetor	4.1, 8.1, 9.1
Backfire through the exhaust	4.1, 8.1, 9.1
Blue exhaust gases	6.1, 7.1
Black exhaust gases	5.1
Running on (after the ignition is shut off)	3.1, 8.1
Susceptible to moisture	4.1
Engine misfires under load	4.1, 7.1, 8.4, 9.1
Engine misfires at speed	4.1, 8.4
Engine misfires at idle	3.1, 4.1, 5.1, 7.1, 8.4

Sample Section

Test and Procedure	Results and Indications	Proceed to
4.1—Check for spark: Hold each spark plug wire approximately ¼" from ground with gloves or a heavy, dry rag. Crank the engine and observe the spark.	→ If no spark is evident:	→4.2
	→ If spark is good in some cases:	→4.3
	→ If spark is good in all cases:	→4.6

Specific Diagnosis

This section is arranged so that following each test, instructions are given to proceed to another, until a problem is diagnosed.

Section 1—Battery

Test and Procedure	Results and Indications	Proceed to
1.1—Inspect the battery visually for case condition (corrosion, cracks) and water level.	If case is cracked, replace battery:	**1.4**
	If the case is intact, remove corrosion with a solution of baking soda and water (**CAUTION**: *do not get the solution into the battery*), and fill with water:	**1.2**

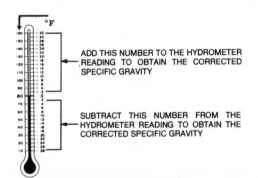

DIRT ON TOP OF BATTERY   PLUGGED VENT
CORROSION
LOOSE CABLE OR POSTS
CRACKS
LOW WATER LEVEL

Inspect the battery case

1.2—Check the battery cable connections: Insert a screwdriver between the battery post and the cable clamp. Turn the headlights on high beam, and observe them as the screwdriver is gently twisted to ensure good metal to metal contact.	If the lights brighten, remove and clean the clamp and post; coat the post with petroleum jelly, install and tighten the clamp:	**1.4**
	If no improvement is noted:	**1.3**

TESTING BATTERY CABLE CONNECTIONS USING A SCREWDRIVER

1.3—Test the state of charge of the battery using an individual cell tester or hydrometer.	If indicated, charge the battery. **NOTE:** *If no obvious reason exists for the low state of charge (i.e., battery age, prolonged storage), proceed to:*	**1.4**

°F

ADD THIS NUMBER TO THE HYDROMETER READING TO OBTAIN THE CORRECTED SPECIFIC GRAVITY

SUBTRACT THIS NUMBER FROM THE HYDROMETER READING TO OBTAIN THE CORRECTED SPECIFIC GRAVITY

Specific Gravity (@ 80° F.)

Minimum	Battery Charge
1.260	100% Charged
1.230	75% Charged
1.200	50% Charged
1.170	25% Charged
1.140	Very Little Power Left
1.110	Completely Discharged

The effects of temperature on battery specific gravity (left) and amount of battery charge in relation to specific gravity (right)

1.4—Visually inspect battery cables for cracking, bad connection to ground, or bad connection to starter.	If necessary, tighten connections or replace the cables:	**2.1**

Section 2—Starting System
See Chapter 3 for service procedures

Test and Procedure	Results and Indications	Proceed to

Note: Tests in Group 2 are performed with coil high tension lead disconnected to prevent accidental starting.

Test and Procedure	Results and Indications	Proceed to
2.1—Test the starter motor and solenoid: Connect a jumper from the battery post of the solenoid (or relay) to the starter post of the solenoid (or relay).	If starter turns the engine normally:	**2.2**
	If the starter buzzes, or turns the engine very slowly:	**2.4**
	If no response, replace the solenoid (or relay).	**3.1**
	If the starter turns, but the engine doesn't, ensure that the flywheel ring gear is intact. If the gear is undamaged, replace the starter drive.	**3.1**
2.2—Determine whether ignition override switches are functioning properly (clutch start switch, neutral safety switch), by connecting a jumper across the switch(es), and turning the ignition switch to "start".	If starter operates, adjust or replace switch:	**3.1**
	If the starter doesn't operate:	**2.3**
2.3—Check the ignition switch "start" position: Connect a 12V test lamp or voltmeter between the starter post of the solenoid (or relay) and ground. Turn the ignition switch to the "start" position, and jiggle the key.	If the lamp doesn't light or the meter needle doesn't move when the switch is turned, check the ignition switch for loose connections, cracked insulation, or broken wires. Repair or replace as necessary:	**3.1**
	If the lamp flickers or needle moves when the key is jiggled, replace the ignition switch.	**3.3**

Checking the ignition switch "start" position

STARTER RELAY
(IF EQUIPPED)

Test and Procedure	Results and Indications	Proceed to
2.4—Remove and bench test the starter, according to specifications in the engine electrical section.	If the starter does not meet specifications, repair or replace as needed:	**3.1**
	If the starter is operating properly:	**2.5**
2.5—Determine whether the engine can turn freely: Remove the spark plugs, and check for water in the cylinders. Check for water on the dipstick, or oil in the radiator. Attempt to turn the engine using an 18″ flex drive and socket on the crankshaft pulley nut or bolt.	If the engine will turn freely only with the spark plugs out, and hydrostatic lock (water in the cylinders) is ruled out, check valve timing:	**9.2**
	If engine will not turn freely, and it is known that the clutch and transmission are free, the engine must be disassembled for further evaluation:	**Chapter 3**

Section 3—Primary Electrical System

Test and Procedure	Results and Indications	Proceed to
3.1—Check the ignition switch "on" position: Connect a jumper wire between the distributor side of the coil and ground, and a 12V test lamp between the switch side of the coil and ground. Remove the high tension lead from the coil. Turn the ignition switch on and jiggle the key.	If the lamp lights:	**3.2**
	If the lamp flickers when the key is jiggled, replace the ignition switch:	**3.3**
	If the lamp doesn't light, check for loose or open connections. If none are found, remove the ignition switch and check for continuity. If the switch is faulty, replace it:	**3.3**

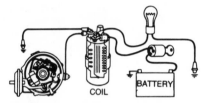

Checking the ignition switch "on" position

3.2—Check the ballast resistor or resistance wire for an open circuit, using an ohmmeter. See Chapter 3 for specific tests.	Replace the resistor or resistance wire if the resistance is zero. **NOTE:** *Some ignition systems have no ballast resistor.*	**3.3**

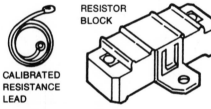

Two types of resistors

3.3—On point-type ignition systems, visually inspect the breaker points for burning, pitting or excessive wear. Gray coloring of the point contact surfaces is normal. Rotate the crankshaft until the contact heel rests on a high point of the distributor cam and adjust the point gap to specifications. On electronic ignition models, remove the distributor cap and visually inspect the armature. Ensure that the armature pin is in place, and that the armature is on tight and rotates when the engine is cranked. Make sure there are no cracks, chips or rounded edges on the armature.	If the breaker points are intact, clean the contact surfaces with fine emery cloth, and adjust the point gap to specifications. If the points are worn, replace them. On electronic systems, replace any parts which appear defective. If condition persists:	**3.4**

Test and Procedure	Results and Indications	Proceed to
3.4—On point-type ignition systems, connect a dwell-meter between the distributor primary lead and ground. Crank the engine and observe the point dwell angle. On electronic ignition systems, conduct a stator (magnetic pickup assembly) test. See Chapter 3.	On point-type systems, adjust the dwell angle if necessary. **NOTE:** *Increasing the point gap decreases the dwell angle and vice-versa.*	**3.6**
	If the dwell meter shows little or no reading;	**3.5**
	On electronic ignition systems, if the stator is bad, replace the stator. If the stator is good, proceed to the other tests in Chapter 3.	

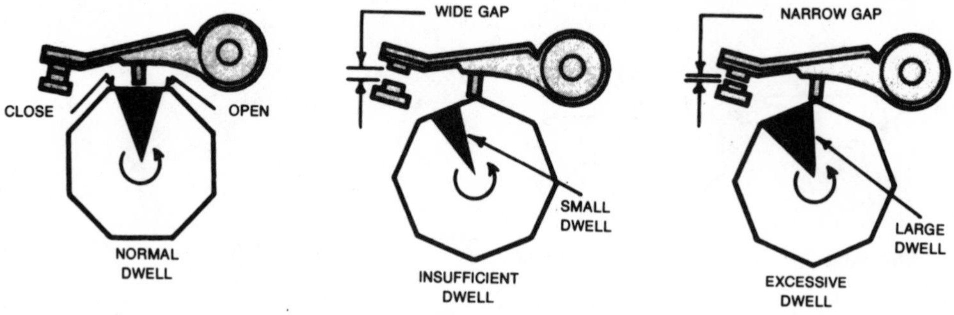

Dwell is a function of point gap

3.5—On the point-type ignition systems, check the condenser for short: connect an ohmeter across the condenser body and the pigtail lead.	If any reading other than infinite is noted, replace the condenser	**3.6**

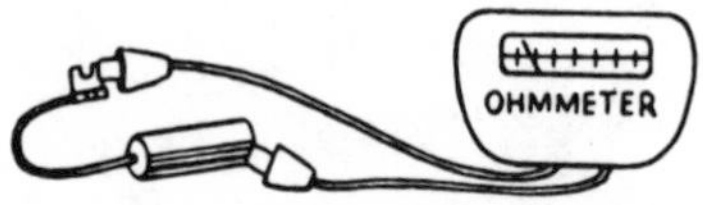

Checking the condenser for short

3.6—Test the coil primary resistance: On point-type ignition systems, connect an ohmmeter across the coil primary terminals, and read the resistance on the low scale. Note whether an external ballast resistor or resistance wire is used. On electronic ignition systems, test the coil primary resistance as in Chapter 3.	Point-type ignition coils utilizing ballast resistors or resistance wires should have approximately 1.0 ohms resistance. Coils with internal resistors should have approximately 4.0 ohms resistance. If values far from the above are noted, replace the coil.	**4.1**

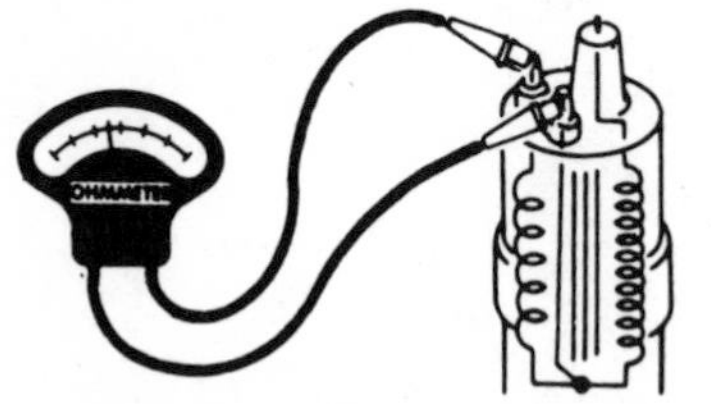

Check the coil primary resistance

Section 4—Secondary Electrical System

See Chapters 2–3 for service procedures

Test and Procedure	Results and Indications	Proceed to
4.1—Check for spark: Hold each spark plug wire approximately ¼″ from ground with gloves or a heavy, dry rag. Crank the engine, and observe the spark.	If no spark is evident:	**4.2**
	If spark is good in some cylinders:	**4.3**
	If spark is good in all cylinders:	**4.6**

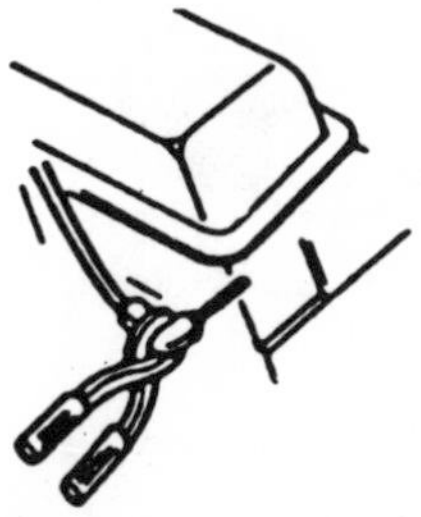

Check for spark at the plugs

4.2—Check for spark at the coil high tension lead: Remove the coil high tension lead from the distributor and position it approximately ¼″ from ground. Crank the engine and observe spark. **CAUTION:** *This test should not be performed on engines equipped with electronic ignition.*	If the spark is good and consistent:	**4.3**
	If the spark is good but intermittent, test the primary electrical system starting at 3.3:	**3.3**
	If the spark is weak or non-existent, replace the coil high tension lead, clean and tighten all connections and retest. If no improvement is noted:	**4.4**
4.3—Visually inspect the distributor cap and rotor for burned or corroded contacts, cracks, carbon tracks, or moisture. Also check the fit of the rotor on the distributor shaft (where applicable).	If moisture is present, dry thoroughly, and retest per 4.1:	**4.1**
	If burned or excessively corroded contacts, cracks, or carbon tracks are noted, replace the defective part(s) and retest per 4.1:	**4.1**
	If the rotor and cap appear intact, or are only slightly corroded, clean the contacts thoroughly (including the cap towers and spark plug wire ends) and retest per 4.1: If the spark is good in all cases:	**4.6**
	If the spark is poor in all cases:	**4.5**

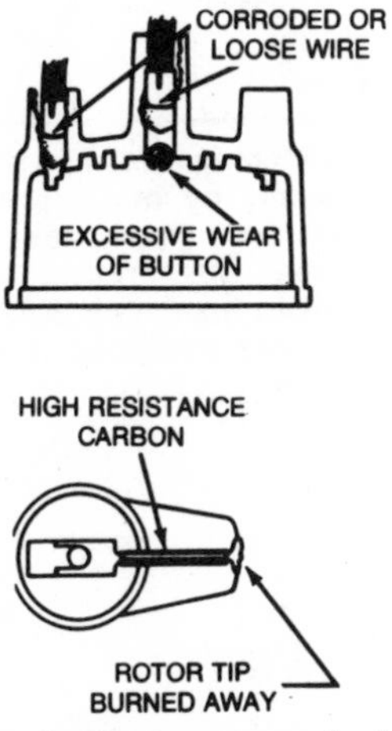

CORRODED OR LOOSE WIRE

EXCESSIVE WEAR OF BUTTON

HIGH RESISTANCE CARBON

ROTOR TIP BURNED AWAY

Inspect the distributor cap and rotor

Test and Procedure	*Results and Indications*	*Proceed to*
4.4—Check the coil secondary resistance: On point-type systems connect an ohmmeter across the distributor side of the coil and the coil tower. Read the resistance on the high scale of the ohmmeter. On electronic ignition systems, see Chapter 3 for specific tests.	The resistance of a satisfactory coil should be between 4,000 and 10,000 ohms. If resistance is considerably higher (i.e., 40,000 ohms) replace the coil and retest per 4.1. **NOTE:** *This does not apply to high performance coils.*	

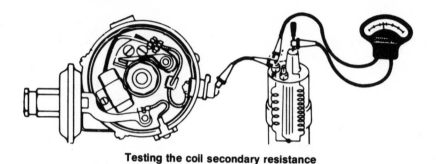

Testing the coil secondary resistance

4.5—Visually inspect the spark plug wires for cracking or brittleness. Ensure that no two wires are positioned so as to cause induction firing (adjacent and parallel). Remove each wire, one by one, and check resistance with an ohmmeter.	Replace any cracked or brittle wires. If any of the wires are defective, replace the entire set. Replace any wires with excessive resistance (over 8000 Ω per foot for suppression wire), and separate any wires that might cause induction firing.	**4.6**

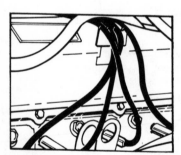

Misfiring can be the result of spark plug leads to adjacent, consecutively firing cylinders running parallel and too close together

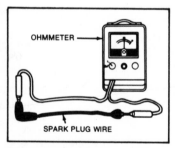

On point-type ignition systems, check the spark plug wires as shown. On electronic ignitions, do not remove the wire from the distributor cap terminal; instead, test through the cap

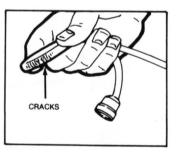

Spark plug wires can be checked visually by bending them in a loop over your finger. This will reveal any cracks, burned or broken insulation. Any wire with cracked insulation should be replaced

4.6—Remove the spark plugs, noting the cylinders from which they were removed, and evaluate according to the color photos in the middle of this book.	See following.	**See following.**

Test and Procedure	Results and Indications	Proceed to
4.7—Examine the location of all the plugs.	The following diagrams illustrate some of the conditions that the location of plugs will reveal.	**4.8**

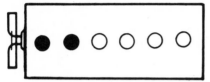

Two adjacent plugs are fouled in a 6-cylinder engine, 4-cylinder engine or either bank of a V-8. This is probably due to a blown head gasket between the two cylinders

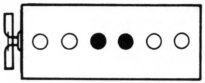

The two center plugs in a 6-cylinder engine are fouled. Raw fuel may be "boiled" out of the carburetor into the intake manifold after the engine is shut-off. Stop-start driving can also foul the center plugs, due to overly rich mixture. Proper float level, a new float needle and seat or use of an insulating spacer may help this problem

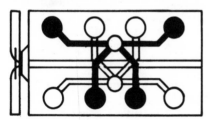

An unbalanced carburetor is indicated. Following the fuel flow on this particular design shows that the cylinders fed by the right-hand barrel are fouled from overly rich mixture, while the cylinders fed by the left-hand barrel are normal

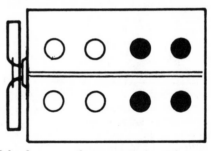

If the four rear plugs are overheated, a cooling system problem is suggested. A thorough cleaning of the cooling system may restore coolant circulation and cure the problem

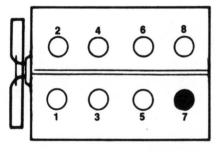

Finding one plug overheated may indicate an intake manifold leak near the affected cylinder. If the overheated plug is the second of two adjacent, consecutively firing plugs, it could be the result of ignition cross-firing. Separating the leads to these two plugs will eliminate cross-fire

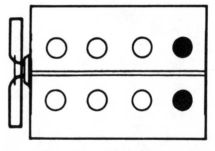

Occasionally, the two rear plugs in large, lightly used V-8's will become oil fouled. High oil consumption and smoky exhaust may also be noticed. It is probably due to plugged oil drain holes in the rear of the cylinder head, causing oil to be sucked in around the valve stems. This usually occurs in the rear cylinders first, because the engine slants that way

Test and Procedure	Results and Indications	Proceed to
4.8—Determine the static ignition timing. Using the crankshaft pulley timing marks as a guide, locate top dead center on the compression stroke of the number one cylinder.	The rotor should be pointing toward the No. 1 tower in the distributor cap, and, on electronic ignitions, the armature spoke for that cylinder should be lined up with the stator.	4.8
4.9—Check coil polarity: Connect a voltmeter negative lead to the coil high tension lead, and the positive lead to ground (**NOTE:** *Reverse the hook-up for positive ground systems*). Crank the engine momentarily. **Checking coil polarity**	If the voltmeter reads up-scale, the polarity is correct: If the voltmeter reads down-scale, reverse the coil polarity (switch the primary leads):	5.1 5.1

Section 5—Fuel System
See Chapter 4 for service procedures

Test and Procedure	Results and Indications	Proceed to
5.1—Determine that the air filter is functioning efficiently: Hold paper elements up to a strong light, and attempt to see light through the filter.	Clean permanent air filters in solvent (or manufacturer's recommendation), and allow to dry. Replace paper elements through which light cannot be seen:	5.2
5.2—Determine whether a flooding condition exists: Flooding is identified by a strong gasoline odor, and excessive gasoline present in the throttle bore(s) of the carburetor. **If the engine floods repeatedly, check the choke butterfly flap**	If flooding is not evident: If flooding is evident, permit the gasoline to dry for a few moments and restart. If flooding doesn't recur: If flooding is persistent:	5.3 5.7 5.5
5.3—Check that fuel is reaching the carburetor: Detach the fuel line at the carburetor inlet. Hold the end of the line in a cup (not styrofoam), and crank the engine. **Check the fuel pump by disconnecting the output line (fuel pump-to-carburetor) at the carburetor and operating the starter briefly**	If fuel flows smoothly: If fuel doesn't flow (**NOTE:** *Make sure that there is fuel in the tank*), or flows erratically:	5.7 5.4

Test and Procedure	Results and Indications	Proceed to
5.4—Test the fuel pump: Disconnect all fuel lines from the fuel pump. Hold a finger over the input fitting, crank the engine (with electric pump, turn the ignition or pump on); and feel for suction.	If suction is evident, blow out the fuel line to the tank with low pressure compressed air until bubbling is heard from the fuel filler neck. Also blow out the carburetor fuel line (both ends disconnected):	**5.7**
	If no suction is evident, replace or repair the fuel pump: **NOTE:** *Repeated oil fouling of the spark plugs, or a no-start condition, could be the result of a ruptured vacuum booster pump diaphragm, through which oil or gasoline is being drawn into the intake manifold (where applicable).*	**5.7**
5.5—Occasionally, small specks of dirt will clog the small jets and orifices in the carburetor. With the engine cold, hold a flat piece of wood or similar material over the carburetor, where possible, and crank the engine.	If the engine starts, but runs roughly the engine is probably not run enough. If the engine won't start:	**5.9**
5.6—Check the needle and seat: Tap the carburetor in the area of the needle and seat.	If flooding stops, a gasoline additive (e.g., Gumout) will often cure the problem:	**5.7**
	If flooding continues, check the fuel pump for excessive pressure at the carburetor (according to specifications). If the pressure is normal, the needle and seat must be removed and checked, and/or the float level adjusted:	**5.7**
5.7—Test the accelerator pump by looking into the throttle bores while operating the throttle.	If the accelerator pump appears to be operating normally:	**5.8**
	If the accelerator pump is not operating, the pump must be reconditioned. Where possible, service the pump with the carburetor(s) installed on the engine. If necessary, remove the carburetor. Prior to removal:	**5.8**

Check for gas at the carburetor by looking down the carburetor throat while someone moves the accelerator

Test and Procedure	Results and Indications	Proceed to
5.8—Determine whether the carburetor main fuel system is functioning: Spray a commercial starting fluid into the carburetor while attempting to start the engine.	If the engine starts, runs for a few seconds, and dies:	**5.9**
	If the engine doesn't start:	**6.1**

Test and Procedure	Results and Indications	Proceed to
5.9—Uncommon fuel system malfunctions: See below:	If the problem is solved: If the problem remains, remove and recondition the carburetor.	6.1

Condition	Indication	Test	Prevailing Weather Conditions	Remedy
Vapor lock	Engine will not restart shortly after running.	Cool the components of the fuel system until the engine starts. Vapor lock can be cured faster by draping a wet cloth over a mechanical fuel pump.	Hot to very hot	Ensure that the exhaust manifold heat control valve is operating. Check with the vehicle manufacturer for the recommended solution to vapor lock on the model in question.
Carburetor icing	Engine will not idle, stalls at low speeds.	Visually inspect the throttle plate area of the throttle bores for frost.	High humidity, 32–40° F.	Ensure that the exhaust manifold heat control valve is operating, and that the intake manifold heat riser is not blocked.
Water in the fuel	Engine sputters and stalls; may not start.	Pump a small amount of fuel into a glass jar. Allow to stand, and inspect for droplets or a layer of water.	High humidity, extreme temperature changes.	For droplets, use one or two cans of commercial gas line anti-freeze. For a layer of water, the tank must be drained, and the fuel lines blown out with compressed air.

Section 6—Engine Compression
See Chapter 3 for service procedures

6.1—Test engine compression: Remove all spark plugs. Block the throttle wide open. Insert a compression gauge into a spark plug port, crank the engine to obtain the maximum reading, and record.	If compression is within limits on all cylinders:	7.1
	If gauge reading is extremely low on all cylinders:	6.2
	If gauge reading is low on one or two cylinders: (If gauge readings are identical and low on two or more adjacent cylinders, the head gasket must be replaced.)	6.2

Checking compression

6.2—Test engine compression (wet): Squirt approximately 30 cc. of engine oil into each cylinder, and retest per 6.1.	If the readings improve, worn or cracked rings or broken pistons are indicated:	See Chapter 3
	If the readings do not improve, burned or excessively carboned valves or a jumped timing chain are indicated: NOTE: *A jumped timing chain is often indicated by difficult cranking.*	7.1

Section 7—Engine Vacuum
See Chapter 3 for service procedures

Test and Procedure	Results and Indications	Proceed to
7.1—Attach a vacuum gauge to the intake manifold beyond the throttle plate. Start the engine, and observe the action of the needle over the range of engine speeds.	See below.	**See below**

INDICATION: normal engine in good condition

Proceed to: 8.1

Normal engine
Gauge reading: steady, from 17–22 in./Hg.

INDICATION: sticking valves or ignition miss

Proceed to: 9.1, 8.3

Sticking valves
Gauge reading: intermittent fluctuation at idle

INDICATION: late ignition or valve timing, low compression, stuck throttle valve, leaking carburetor or manifold gasket

Proceed to: 6.1

Incorrect valve timing
Gauge reading: low (10–15 in./Hg) but steady

INDICATION: improper carburetor adjustment or minor intake leak.

Proceed to: 7.2

Carburetor requires adjustment
Gauge reading: drifting needle

INDICATION: ignition miss, blown cylinder head gasket, leaking valve or weak valve spring

Proceed to: 8.3, 6.1

Blown head gasket
Gauge reading: needle fluctuates as engine speed increases

INDICATION: burnt valve or faulty valve clearance. Needle will fall when defective valve operates

Proceed to: 9.1

Burnt or leaking valves
Gauge reading: steady needle, but drops regularly

INDICATION: choked muffler, excessive back pressure in system

Proceed to: 10.1

Clogged exhaust system
Gauge reading: gradual drop in reading at idle

INDICATION: worn valve guides

Proceed to: 9.1

Worn valve guides
Gauge reading: needle vibrates excessively at idle, but steadies as engine speed increases

White pointer = steady gauge hand

Black pointer = fluctuating gauge hand

Test and Procedure	Results and Indications	Proceed to
7.2—Attach a vacuum gauge per 7.1, and test for an intake manifold leak. Squirt a small amount of oil around the intake manifold gaskets, carburetor gaskets, plugs and fittings. Observe the action of the vacuum gauge.	If the reading improves, replace the indicated gasket, or seal the indicated fitting or plug: If the reading remains low:	8.1 7.3
7.3—Test all vacuum hoses and accessories for leaks as described in 7.2. Also check the carburetor body (dashpots, automatic choke mechanism, throttle shafts) for leaks in the same manner.	If the reading improves, service or replace the offending part(s): If the reading remains low:	8.1 6.1

Section 8—Secondary Electrical System
See Chapter 2 for service procedures

Test and Procedure	Results and Indications	Proceed to
8.1—Remove the distributor cap and check to make sure that the rotor turns when the engine is cranked. Visually inspect the distributor components.	Clean, tighten or replace any components which appear defective.	8.2
8.2—Connect a timing light (per manufacturer's recommendation) and check the dynamic ignition timing. Disconnect and plug the vacuum hose(s) to the distributor if specified, start the engine, and observe the timing marks at the specified engine speed.	If the timing is not correct, adjust to specifications by rotating the distributor in the engine: (Advance timing by rotating distributor opposite normal direction of rotor rotation, retard timing by rotating distributor in same direction as rotor rotation.)	8.3
8.3—Check the operation of the distributor advance mechanism(s): To test the mechanical advance, disconnect the vacuum lines from the distributor advance unit and observe the timing marks with a timing light as the engine speed is increased from idle. If the mark moves smoothly, without hesitation, it may be assumed that the mechanical advance is functioning properly. To test vacuum advance and/or retard systems, alternately crimp and release the vacuum line, and observe the timing mark for movement. If movement is noted, the system is operating.	If the systems are functioning: If the systems are not functioning, remove the distributor, and test on a distributor tester:	8.4 8.4
8.4—Locate an ignition miss: With the engine running, remove each spark plug wire, one at a time, until one is found that doesn't cause the engine to roughen and slow down.	When the missing cylinder is identified:	4.1

Section 9—Valve Train
See Chapter 3 for service procedures

Test and Procedure	Results and Indications	Proceed to
9.1—Evaluate the valve train: Remove the valve cover, and ensure that the valves are adjusted to specifications. A mechanic's stethoscope may be used to aid in the diagnosis of the valve train. By pushing the probe on or near push rods or rockers, valve noise often can be isolated. A timing light also may be used to diagnose valve problems. Connect the light according to manufacturer's recommendations, and start the engine. Vary the firing moment of the light by increasing the engine speed (and therefore the ignition advance), and moving the trigger from cylinder to cylinder. Observe the movement of each valve.	Sticking valves or erratic valve train motion can be observed with the timing light. The cylinder head must be disassembled for repairs.	**See Chapter 3**
9.2—Check the valve timing: Locate top dead center of the No. 1 piston, and install a degree wheel or tape on the crankshaft pulley or damper with zero corresponding to an index mark on the engine. Rotate the crankshaft in its direction of rotation, and observe the opening of the No. 1 cylinder intake valve. The opening should correspond with the correct mark on the degree wheel according to specifications.	If the timing is not correct, the timing cover must be removed for further investigation.	**See Chapter 3**

Section 10—Exhaust System

Test and Procedure	Results and Indications	Proceed to
10.1—Determine whether the exhaust manifold heat control valve is operating: Operate the valve by hand to determine whether it is free to move. If the valve is free, run the engine to operating temperature and observe the action of the valve, to ensure that it is opening.	If the valve sticks, spray it with a suitable solvent, open and close the valve to free it, and retest. If the valve functions properly: If the valve does not free, or does not operate, replace the valve:	**10.2** **10.2**
10.2—Ensure that there are no exhaust restrictions: Visually inspect the exhaust system for kinks, dents, or crushing. Also note that gases are flowing freely from the tailpipe at all engine speeds, indicating no restriction in the muffler or resonator.	Replace any damaged portion of the system:	**11.1**

Section 11—Cooling System
See Chapter 3 for service procedures

Test and Procedure	Results and Indications	Proceed to
11.1—Visually inspect the fan belt for glazing, cracks, and fraying, and replace if necessary. Tighten the belt so that the longest span has approximately ½″ play at its midpoint under thumb pressure (see Chapter 1).	Replace or tighten the fan belt as necessary:	**11.2**

Checking belt tension

11.2—Check the fluid level of the cooling system.	If full or slightly low, fill as necessary:	**11.5**
	If extremely low:	**11.3**
11.3—Visually inspect the external portions of the cooling system (radiator, radiator hoses, thermostat elbow, water pump seals, heater hoses, etc.) for leaks. If none are found, pressurize the cooling system to 14–15 psi.	If cooling system holds the pressure:	**11.5**
	If cooling system loses pressure rapidly, reinspect external parts of the system for leaks under pressure. If none are found, check dipstick for coolant in crankcase. If no coolant is present, but pressure loss continues:	**11.4**
	If coolant is evident in crankcase, remove cylinder head(s), and check gasket(s). If gaskets are intact, block and cylinder head(s) should be checked for cracks or holes. If the gasket(s) is blown, replace, and purge the crankcase of coolant: **NOTE:** *Occasionally, due to atmospheric and driving conditions, condensation of water can occur in the crankcase. This causes the oil to appear milky white. To remedy, run the engine until hot, and change the oil and oil filter.*	**12.6**
11.4—Check for combustion leaks into the cooling system: Pressurize the cooling system as above. Start the engine, and observe the pressure gauge. If the needle fluctuates, remove each spark plug wire, one at a time, noting which cylinder(s) reduce or eliminate the fluctuation.	Cylinders which reduce or eliminate the fluctuation, when the spark plug wire is removed, are leaking into the cooling system. Replace the head gasket on the affected cylinder bank(s).	

Pressurizing the cooling system

Test and Procedure	Results and Indications	Proceed to
11.5—Check the radiator pressure cap: Attach a radiator pressure tester to the radiator cap (wet the seal prior to installation). Quickly pump up the pressure, noting the point at which the cap releases.	If the cap releases within ± 1 psi of the specified rating, it is operating properly:	**11.6**
	If the cap releases at more than ± 1 psi of the specified rating, it should be replaced:	**11.6**

Checking radiator pressure cap

Test and Procedure	Results and Indications	Proceed to
11.6—Test the thermostat: Start the engine cold, remove the radiator cap, and insert a thermometer into the radiator. Allow the engine to idle. After a short while, there will be a sudden, rapid increase in coolant temperature. The temperature at which this sharp rise stops is the thermostat opening temperature.	If the thermostat opens at or about the specified temperature:	**11.7**
	If the temperature doesn't increase: (If the temperature increases slowly and gradually, replace the thermostat.)	**11.7**
11.7—Check the water pump: Remove the thermostat elbow and the thermostat, disconnect the coil high tension lead (to prevent starting), and crank the engine momentarily.	If coolant flows, replace the thermostat and retest per 11.6:	**11.6**
	If coolant doesn't flow, reverse flush the cooling system to alleviate any blockage that might exist. If system is not blocked, and coolant will not flow, replace the water pump.	

Section 12—Lubrication
See Chapter 3 for service procedures

Test and Procedure	Results and Indications	Proceed to
12.1—Check the oil pressure gauge or warning light: If the gauge shows low pressure, or the light is on for no obvious reason, remove the oil pressure sender. Install an accurate oil pressure gauge and run the engine momentarily.	If oil pressure builds normally, run engine for a few moments to determine that it is functioning normally, and replace the sender.	—
	If the pressure remains low:	**12.2**
	If the pressure surges:	**12.3**
	If the oil pressure is zero:	**12.3**
12.2—Visually inspect the oil: If the oil is watery or very thin, milky, or foamy, replace the oil and oil filter.	If the oil is normal:	**12.3**
	If after replacing oil the pressure remains low:	**12.3**
	If after replacing oil the pressure becomes normal:	—

Test and Procedure	Results and Indications	Proceed to
12.3—Inspect the oil pressure relief valve and spring, to ensure that it is not sticking or stuck. Remove and thoroughly clean the valve, spring, and the valve body.	If the oil pressure improves: If no improvement is noted:	— **12.4**
12.4—Check to ensure that the oil pump is not cavitating (sucking air instead of oil): See that the crankcase is neither over nor underfull, and that the pickup in the sump is in the proper position and free from sludge.	Fill or drain the crankcase to the proper capacity, and clean the pickup screen in solvent if necessary. If no improvement is noted:	**12.5**
12.5—Inspect the oil pump drive and the oil pump:	If the pump drive or the oil pump appear to be defective, service as necessary and retest per 12.1: If the pump drive and pump appear to be operating normally, the engine should be disassembled to determine where blockage exists:	**12.1** **See Chapter 3**
12.6—Purge the engine of ethylene glycol coolant: Completely drain the crankcase and the oil filter. Obtain a commercial butyl cellosolve base solvent, designated for this purpose, and follow the instructions precisely. Following this, install a new oil filter and refill the crankcase with the proper weight oil. The next oil and filter change should follow shortly thereafter (1000 miles).		

TROUBLESHOOTING EMISSION CONTROL SYSTEMS

See Chapter 4 for procedures applicable to individual emission control systems used on specific combinations of engine/transmission/model.

TROUBLESHOOTING THE CARBURETOR
See Chapter 4 for service procedures

Carburetor problems cannot be effectively isolated unless all other engine systems (particularly ignition and emission) are functioning properly and the engine is properly tuned.

Condition	Possible Cause
Engine cranks, but does not start	1. Improper starting procedure 2. No fuel in tank 3. Clogged fuel line or filter 4. Defective fuel pump 5. Choke valve not closing properly 6. Engine flooded 7. Choke valve not unloading 8. Throttle linkage not making full travel 9. Stuck needle or float 10. Leaking float needle or seat 11. Improper float adjustment
Engine stalls	1. Improperly adjusted idle speed or mixture **Engine hot** 2. Improperly adjusted dashpot 3. Defective or improperly adjusted solenoid 4. Incorrect fuel level in fuel bowl 5. Fuel pump pressure too high 6. Leaking float needle seat 7. Secondary throttle valve stuck open 8. Air or fuel leaks 9. Idle air bleeds plugged or missing 10. Idle passages plugged **Engine Cold** 11. Incorrectly adjusted choke 12. Improperly adjusted fast idle speed 13. Air leaks 14. Plugged idle or idle air passages 15. Stuck choke valve or binding linkage 16. Stuck secondary throttle valves 17. Engine flooding—high fuel level 18. Leaking or misaligned float
Engine hesitates on acceleration	1. Clogged fuel filter 2. Leaking fuel pump diaphragm 3. Low fuel pump pressure 4. Secondary throttle valves stuck, bent or misadjusted 5. Sticking or binding air valve 6. Defective accelerator pump 7. Vacuum leaks 8. Clogged air filter 9. Incorrect choke adjustment (engine cold)
Engine feels sluggish or flat on acceleration	1. Improperly adjusted idle speed or mixture 2. Clogged fuel filter 3. Defective accelerator pump 4. Dirty, plugged or incorrect main metering jets 5. Bent or sticking main metering rods 6. Sticking throttle valves 7. Stuck heat riser 8. Binding or stuck air valve 9. Dirty, plugged or incorrect secondary jets 10. Bent or sticking secondary metering rods. 11. Throttle body or manifold heat passages plugged 12. Improperly adjusted choke or choke vacuum break.
Carburetor floods	1. Defective fuel pump. Pressure too high. 2. Stuck choke valve 3. Dirty, worn or damaged float or needle valve/seat 4. Incorrect float/fuel level 5. Leaking float bowl

Condition	Possible Cause
Engine idles roughly and stalls	1. Incorrect idle speed 2. Clogged fuel filter 3. Dirt in fuel system or carburetor 4. Loose carburetor screws or attaching bolts 5. Broken carburetor gaskets 6. Air leaks 7. Dirty carburetor 8. Worn idle mixture needles 9. Throttle valves stuck open 10. Incorrectly adjusted float or fuel level 11. Clogged air filter
Engine runs unevenly or surges	1. Defective fuel pump 2. Dirty or clogged fuel filter 3. Plugged, loose or incorrect main metering jets or rods 4. Air leaks 5. Bent or sticking main metering rods 6. Stuck power piston 7. Incorrect float adjustment 8. Incorrect idle speed or mixture 9. Dirty or plugged idle system passages 10. Hard, brittle or broken gaskets 11. Loose attaching or mounting screws 12. Stuck or misaligned secondary throttle valves
Poor fuel economy	1. Poor driving habits 2. Stuck choke valve 3. Binding choke linkage 4. Stuck heat riser 5. Incorrect idle mixture 6. Defective accelerator pump 7. Air leaks 8. Plugged, loose or incorrect main metering jets 9. Improperly adjusted float or fuel level 10. Bent, misaligned or fuel-clogged float 11. Leaking float needle seat 12. Fuel leak 13. Accelerator pump discharge ball not seating properly 14. Incorrect main jets
Engine lacks high speed performance or power	1. Incorrect throttle linkage adjustment 2. Stuck or binding power piston 3. Defective accelerator pump 4. Air leaks 5. Incorrect float setting or fuel level 6. Dirty, plugged, worn or incorrect main metering jets or rods 7. Binding or sticking air valve 8. Brittle or cracked gaskets 9. Bent, incorrect or improperly adjusted secondary metering rods 10. Clogged fuel filter 11. Clogged air filter 12. Defective fuel pump

TROUBLESHOOTING FUEL INJECTION PROBLEMS

Each fuel injection system has its own unique components and test procedures, for which it is impossible to generalize. Refer to Chapter 4 of this Repair & Tune-Up Guide for specific test and repair procedures, if the vehicle is equipped with fuel injection.

TROUBLESHOOTING ELECTRICAL PROBLEMS

See Chapter 5 for service procedures

For any electrical system to operate, it must make a complete circuit. This simply means that the power flow from the battery must make a complete circle. When an electrical component is operating, power flows from the battery to the component, passes through the component causing it to perform its function (lighting a light bulb), and then returns to the battery through the ground of the circuit. This ground is usually (but not always) the metal part of the car or truck on which the electrical component is mounted.

Perhaps the easiest way to visualize this is to think of connecting a light bulb with two wires attached to it to the battery. If one of the two wires attached to the light bulb were attached to the negative post of the battery and the other were attached to the positive post of the battery, you would have a complete circuit. Current from the battery would flow to the light bulb, causing it to light, and return to the negative post of the battery.

The normal automotive circuit differs from this simple example in two ways. First, instead of having a return wire from the bulb to the battery, the light bulb returns the current to the battery through the chassis of the vehicle. Since the negative battery cable is attached to the chassis and the chassis is made of electrically conductive metal, the chassis of the vehicle can serve as a ground wire to complete the circuit. Secondly, most automotive circuits contain switches to turn components on and off as required.

Every complete circuit from a power source must include a component which is using the power from the power source. If you were to disconnect the light bulb from the wires and touch the two wires together (don't do this) the power supply wire to the component would be grounded before the normal ground connection for the circuit.

Because grounding a wire from a power source makes a complete circuit—less the required component to use the power—this phenomenon is called a short circuit. Common causes are: broken insulation (exposing the metal wire to a metal part of the car or truck), or a shorted switch.

Some electrical components which require a large amount of current to operate also have a relay in their circuit. Since these circuits carry a large amount of current, the thickness of the wire in the circuit (gauge size) is also greater. If this large wire were connected from the component to the control switch on the instrument panel, and then back to the component, a voltage drop would occur in the circuit. To prevent this potential drop in voltage, an electromagnetic switch (relay) is used. The large wires in the circuit are connected from the battery to one side of the relay, and from the opposite side of the relay to the component. The relay is normally open, preventing current from passing through the circuit. An additional, smaller, wire is connected from the relay to the control switch for the circuit. When the control switch is turned on, it grounds the smaller wire from the relay and completes the circuit. This closes the relay and allows current to flow from the battery to the component. The horn, headlight, and starter circuits are three which use relays.

It is possible for larger surges of current to pass through the electrical system of your car or truck. If this surge of current were to reach an electrical component, it could burn it out. To prevent this, fuses, circuit breakers or fusible links are connected into the current supply wires of most of the major electrical systems. When an electrical current of excessive power passes through the component's fuse, the fuse blows out and breaks the circuit, saving the component from destruction.

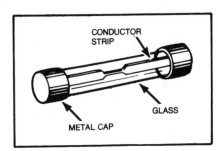

CONDUCTOR STRIP
GLASS
METAL CAP

Typical automotive fuse

A circuit breaker is basically a self-repairing fuse. The circuit breaker opens the circuit the same way a fuse does. However, when either the short is removed from the circuit or the surge subsides, the circuit breaker resets itself and does not have to be replaced as a fuse does.

A fuse link is a wire that acts as a fuse. It is normally connected between the starter relay and the main wiring harness. This connection is usually under the hood. The fuse link (if installed) protects all the

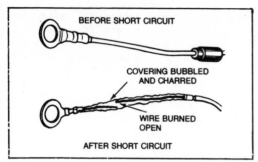

Most fusible links show a charred, melted insulation when they burn out

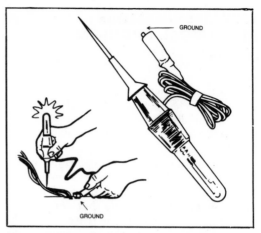

The test light will show the presence of current when touched to a hot wire and grounded at the other end

chassis electrical components, and is the probable cause of trouble when none of the electrical components function, unless the battery is disconnected or dead.

Electrical problems generally fall into one of three areas:

1. The component that is not functioning is not receiving current.

2. The component itself is not functioning.

3. The component is not properly grounded.

The electrical system can be checked with a test light and a jumper wire. A test light is a device that looks like a pointed screwdriver with a wire attached to it and has a light bulb in its handle. A jumper wire is a piece of insulated wire with an alligator clip attached to each end.

If a component is not working, you must follow a systematic plan to determine which of the three causes is the villain.

1. Turn on the switch that controls the inoperable component.

2. Disconnect the power supply wire from the component.

3. Attach the ground wire on the test light to a good metal ground.

4. Touch the probe end of the test light to the end of the power supply wire that was disconnected from the component. If the component is receiving current, the test light will go on.

NOTE: *Some components work only when the ignition switch is turned on.*

If the test light does not go on, then the problem is in the circuit between the battery and the component. This includes all the switches, fuses, and relays in the system. Follow the wire that runs back to the battery. The problem is an open circuit between the

battery and the component. If the fuse is blown and, when replaced, immediately blows again, there is a short circuit in the system which must be located and repaired. If there is a switch in the system, bypass it with a jumper wire. This is done by connecting one end of the jumper wire to the power supply wire into the switch and the other end of the jumper wire to the wire coming out of the switch. If the test light lights with the jumper wire installed, the switch or whatever was bypassed is defective.

NOTE: *Never substitute the jumper wire for the component, since it is required to use the power from the power source.*

5. If the bulb in the test light goes on, then the current is getting to the component that is not working. This eliminates the first of the three possible causes. Connect the power supply wire and connect a jumper wire from the component to a good metal ground. Do this with the switch which controls the component turned on, and also the ignition switch turned on if it is required for the component to work. If the component works with the jumper wire installed, then it has a bad ground. This is usually caused by the metal area on which the component mounts to the chassis being coated with some type of foreign matter.

6. If neither test located the source of the trouble, then the component itself is defective. Remember that for any electrical system to work, all connections must be clean and tight.

Troubleshooting Basic Turn Signal and Flasher Problems
See Chapter 5 for service procedures

Most problems in the turn signals or flasher system can be reduced to defective flashers or bulbs, which are easily replaced. Occasionally, the turn signal switch will prove defective.

F = Front   R = Rear   ● = Lights off   ○ = Lights on

Condition		Possible Cause
Turn signals light, but do not flash	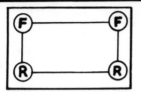	Defective flasher
No turn signals light on either side	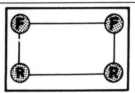	Blown fuse. Replace if defective. Defective flasher. Check by substitution. Open circuit, short circuit or poor ground.
Both turn signals on one side don't work	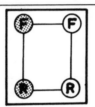	Bad bulbs. Bad ground in both (or either) housings.
One turn signal light on one side doesn't work	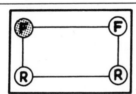	Defective bulb. Corrosion in socket. Clean contacts. Poor ground at socket.
Turn signal flashes too fast or too slowly	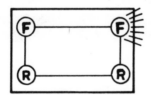	Check any bulb on the side flashing too fast. A heavy-duty bulb is probably installed in place of a regular bulb. Check the bulb flashing too slowly. A standard bulb was probably installed in place of a heavy-duty bulb. Loose connections or corrosion at the bulb socket.
Indicator lights don't work in either direction		Check if the turn signals are working. Check the dash indicator lights. Check the flasher by substitution.
One indicator light doesn't light		On systems with one dash indicator: See if the lights work on the same side. Often the filaments have been reversed in systems combining stoplights with taillights and turn signals. Check the flasher by substitution. On systems with two indicators: Check the bulbs on the same side. Check the indicator light bulb. Check the flasher by substitution.

Troubleshooting Lighting Problems

See Chapter 5 for service procedures

Condition	Possible Cause
One or more lights don't work, but others do	1. Defective bulb(s) 2. Blown fuse(s) 3. Dirty fuse clips or light sockets 4. Poor ground circuit
Lights burn out quickly	1. Incorrect voltage regulator setting or defective regulator 2. Poor battery/alternator connections
Lights go dim	1. Low/discharged battery 2. Alternator not charging 3. Corroded sockets or connections 4. Low voltage output
Lights flicker	1. Loose connection 2. Poor ground. (Run ground wire from light housing to frame) 3. Circuit breaker operating (short circuit)
Lights "flare"—Some flare is normal on acceleration—If excessive, see "Lights Burn Out Quickly"	High voltage setting
Lights glare—approaching drivers are blinded	1. Lights adjusted too high 2. Rear springs or shocks sagging 3. Rear tires soft

Troubleshooting Dash Gauge Problems

Most problems can be traced to a defective sending unit or faulty wiring. Occasionally, the gauge itself is at fault. See Chapter 5 for service procedures.

Condition	Possible Cause
COOLANT TEMPERATURE GAUGE	
Gauge reads erratically or not at all	1. Loose or dirty connections 2. Defective sending unit. 3. Defective gauge. To test a bi-metal gauge, remove the wire from the sending unit. Ground the wire for an instant. If the gauge registers, replace the sending unit. To test a magnetic gauge, disconnect the wire at the sending unit. With ignition ON gauge should register COLD. Ground the wire; gauge should register HOT.
AMMETER GAUGE—TURN HEADLIGHTS ON (DO NOT START ENGINE). NOTE REACTION	
Ammeter shows charge Ammeter shows discharge Ammeter does not move	1. Connections reversed on gauge 2. Ammeter is OK 3. Loose connections or faulty wiring 4. Defective gauge

Condition	Possible Cause

OIL PRESSURE GAUGE

Condition	Possible Cause
Gauge does not register or is inaccurate	1. On mechanical gauge, Bourdon tube may be bent or kinked. 2. Low oil pressure. Remove sending unit. Idle the engine briefly. If no oil flows from sending unit hole, problem is in engine. 3. Defective gauge. Remove the wire from the sending unit and ground it for an instant with the ignition ON. A good gauge will go to the top of the scale. 4. Defective wiring. Check the wiring to the gauge. If it's OK and the gauge doesn't register when grounded, replace the gauge. 5. Defective sending unit.

ALL GAUGES

Condition	Possible Cause
All gauges do not operate All gauges read low or erratically All gauges pegged	1. Blown fuse 2. Defective instrument regulator 3. Defective or dirty instrument voltage regulator 4. Loss of ground between instrument voltage regulator and frame 5. Defective instrument regulator

WARNING LIGHTS

Condition	Possible Cause
Light(s) do not come on when ignition is ON, but engine is not started Light comes on with engine running	1. Defective bulb 2. Defective wire 3. Defective sending unit. Disconnect the wire from the sending unit and ground it. Replace the sending unit if the light comes on with the ignition ON. 4. Problem in individual system 5. Defective sending unit

Troubleshooting Clutch Problems

It is false economy to replace individual clutch components. The pressure plate, clutch plate and throwout bearing should be replaced as a set, and the flywheel face inspected, whenever the clutch is overhauled. See Chapter 6 for service procedures.

Condition	Possible Cause
Clutch chatter	1. Grease on driven plate (disc) facing 2. Binding clutch linkage or cable 3. Loose, damaged facings on driven plate (disc) 4. Engine mounts loose 5. Incorrect height adjustment of pressure plate release levers 6. Clutch housing or housing to transmission adapter misalignment 7. Loose driven plate hub
Clutch grabbing	1. Oil, grease on driven plate (disc) facing 2. Broken pressure plate 3. Warped or binding driven plate. Driven plate binding on clutch shaft
Clutch slips	1. Lack of lubrication in clutch linkage or cable (linkage or cable binds, causes incomplete engagement) 2. Incorrect pedal, or linkage adjustment 3. Broken pressure plate springs 4. Weak pressure plate springs 5. Grease on driven plate facings (disc)

Troubleshooting Clutch Problems (cont.)

Condition	Possible Cause
Incomplete clutch release	1. Incorrect pedal or linkage adjustment or linkage or cable binding 2. Incorrect height adjustment on pressure plate release levers 3. Loose, broken facings on driven plate (disc) 4. Bent, dished, warped driven plate caused by overheating
Grinding, whirring grating noise when pedal is depressed	1. Worn or defective throwout bearing 2. Starter drive teeth contacting flywheel ring gear teeth. Look for milled or polished teeth on ring gear.
Squeal, howl, trumpeting noise when pedal is being released (occurs during first inch to inch and one-half of pedal travel)	Pilot bushing worn or lack of lubricant. If bushing appears OK, polish bushing with emery cloth, soak lube wick in oil, lube bushing with oil, apply film of chassis grease to clutch shaft pilot hub, reassemble. NOTE: Bushing wear may be due to misalignment of clutch housing or housing to transmission adapter
Vibration or clutch pedal pulsation with clutch disengaged (pedal fully depressed)	1. Worn or defective engine transmission mounts 2. Flywheel run out. (Flywheel run out at face not to exceed 0.005") 3. Damaged or defective clutch components

Troubleshooting Manual Transmission Problems
See Chapter 6 for service procedures

Condition	Possible Cause
Transmission jumps out of gear	1. Misalignment of transmission case or clutch housing. 2. Worn pilot bearing in crankshaft. 3. Bent transmission shaft. 4. Worn high speed sliding gear. 5. Worn teeth or end-play in clutch shaft. 6. Insufficient spring tension on shifter rail plunger. 7. Bent or loose shifter fork. 8. Gears not engaging completely. 9. Loose or worn bearings on clutch shaft or mainshaft. 10. Worn gear teeth. 11. Worn or damaged detent balls.
Transmission sticks in gear	1. Clutch not releasing fully. 2. Burred or battered teeth on clutch shaft, or sliding sleeve. 3. Burred or battered transmission mainshaft. 4. Frozen synchronizing clutch. 5. Stuck shifter rail plunger. 6. Gearshift lever twisting and binding shifter rail. 7. Battered teeth on high speed sliding gear or on sleeve. 8. Improper lubrication, or lack of lubrication. 9. Corroded transmission parts. 10. Defective mainshaft pilot bearing. 11. Locked gear bearings will give same effect as stuck in gear.
Transmission gears will not synchronize	1. Binding pilot bearing on mainshaft, will synchronize in high gear only. 2. Clutch not releasing fully. 3. Detent spring weak or broken. 4. Weak or broken springs under balls in sliding gear sleeve. 5. Binding bearing on clutch shaft, or binding countershaft. 6. Binding pilot bearing in crankshaft. 7. Badly worn gear teeth. 8. Improper lubrication. 9. Constant mesh gear not turning freely on transmission mainshaft. Will synchronize in that gear only.

Condition	Possible Cause
Gears spinning when shifting into gear from neutral	1. Clutch not releasing fully. 2. In some cases an extremely light lubricant in transmission will cause gears to continue to spin for a short time after clutch is released. 3. Binding pilot bearing in crankshaft.
Transmission noisy in all gears	1. Insufficient lubricant, or improper lubricant. 2. Worn countergear bearings. 3. Worn or damaged main drive gear or countergear. 4. Damaged main drive gear or mainshaft bearings. 5. Worn or damaged countergear anti-lash plate.
Transmission noisy in neutral only	1. Damaged main drive gear bearing. 2. Damaged or loose mainshaft pilot bearing. 3. Worn or damaged countergear anti-lash plate. 4. Worn countergear bearings.
Transmission noisy in one gear only	1. Damaged or worn constant mesh gears. 2. Worn or damaged countergear bearings. 3. Damaged or worn synchronizer.
Transmission noisy in reverse only	1. Worn or damaged reverse idler gear or idler bushing. 2. Worn or damaged mainshaft reverse gear. 3. Worn or damaged reverse countergear. 4. Damaged shift mechanism.

TROUBLESHOOTING AUTOMATIC TRANSMISSION PROBLEMS

Keeping alert to changes in the operating characteristics of the transmission (changing shift points, noises, etc.) can prevent small problems from becoming large ones. If the problem cannot be traced to loose bolts, fluid level, misadjusted linkage, clogged filters or similar problems, you should probably seek professional service.

Transmission Fluid Indications

The appearance and odor of the transmission fluid can give valuable clues to the overall condition of the transmission. Always note the appearance of the fluid when you check the fluid level or change the fluid. Rub a small amount of fluid between your fingers to feel for grit and smell the fluid on the dipstick.

If the fluid appears:	It indicates:
Clear and red colored	Normal operation
Discolored (extremely dark red or brownish) or smells burned	Band or clutch pack failure, usually caused by an overheated transmission. Hauling very heavy loads with insufficient power or failure to change the fluid often result in overheating. Do not confuse this appearance with newer fluids that have a darker red color and a strong odor (though not a burned odor).
Foamy or aerated (light in color and full of bubbles)	1. The level is too high (gear train is churning oil) 2. An internal air leak (air is mixing with the fluid). Have the transmission checked professionally.
Solid residue in the fluid	Defective bands, clutch pack or bearings. Bits of band material or metal abrasives are clinging to the dipstick. Have the transmission checked professionally.
Varnish coating on the dipstick	The transmission fluid is overheating

TROUBLESHOOTING DRIVE AXLE PROBLEMS

First, determine when the noise is most noticeable.

Drive Noise: Produced under vehicle acceleration.

Coast Noise: Produced while coasting with a closed throttle.

Float Noise: Occurs while maintaining constant speed (just enough to keep speed constant) on a level road.

External Noise Elimination

It is advisable to make a thorough road test to determine whether the noise originates in the rear axle or whether it originates from the tires, engine, transmission, wheel bearings or road surface. Noise originating from other places cannot be corrected by servicing the rear axle.

ROAD NOISE

Brick or rough surfaced concrete roads produce noises that seem to come from the rear axle. Road noise is usually identical in Drive or Coast and driving on a different type of road will tell whether the road is the problem.

TIRE NOISE

Tire noise can be mistaken as rear axle noise, even though the tires on the front are at fault. Snow tread and mud tread tires or tires worn unevenly will frequently cause vibrations which seem to originate elsewhere; *temporarily, and for test purposes only,* inflate the tires to 40–50 lbs. This will significantly alter the noise produced by the tires, but will not alter noise from the rear axle. Noises from the rear axle will normally cease at speeds below 30 mph on coast, while tire noise will continue at lower tone as speed is decreased. The rear axle noise will usually change from drive conditions to coast conditions, while tire noise will not. Do not forget to lower the tire pressure to normal after the test is complete.

ENGINE/TRANSMISSION NOISE

Determine at what speed the noise is most pronounced, then stop in a quiet place. With the transmission in Neutral, run the engine through speeds corresponding to road speeds where the noise was noticed. Noises produced with the vehicle standing still are coming from the engine or transmission.

FRONT WHEEL BEARINGS

Front wheel bearing noises, sometimes confused with rear axle noises, will not change when comparing drive and coast conditions. While holding the speed steady, lightly apply the footbrake. This will often cause wheel bearing noise to lessen, as some of the weight is taken off the bearing. Front wheel bearings are easily checked by jacking up the wheels and spinning the wheels. Shaking the wheels will also determine if the wheel bearings are excessively loose.

REAR AXLE NOISES

Eliminating other possible sources can narrow the cause to the rear axle, which normally produces noise from worn gears or bearings. Gear noises tend to peak in a narrow speed range, while bearing noises will usually vary in pitch with engine speeds.

Noise Diagnosis

The Noise Is:	Most Probably Produced By:
1. Identical under Drive or Coast	Road surface, tires or front wheel bearings
2. Different depending on road surface	Road surface or tires
3. Lower as speed is lowered	Tires
4. Similar when standing or moving	Engine or transmission
5. A vibration	Unbalanced tires, rear wheel bearing, unbalanced driveshaft or worn U-joint
6. A knock or click about every two tire revolutions	Rear wheel bearing
7. Most pronounced on turns	Damaged differential gears
8. A steady low-pitched whirring or scraping, starting at low speeds	Damaged or worn pinion bearing
9. A chattering vibration on turns	Wrong differential lubricant or worn clutch plates (limited slip rear axle)
10. Noticed only in Drive, Coast or Float conditions	Worn ring gear and/or pinion gear

Troubleshooting Steering & Suspension Problems

Condition	Possible Cause
Hard steering (wheel is hard to turn)	1. Improper tire pressure 2. Loose or glazed pump drive belt 3. Low or incorrect fluid 4. Loose, bent or poorly lubricated front end parts 5. Improper front end alignment (excessive caster) 6. Bind in steering column or linkage 7. Kinked hydraulic hose 8. Air in hydraulic system 9. Low pump output or leaks in system 10. Obstruction in lines 11. Pump valves sticking or out of adjustment 12. Incorrect wheel alignment
Loose steering (too much play in steering wheel)	1. Loose wheel bearings 2. Faulty shocks 3. Worn linkage or suspension components 4. Loose steering gear mounting or linkage points 5. Steering mechanism worn or improperly adjusted 6. Valve spool improperly adjusted 7. Worn ball joints, tie-rod ends, etc.
Veers or wanders (pulls to one side with hands off steering wheel)	1. Improper tire pressure 2. Improper front end alignment 3. Dragging or improperly adjusted brakes 4. Bent frame 5. Improper rear end alignment 6. Faulty shocks or springs 7. Loose or bent front end components 8. Play in Pitman arm 9. Steering gear mountings loose 10. Loose wheel bearings 11. Binding Pitman arm 12. Spool valve sticking or improperly adjusted 13. Worn ball joints
Wheel oscillation or vibration transmitted through steering wheel	1. Low or uneven tire pressure 2. Loose wheel bearings 3. Improper front end alignment 4. Bent spindle 5. Worn, bent or broken front end components 6. Tires out of round or out of balance 7. Excessive lateral runout in disc brake rotor 8. Loose or bent shock absorber or strut
Noises (see also "Troubleshooting Drive Axle Problems")	1. Loose belts 2. Low fluid, air in system 3. Foreign matter in system 4. Improper lubrication 5. Interference or chafing in linkage 6. Steering gear mountings loose 7. Incorrect adjustment or wear in gear box 8. Faulty valves or wear in pump 9. Kinked hydraulic lines 10. Worn wheel bearings
Poor return of steering	1. Over-inflated tires 2. Improperly aligned front end (excessive caster) 3. Binding in steering column 4. No lubrication in front end 5. Steering gear adjusted too tight
Uneven tire wear (see "How To Read Tire Wear")	1. Incorrect tire pressure 2. Improperly aligned front end 3. Tires out-of-balance 4. Bent or worn suspension parts

HOW TO READ TIRE WEAR

The way your tires wear is a good indicator of other parts of the suspension. Abnormal wear patterns are often caused by the need for simple tire maintenance, or for front end alignment.

Excessive wear at the center of the tread indicates that the air pressure in the tire is consistently too high. The tire is riding on the center of the tread and wearing it prematurely. Occasionally, this wear pattern can result from outrageously wide tires on narrow rims. The cure for this is to replace either the tires or the wheels.

This type of wear usually results from consistent under-inflation. When a tire is under-inflated, there is too much contact with the road by the outer treads, which wear prematurely. When this type of wear occurs, and the tire pressure is known to be consistently correct, a bent or worn steering component or the need for wheel alignment could be indicated.

Feathering is a condition when the edge of each tread rib develops a slightly rounded edge on one side and a sharp edge on the other. By running your hand over the tire, you can usually feel the sharper edges before you'll be able to see them. The most common causes of feathering are incorrect toe-in setting or deteriorated bushings in the front suspension.

When an inner or outer rib wears faster than the rest of the tire, the need for wheel alignment is indicated. There is excessive camber in the front suspension, causing the wheel to lean too much putting excessive load on one side of the tire. Misalignment could also be due to sagging springs, worn ball joints, or worn control arm bushings. Be sure the vehicle is loaded the way it's normally driven when you have the wheels aligned.

Cups or scalloped dips appearing around the edge of the tread almost always indicate worn (sometimes bent) suspension parts. Adjustment of wheel alignment alone will seldom cure the problem. Any worn component that connects the wheel to the suspension can cause this type of wear. Occasionally, wheels that are out of balance will wear like this, but wheel imbalance usually shows up as bald spots between the outside edges and center of the tread.

Second-rib wear is usually found only in radial tires, and appears where the steel belts end in relation to the tread. It can be kept to a minimum by paying careful attention to tire pressure and frequently rotating the tires. This is often considered normal wear but excessive amounts indicate that the tires are too wide for the wheels.

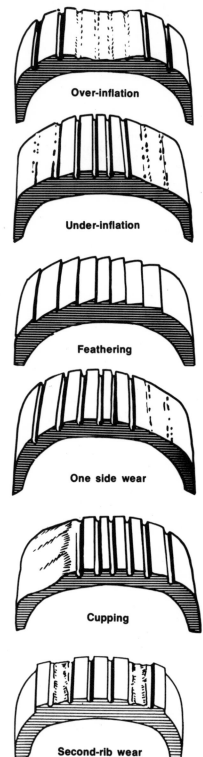

Over-inflation

Under-inflation

Feathering

One side wear

Cupping

Second-rib wear

Troubleshooting Disc Brake Problems

Condition	Possible Cause
Noise—groan—brake noise emanating when slowly releasing brakes (creep-groan)	Not detrimental to function of disc brakes—no corrective action required. (This noise may be eliminated by slightly increasing or decreasing brake pedal efforts.)
Rattle—brake noise or rattle emanating at low speeds on rough roads, (front wheels only).	1. Shoe anti-rattle spring missing or not properly positioned. 2. Excessive clearance between shoe and caliper. 3. Soft or broken caliper seals. 4. Deformed or misaligned disc. 5. Loose caliper.
Scraping	1. Mounting bolts too long. 2. Loose wheel bearings. 3. Bent, loose, or misaligned splash shield.
Front brakes heat up during driving and fail to release	1. Operator riding brake pedal. 2. Stop light switch improperly adjusted. 3. Sticking pedal linkage. 4. Frozen or seized piston. 5. Residual pressure valve in master cylinder. 6. Power brake malfunction. 7. Proportioning valve malfunction.
Leaky brake caliper	1. Damaged or worn caliper piston seal. 2. Scores or corrosion on surface of cylinder bore.
Grabbing or uneven brake action—Brakes pull to one side	1. Causes listed under "Brakes Pull". 2. Power brake malfunction. 3. Low fluid level in master cylinder. 4. Air in hydraulic system. 5. Brake fluid, oil or grease on linings. 6. Unmatched linings. 7. Distorted brake pads. 8. Frozen or seized pistons. 9. Incorrect tire pressure. 10. Front end out of alignment. 11. Broken rear spring. 12. Brake caliper pistons sticking. 13. Restricted hose or line. 14. Caliper not in proper alignment to braking disc. 15. Stuck or malfunctioning metering valve. 16. Soft or broken caliper seals. 17. Loose caliper.
Brake pedal can be depressed without braking effect	1. Air in hydraulic system or improper bleeding procedure. 2. Leak past primary cup in master cylinder. 3. Leak in system. 4. Rear brakes out of adjustment. 5. Bleeder screw open.
Excessive pedal travel	1. Air, leak, or insufficient fluid in system or caliper. 2. Warped or excessively tapered shoe and lining assembly. 3. Excessive disc runout. 4. Rear brake adjustment required. 5. Loose wheel bearing adjustment. 6. Damaged caliper piston seal. 7. Improper brake fluid (boil). 8. Power brake malfunction. 9. Weak or soft hoses.

Troubleshooting Disc Brake Problems (cont.)

Condition	Possible Cause
Brake roughness or chatter (pedal pumping)	1. Excessive thickness variation of braking disc. 2. Excessive lateral runout of braking disc. 3. Rear brake drums out-of-round. 4. Excessive front bearing clearance.
Excessive pedal effort	1. Brake fluid, oil or grease on linings. 2. Incorrect lining. 3. Frozen or seized pistons. 4. Power brake malfunction. 5. Kinked or collapsed hose or line. 6. Stuck metering valve. 7. Scored caliper or master cylinder bore. 8. Seized caliper pistons.
Brake pedal fades (pedal travel increases with foot on brake)	1. Rough master cylinder or caliper bore. 2. Loose or broken hydraulic lines/connections. 3. Air in hydraulic system. 4. Fluid level low. 5. Weak or soft hoses. 6. Inferior quality brake shoes or fluid. 7. Worn master cylinder piston cups or seals.

Troubleshooting Drum Brakes

Condition	Possible Cause
Pedal goes to floor	1. Fluid low in reservoir. 2. Air in hydraulic system. 3. Improperly adjusted brake. 4. Leaking wheel cylinders. 5. Loose or broken brake lines. 6. Leaking or worn master cylinder. 7. Excessively worn brake lining.
Spongy brake pedal	1. Air in hydraulic system. 2. Improper brake fluid (low boiling point). 3. Excessively worn or cracked brake drums. 4. Broken pedal pivot bushing.
Brakes pulling	1. Contaminated lining. 2. Front end out of alignment. 3. Incorrect brake adjustment. 4. Unmatched brake lining. 5. Brake drums out of round. 6. Brake shoes distorted. 7. Restricted brake hose or line. 8. Broken rear spring. 9. Worn brake linings. 10. Uneven lining wear. 11. Glazed brake lining. 12. Excessive brake lining dust. 13. Heat spotted brake drums. 14. Weak brake return springs. 15. Faulty automatic adjusters. 16. Low or incorrect tire pressure.

Condition	Possible Cause
Squealing brakes	1. Glazed brake lining. 2. Saturated brake lining. 3. Weak or broken brake shoe retaining spring. 4. Broken or weak brake shoe return spring. 5. Incorrect brake lining. 6. Distorted brake shoes. 7. Bent support plate. 8. Dust in brakes or scored brake drums. 9. Linings worn below limit. 10. Uneven brake lining wear. 11. Heat spotted brake drums.
Chirping brakes	1. Out of round drum or eccentric axle flange pilot.
Dragging brakes	1. Incorrect wheel or parking brake adjustment. 2. Parking brakes engaged or improperly adjusted. 3. Weak or broken brake shoe return spring. 4. Brake pedal binding. 5. Master cylinder cup sticking. 6. Obstructed master cylinder relief port. 7. Saturated brake lining. 8. Bent or out of round brake drum. 9. Contaminated or improper brake fluid. 10. Sticking wheel cylinder pistons. 11. Driver riding brake pedal. 12. Defective proportioning valve. 13. Insufficient brake shoe lubricant.
Hard pedal	1. Brake booster inoperative. 2. Incorrect brake lining. 3. Restricted brake line or hose. 4. Frozen brake pedal linkage. 5. Stuck wheel cylinder. 6. Binding pedal linkage. 7. Faulty proportioning valve.
Wheel locks	1. Contaminated brake lining. 2. Loose or torn brake lining. 3. Wheel cylinder cups sticking. 4. Incorrect wheel bearing adjustment. 5. Faulty proportioning valve.
Brakes fade (high speed)	1. Incorrect lining. 2. Overheated brake drums. 3. Incorrect brake fluid (low boiling temperature). 4. Saturated brake lining. 5. Leak in hydraulic system. 6. Faulty automatic adjusters.
Pedal pulsates	1. Bent or out of round brake drum.
Brake chatter and shoe knock	1. Out of round brake drum. 2. Loose support plate. 3. Bent support plate. 4. Distorted brake shoes. 5. Machine grooves in contact face of brake drum (Shoe Knock). 6. Contaminated brake lining. 7. Missing or loose components. 8. Incorrect lining material. 9. Out-of-round brake drums. 10. Heat spotted or scored brake drums. 11. Out-of-balance wheels.

Troubleshooting Drum Brakes (cont.)

Condition	Possible Cause
Brakes do not self adjust	1. Adjuster screw frozen in thread. 2. Adjuster screw corroded at thrust washer. 3. Adjuster lever does not engage star wheel. 4. Adjuster installed on wrong wheel.
Brake light glows	1. Leak in the hydraulic system. 2. Air in the system. 3. Improperly adjusted master cylinder pushrod. 4. Uneven lining wear. 5. Failure to center combination valve or proportioning valve.

Appendix

General Conversion Table

Multiply by	To convert	To	
2.54	Inches	Centimeters	.3937
30.48	Feet	Centimeters	.0328
.914	Yards	Meters	1.094
1.609	Miles	Kilometers	.621
.645	Square inches	Square cm.	.155
.836	Square yards	Square meters	1.196
16.39	Cubic inches	Cubic cm.	.061
28.3	Cubic feet	Liters	.0353
.4536	Pounds	Kilograms	2.2045
4.226	Gallons	Liters	.264
.068	Lbs./sq. in. (psi)	Atmospheres	14.7
.138	Foot pounds	Kg. m.	7.23
1.014	H.P. (DIN)	H.P. (SAE)	.9861
—	To obtain	From	Multiply by

Note: 1 cm. equals 10 mm.; 1 mm. equals .0394″.

Conversion—Common Fractions to Decimals and Millimeters

Common Fractions	Decimal Fractions	Millimeters (approx.)	Common Fractions	Decimal Fractions	Millimeters (approx.)	Common Fractions	Decimal Fractions	Millimeters (approx.)
1/128	.008	0.20	11/32	.344	8.73	43/64	.672	17.07
1/64	.016	0.40	23/64	.359	9.13	11/16	.688	17.46
1/32	.031	0.79	3/8	.375	9.53	45/64	.703	17.86
3/64	.047	1.19	25/64	.391	9.92	23/32	.719	18.26
1/16	.063	1.59	13/32	.406	10.32	47/64	.734	18.65
5/64	.078	1.98	27/64	.422	10.72	3/4	.750	19.05
3/32	.094	2.38	7/16	.438	11.11	49/64	.766	19.45
7/64	.109	2.78	29/64	.453	11.51	25/32	.781	19.84
1/8	.125	3.18	15/32	.469	11.91	51/64	.797	20.24
9/64	.141	3.57	31/64	.484	12.30	13/16	.813	20.64
5/32	.156	3.97	1/2	.500	12.70	53/64	.828	21.03
11/64	.172	4.37	33/64	.516	13.10	27/32	.844	21.43
3/16	.188	4.76	17/32	.531	13.49	55/64	.859	21.83
13/64	.203	5.16	35/64	.547	13.89	7/8	.875	22.23
7/32	.219	5.56	9/16	.563	14.29	57/64	.891	22.62
15/64	.234	5.95	37/64	.578	14.68	29/32	.906	23.02
1/4	.250	6.35	19/32	.594	15.08	59/64	.922	23.42
17/64	.266	6.75	39/64	.609	15.48	15/16	.938	23.81
9/32	.281	7.14	5/8	.625	15.88	61/64	.953	24.21
19/64	.297	7.54	41/64	.641	16.27	31/32	.969	24.61
5/16	.313	7.94	21/32	.656	16.67	63/64	.984	25.00
21/64	.328	8.33						

Conversion—Millimeters to Decimal Inches

mm	inches	mm	inches	mm	inches	mm	inches	mm	inches
1	.039 370	31	1.220 470	61	2.401 570	91	3.582 670	210	8.267 700
2	.078 740	32	1.259 840	62	2.440 940	92	3.622 040	220	8.661 400
3	.118 110	33	1.299 210	63	2.480 310	93	3.661 410	230	9.055 100
4	.157 480	34	1.338 580	64	2.519 680	94	3.700 780	240	9.448 800
5	.196 850	35	1.377 949	65	2.559 050	95	3.740 150	250	9.842 500
6	.236 220	36	1.417 319	66	2.598 420	96	3.779 520	260	10.236 200
7	.275 590	37	1.456 689	67	2.637 790	97	3.818 890	270	10.629 900
8	.314 960	38	1.496 050	68	2.677 160	98	3.858 260	280	11.032 600
9	.354 330	39	1.535 430	69	2.716 530	99	3.897 630	290	11.417 300
10	.393 700	40	1.574 800	70	2.755 900	100	3.937 000	300	11.811 000
11	.433 070	41	1.614 170	71	2.795 270	105	4.133 848	310	12.204 700
12	.472 440	42	1.653 540	72	2.834 640	110	4.330 700	320	12.598 400
13	.511 810	43	1.692 910	73	2.874 010	115	4.527 550	330	12.992 100
14	.551 180	44	1.732 280	74	2.913 380	120	4.724 400	340	13.385 800
15	.590 550	45	1.771 650	75	2.952 750	125	4.921 250	350	13.779 500
16	.629 920	46	1.811 020	76	2.992 120	130	5.118 100	360	14.173 200
17	.669 290	47	1.850 390	77	3.031 490	135	5.314 950	370	14.566 900
18	.708 660	48	1.889 760	78	3.070 860	140	5.511 800	380	14.960 600
19	.748 030	49	1.929 130	79	3.110 230	145	5.708 650	390	15.354 300
20	.787 400	50	1.968 500	80	3.149 600	150	5.905 500	400	15.748 000
21	.826 770	51	2.007 870	81	3.188 970	155	6.102 350	500	19.685 000
22	.866 140	52	2.047 240	82	3.228 340	160	6.299 200	600	23.622 000
23	.905 510	53	2.086 610	83	3.267 710	165	6.496 050	700	27.559 000
24	.944 880	54	2.125 980	84	3.307 080	170	6.692 900	800	31.496 000
25	.984 250	55	2.165 350	85	3.346 450	175	6.889 750	900	35.433 000
26	1.023 620	56	2.204 720	86	3.385 820	180	7.086 600	1000	39.370 000
27	1.062 990	57	2.244 090	87	3.425 190	185	7.283 450	2000	78.740 000
28	1.102 360	58	2.283 460	88	3.464 560	190	7.480 300	3000	118.110 000
29	1.141 730	59	2.322 830	89	3.503 903	195	7.677 150	4000	157.480 000
30	1.181 100	60	2.362 200	90	3.543 300	200	7.874 000	5000	196.850 000

To change decimal millimeters to decimal inches, position the decimal point where desired on either side of the millimeter measurement shown and reset the inches decimal by the same number of digits in the same direction. For example, to convert 0.001 mm to decimal inches, reset the decimal behind the 1 mm (shown on the chart) to 0.001; change the decimal inch equivalent (0.039″ shown) to 0.000039″.

Tap Drill Sizes

National Fine or S.A.E.

Screw & Tap Size	Threads Per Inch	Use Drill Number
No. 5	44	37
No. 6	40	33
No. 8	36	29
No. 10	32	21
No. 12	28	15
1/4	28	3
5/16	24	1
3/8	24	Q
7/16	20	W
1/2	20	29/64
9/16	18	33/64
5/8	18	37/64
3/4	16	11/16
7/8	14	13/16
1 1/8	12	1 3/64
1 1/4	12	1 11/64
1 1/2	12	1 27/64

Tap Drill Sizes

National Coarse or U.S.S.

Screw & Tap Size	Threads Per Inch	Use Drill Number
No. 5	40	39
No. 6	32	36
No. 8	32	29
No. 10	24	25
No. 12	24	17
1/4	20	8
5/16	18	F
3/8	16	5/16
7/16	14	U
1/2	13	27/64
9/16	12	31/64
5/8	11	17/32
3/4	10	21/32
7/8	9	49/64
1	8	7/8
1 1/8	7	63/64
1 1/4	7	1 7/64
1 1/2	6	1 11/32

Decimal Equivalent Size of the Number Drills

Drill No.	Decimal Equivalent	Drill No.	Decimal Equivalent	Drill No.	Decimal Equivalent
80	.0135	53	.0595	26	.1470
79	.0145	52	.0635	25	.1495
78	.0160	51	.0670	24	.1520
77	.0180	50	.0700	23	.1540
76	.0200	49	.0730	22	.1570
75	.0210	48	.0760	21	.1590
74	.0225	47	.0785	20	.1610
73	.0240	46	.0810	19	.1660
72	.0250	45	.0820	18	.1695
71	.0260	44	.0860	17	.1730
70	.0280	43	.0890	16	.1770
69	.0292	42	.0935	15	.1800
68	.0310	41	.0960	14	.1820
67	.0320	40	.0980	13	.1850
66	.0330	39	.0995	12	.1890
65	.0350	38	.1015	11	.1910
64	.0360	37	.1040	10	.1935
63	.0370	36	.1065	9	.1960
62	.0380	35	.1100	8	.1990
61	.0390	34	.1110	7	.2010
60	.0400	33	.1130	6	.2040
59	.0410	32	.1160	5	.2055
58	.0420	31	.1200	4	.2090
57	.0430	30	.1285	3	.2130
56	.0465	29	.1360	2	.2210
55	.0520	28	.1405	1	.2280
54	.0550	27	.1440		

Decimal Equivalent Size of the Letter Drills

Letter Drill	Decimal Equivalent	Letter Drill	Decimal Equivalent	Letter Drill	Decimal Equivalent
A	.234	J	.277	S	.348
B	.238	K	.281	T	.358
C	.242	L	.290	U	.368
D	.246	M	.295	V	.377
E	.250	N	.302	W	.386
F	.257	O	.316	X	.397
G	.261	P	.323	Y	.404
H	.266	Q	.332	Z	.413
I	.272	R	.339		

Anti-Freeze Chart

Temperatures Shown in Degrees Fahrenheit +32 is Freezing

Cooling System Capacity Quarts	Quarts of ETHYLENE GLYCOL Needed for Protection to Temperatures Shown Below													
	1	2	3	4	5	6	7	8	9	10	11	12	13	14
10	+24°	+16°	+4°	−12°	−34°	−62°								
11	+25	+18	+8	−6	−23	−47								
12	+26	+19	+10	0	−15	−34	−57°							
13	+27	+21	+13	+3	−9	−25	−45							
14			+15	+6	−5	−18	−34							
15			+16	+8	0	−12	−26							
16		+17	+10	+2	−8	−19	−34	−52°						
17		+18	+12	+5	−4	−14	−27	−42						
18		+19	+14	+7	0	−10	−21	−34	−50°					
19		+20	+15	+9	+2	−7	−16	−28	−42					
20			+16	+10	+4	−3	−12	−22	−34	−48°				
21				+17	+12	+6	0	−9	−17	−28	−41			
22				+18	+13	+8	+2	−6	−14	−23	−34	−47°		
23				+19	+14	+9	+4	−3	−10	−19	−29	−40		
24				+19	+15	+10	+5	0	−8	−15	−23	−34	−46°	
25				+20	+16	+12	+7	+1	−5	−12	−20	−29	−40	−50°
26				+17	+13	+8	+3	−3	−9	−16	−25	−34	−44	
27				+18	+14	+9	+5	−1	−7	−13	−21	−29	−39	
28				+18	+15	+10	+6	+1	−5	−11	−18	−25	−34	
29				+19	+16	+12	+7	+2	−3	−8	−15	−22	−29	
30				+20	+17	+13	+8	+4	−1	−6	−12	−18	−25	

For capacities over 30 quarts divide true capacity by 3. Find quarts Anti-Freeze for the 1/3 and multiply by 3 for quarts to add.

For capacities under 10 quarts multiply true capacity by 3. Find quarts Anti-Freeze for the tripled volume and divide by 3 for quarts to add.

To Increase the Freezing Protection of Anti-Freeze Solutions Already Installed

Cooling System Capacity Quarts	Number of Quarts of ETHYLENE GLYCOL Anti-Freeze Required to Increase Protection													
	From +20° F. to					From +10° F. to					From 0° F. to			
	0°	−10°	−20°	−30°	−40°	0°	−10°	−20°	−30°	−40°	−10°	−20°	−30°	−40°
10	1¾	2¼	3	3½	3¾	¾	1½	2¼	2¾	3¼	¾	1½	2	2½
12	2	2¾	3½	4	4½	1	1¾	2½	3¼	3¾	1	1¾	2½	3¼
14	2¼	3¼	4	4¾	5½	1¼	2	3	3¾	4½	1	2	3	3½
16	2½	3½	4½	5¼	6	1¼	2½	3½	4¼	5¼	1¼	2¼	3¼	4
18	3	4	5	6	7	1½	2¾	4	5	5¾	1½	2½	3¾	4¾
20	3¼	4½	5¾	6¾	7½	1¾	3	4¼	5½	6½	1½	2¾	4¼	5¼
22	3½	5	6¼	7¼	8¼	1¾	3¼	4¾	6	7¼	1¾	3¼	4½	5½
24	4	5½	7	8	9	2	3½	5	6½	7½	1¾	3½	5	6
26	4¼	6	7½	8¾	10	2	4	5½	7	8¼	2	3¾	5½	6¾
28	4½	6¼	8	9½	10½	2¼	4¼	6	7½	9	2	4	5¾	7¼
30	5	6¾	8½	10	11½	2½	4½	6½	8	9½	2¼	4¼	6¼	7¾

Test radiator solution with proper hydrometer. Determine from the table the number of quarts of solution to be drawn off from a full cooling system and replace with undiluted anti-freeze, to give the desired increased protection. For example, to increase protection of a 22-quart cooling system containing Ethylene Glycol (permanent type) anti-freeze, from +20° F. to −20° F. will require the replacement of 6¼ quarts of solution with undiluted anti-freeze.

Index

Chilton's Repair & Tune-Up Guides

The complete line covers domestic cars, imports, trucks, vans, RV's and 4-wheel drive vehicles.

BOOK CODE	TITLE	BOOK CODE	TITLE
#7032	Arrow & D-50 Pick-Ups 79-81	#5984	Gremlin & Hornet 70-74
#6637	Aspen & Volare 76-78	#6980	Honda 73-80
#5902	Audi 70-73	#5912	International Scout 67-73
#7028	Audi 4000 & 5000 77-81	#5998	Jaguar 69-74
#6337	Audi Fox 73-75	#6817	Jeep CJ 53-79
#5807	Barracuda and Challenger 65-72	#6739	Jeep Wagoneer, Commando, and Cherokee 66-79
#6931	Blazer & Jimmy 69-80		
#5576	BMW 59-70	#6634	Maverick/Comet 70-77
#6844	BMW 70-79	#6981	Mazda 71-80
#6735	Camaro 67-79	#7031	Mazda RX-7 78-81
#6695	Capri 70-77	#6065	Mercedes-Benz 59-70
#6316	Charger, Coronet 71-75	#5907	Mercedes-Benz 68-73
#6836	Chevette 76-80	#6809	Mercedes-Benz 74-79
#6840	Chevrolet Mid Size 64-79 Covers Chevelle, Laguna, El Camino, Monte Carlo & Malibu	#6780	MG 61-79
		#6542	Mustang 65-73
		#6812	Mustang II 74-78
#6839	Chevrolet 68-79 All Full-Size Chevrolet Models	#6963	Mustang & Capri 79-80 Inc. Turbo.
		#6845	Omni/Horizon 78-80
#6936	Chevrolet & GMC Pick-Ups 70-80	#5792	Opel 64-70
#6930	Chevrolet & GMC Vans 67-80	#6575	Opel 71-75
#6815	Chevrolet LUV 72-79 Inc. 4 x 4 Models	#6473	Pacer 75-76
#6841	Chevy II, Nova 62-79	#5982	Peugeot 70-74
#7037	Colt & Challenger 71-80	#7027	Pinto & Bobcat 71-80
#6691	Corvair 60-69 All Models and Engines, Inc. Turbo.	#6552	Plymouth 68-76
		#5822	Porsche 69-73
#6576	Corvette 53-62	#6331	Ramcharger & Trail Duster 74-75
#6843	Corvette 63-79	#5985	Rebel/Matador 67-74
#6933	Cutlass 70-80	#5821	Road Runner, Satellite, Belvedere, GTX 68-73
#6962	Dasher, Rabbit, Scirocco, Jetta 74-80		
#5790	Datsun 61-72	#5988	Saab 99 69-75
#6960	Datsun 73-80	#6978	Snowmobiles 76-80
#6816	Datsun Pick-Ups 70-79	#6982	Subaru 70-80
#6932	Datsun Z and ZX 70-80	#5905	Tempest, GTO and Le Mans 68-73
#6554	Dodge 68-77	#5795	Toyota 66-70
#6486	Dodge Charger 67-70	#6838	Toyota 70-79
#5720	Dodge Dart and Demon 65-72	#7036	Toyota Carolla/Carina/Tercel 79-81
#6934	Dodge & Plymouth Vans 67-80	#7043	Toyota Celica & Supra 71-81
#6320	Fairlane and Torino 62-75	#6276	Toyota Land Cruiser 66-74
#6965	Fairmont & Zephyr 78-80	#7035	Toyota Pick-Ups 70-81
#6485	Fiat 64-70	#5910	Triumph 69-73
#7042	Fiat 69-81	#6326	Valiant and Duster 68-76
#6846	Fiesta 78-80	#5796	Volkswagen 49-71
#5996	Firebird 67-74	#6837	Volkswagen 70-81
#6961	Ford Bronco 66-80	#6529	Volvo 56-69
#6983	Ford Courier 72-80	#7040	Volvo 70-81
#6842	Ford and Mercury 68-79 All Full-Size Models		
#6696	Ford and Mercury Mid-Size 71-78 Covers Torino, Gran Torino, Ranchero, Elite, LTD II, Thunderbird, Montego, and Cougar		**AUTOMOTIVE SPECIALITY BOOKS**
		#6754	Chilton's Diesel Guide
		#6942	Chilton's Guide to Consumers' Auto Repairs and Prices
#6935	GM Subcompact 71-80 Covers Vega, Monza, Astre, Sunbird, Starfire, Skyhawk	#6940	Chilton's Minor Auto Body Repair
		#6908	Chilton's More Miles Per Gallon
		#6867	Chilton's Motorcycle Owner's Handbook
#6909	GM X-Body 80 Covers Citation, Omega, Phoenix and Skylark	#6727	Chilton's Off-Roading Guide
		#6811	Chilton's Repair Guide for Small Engines - Covers 2 and 4-stroke air cooled gasoline engines up to 20 hp.
#6937	Granada/Monarch 75-80		

Chilton's Repair & Tune-Up Guides are available at your local retailer or by mailing a check or money order for **$8.95** plus **$1.00** to cover postage and handling to:

Chilton Book Company
Dept. DM,
Radnor, PA 19089

NOTE: When ordering be sure to include name & address, book code & title.